INSPIRE / PLAN / DISCOVER / EXPERIENCE

BERLIN

BERLIN

CONTENTS

DISCOVER 6

EXPERIENCE 60

NEED TO KNOW 268

Left: Inside the Reichstag dome
Previous page: Ferries passing by the Berliner Dom
Front cover: The Fernsehturm and Bode-Museum

DISCOVER

The Mitte district divided by the Spree

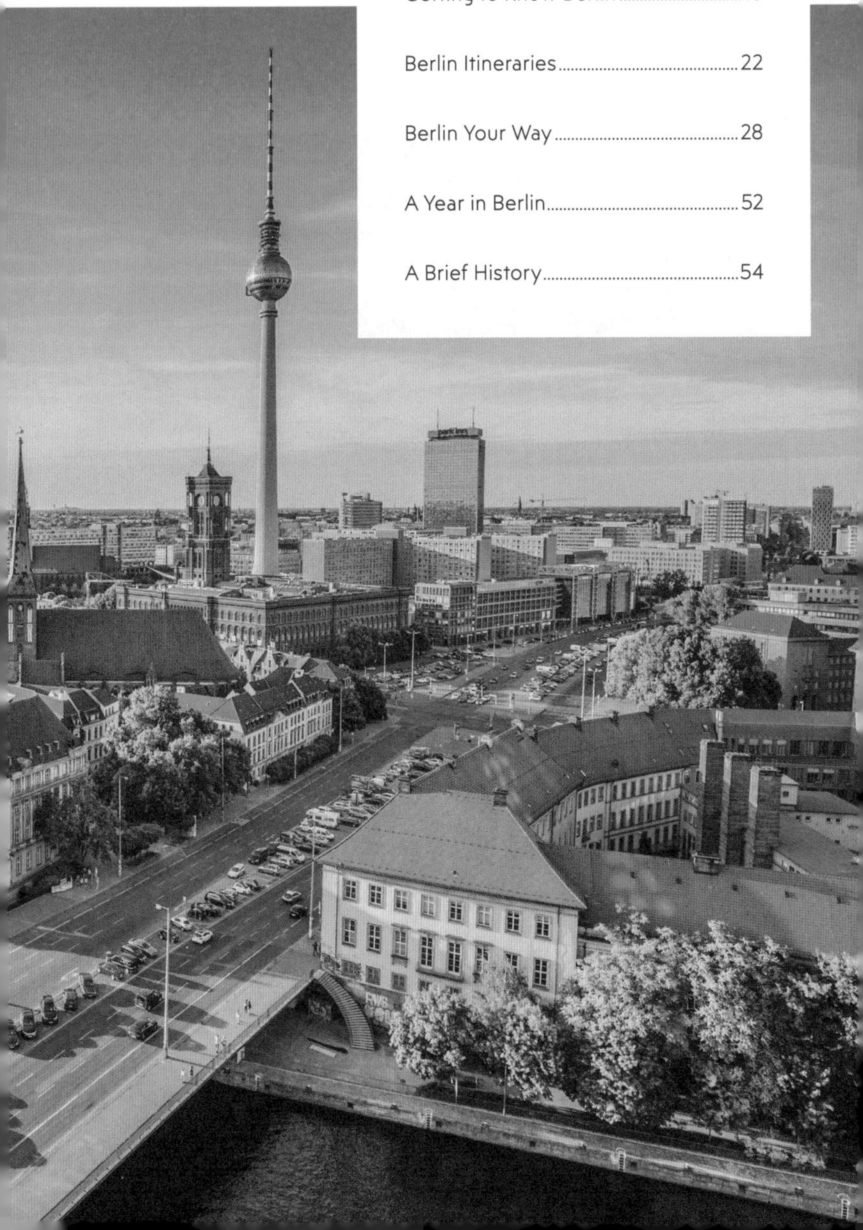

WELCOME TO
BERLIN

Berlin has it all, from inspiring cultural sights to endless examples of its role in world history. But Berlin also has something many major cities lack: a vibrant alternative spirit, thrillingly manifest in its edgy nightlife and art scenes. Whatever your dream trip to Berlin includes, this DK Eyewitness Guide is the perfect travel companion.

1 The sombre Memorial to the Murdered Jews of Europe.

2 The Fernsehturm towering above the cityscape.

3 The Brandenburg Gate bathed by the setting sun.

Many of Berlin's key sights are conveniently located in the city centre, and grouped together in a way that makes them ideal for easy walking tours. A stroll along the grand avenue Unter den Linden will bring you directly to the Brandenburg Gate and the Reichstag. And a visit to bustling Alexanderplatz can easily be combined with a walk around the reconstructed old town of Nikolaiviertel or the Soviet boulevard Karl-Marx-Allee.

Berlin's residential neighbourhoods – especially Friedrichshain, Kreuzberg and Neukölln – should not be missed either. They're key to understanding the city's infamously cool appeal, and exploring their laid-back streets will often lead to a delightful array of independent cafés, shops, bars and more. These neighbourhoods eventually give way to the city's green spaces and lakes beyond the centre, as well as more fascinating cultural and historical sights. Venture further and you'll discover the grand Park Sanssouci in Potsdam, sprinkled with decadent buildings like the Neues Palais that brings to life the Prussian Baroque era of the 18th century.

A city made up of so many unique districts can seem overwhelming at first. This guide-book breaks Berlin down into easily navigable chapters, full of expert local knowledge on the sights and simple yet comprehensive maps to help you get around and find even the most secluded hidden gems. With the Need to Know section providing all the key facts for those new to Berlin, this Eyewitness guide will help you make the most of all that the city has to offer. Enjoy the book, and enjoy Berlin.

3

REASONS TO LOVE
BERLIN

As a modern metropolis that has evolved over hundreds of years of change, Berlin is overflowing with fascinating sights and attractions. Here are the highlights that no visitor should miss.

1 MARKETS

Head outside at the weekend and you'll hear the buzz of flea markets across the city. Or follow the aromas of hot food and fresh fruit to one of the many Saturday food markets.

EAST SIDE GALLERY 2

History is everywhere here, but don't miss this heritage-protected stretch of the Berlin Wall *(p150)* – an anarchic collection of street art, graffiti and social commentary.

MUSEUMSINSEL 3

One of Prussia's finest legacies, Museum Island *(p82)* is a UNESCO-heritage ensemble of five museums that take you on a cultural journey through 2,000 years of world history.

NIGHTLIFE 4

No city parties quite like Berlin. Not only does it have some of the best techno clubs in the world *(p47)*, but entry fees are low and the bars stay open all night.

KAFFEE UND KUCHEN 5

Enjoy the German tradition of coffee and cake with a classic treat like apple strudel, or join the hipsters for the modern alternative: a barista-grade brew in a cool new coffee shop.

MUSIC 6

Whatever your genre, you'll find it here. From intimate clubs to big open-air festivals, music is celebrated all year long in every corner of the city.

KU'DAMM 7

Berlin's best-known boulevard *(p206)* is lined with high-end boutiques, glamorous restaurants and historic cafés. Explore the side streets for local brands and cute coffee shops.

8 CHEAP STREET EATS

Berlin's cheap eats are legendary. For every hip new restaurant opening there are several delicious doner kebab and falafel spots. (Don't miss out on the city's Currywurst.)

9 RIVERS AND LAKES

The tranquil canals and meandering rivers that crisscross the city are perfect for a peaceful stroll or a boat ride. More many scenic stops await outside the city centre.

STREET ART 10

Berlin can sometimes feel like one giant canvas. As well as famous paintings on buildings around the city, you can visit dedicated street art galleries like Urban Spree *(p151)*.

THE REICHSTAG 11

Berlin's official parliamentary building *(p173)* has survived arson, revolution and war, and a tour through its remarkable interior is a fine way to learn about modern German history.

EXPLORE
BERLIN

This guide divides Berlin into nine
colour-coded sightseeing areas,
as shown on the map below.
Find out more about each area
on the following pages. For areas
beyond the centre see p220.

WEDDING

MOABIT

Fritz-Schloss-
Park

Hamburger
Bahnhof

Schlosspark

Schloss
Charlottenburg

Spree

Englischer
Garten

Reichstag

**AROUND SCHLOSS
CHARLOTTENBURG**
p208

Grosser
Stern

Tiergarten

Ernst-Reuter-
Platz

Sophie-
Charlotte-
Platz

Kunstgewerbemuseum

Patsdamer
Platz

Zoologischer
Garten

Gemäldegalerie

CHARLOTTENBURG

Kaiser Wilhelm
Gedächtnis Kirche

Breitscheid-
platz

Lutzow-
platz

TIERGARTEN
p152

Adenauer-
platz

**AROUND
KURFÜRSTENDAMM**
p196

Wittenberg-
platz

Nollendorf-
platz

Deutsches
Technikmuseum
Berlin

Winterfeldt-
platz

Fehrbelliner
Platz

WILMERSDORF

Volkspark
Wilmersdorf

SCHMARGENDORF

FRIEDENAU

GESUNDBRUNNEN

WEISSENSEE

Mauerpark

Kollwitz-platz

Gedenkstätte
Berliner Mauer

Zionskirche

*Jüdischer
Friedhof*

*Volkspark
Prenzlauer
Berg*

**NORTH MITTE AND
PRENZLAUER BERG**
p118

*Oranienburger
Tor*

Volksbühne

*Volkspark
Friedrichshain*

Alexander-platz

Marienkirche

Berliner Dom

Zeughaus

ALEXANDERPLATZ
p102

*Strausberger
Platz*

**AROUND UNTER
DEN LINDEN**
p62

**MUSEUMS-
INSEL**
p82

FRIEDRICHSHAIN
p142

Holocaust
Denkmal

*Boxhagener-
Platz*

Spree

KREUZBERG
p178

Jüdisches
Museum Berlin

*Oranien-
platz*

*Mehring-
platz*

*Wassertor-
platz*

ALT-
TREPTOW

*Viktoria-
park*

*Platz der
Luftbrücke*

*Volkspark
Hasenheide*

*Tempelhofer
Feld*

TEMPELHOF

CENTRAL EUROPE

*North
Sea*

DENMARK

Hamburg

NETHERLANDS

Hannover

BERLIN

POLAND

Düsseldorf

Leipzig

GERMANY

BELGIUM

CZECH
REPUBLIC

Frankfurt

Stuttgart

Munich

SLOVAKIA

FRANCE

SWITZERLAND

AUSTRIA

HUNGARY

ITALY

GETTING TO KNOW
BERLIN

Berlin is made up of 12 boroughs which group together the city's 96 *Ortsteile* (localities), each one with its own character, history and highlights. The most famous sights are located in the dozen or so inner-city *Ortsteile*, but there's plenty more to see beyond the centre in Greater Berlin *(p220)*.

PAGE 62

AROUND UNTER DEN LINDEN

Berlin's most stately street still fulfils its role as a connecting artery between Museumsinsel and Tiergarten park. Lined with some of the city's most impressive baroque and Neo-Classical buildings, this is the boulevard you'll want to stroll down for a first impression of Berlin: both its Prussian past and its cosmopolitan present.

Best for
Culture, architecture, history

Home to
Zeughaus (DHM), Brandenburger Tor, Bebelplatz

Experience
Prussian-era architecture and iconic landmarks, plus coffee and cake in Café Einstein

PAGE 82

MUSEUMSINSEL

At the heart of Berlin's central Mitte district is a long island nestled in the tributaries of the winding river Spree. The UNESCO-listed museum complex on this island is one of Berlin's unique landmarks and a must-see for anyone interested in art and history. And when you're done exploring the museums, the rest of the city is only a short walk away.

Best for
Culture, architecture, history

Home to
Berliner Dom, Pergamonmuseum, Neues Museum, Altes Museum, Alte Nationalgalerie, Bode-Museum

Experience
Antiquities from the Middle East and European artworks from the Middle Ages to the 18th century

PAGE 102

ALEXANDERPLATZ

Berlin's most famous square is synonymous with one of the city's most iconic landmarks: the looming GDR-era Fernsehturm. The whole area is characterized by the somewhat dreary – and heritage-protected – Communist buildings that surround it, but it's still the beating heart of Berlin, a place where locals rush by on their morning commute or meet up with friends at the weekend.

Best for
Shopping, architecture

Home to
Fernsehturm, Marienkirche

Experience
Shopping at the the Alexa Mall then heading to the Fernsehturm to check out the stunning views from the 203-m- (666-ft-) high observation deck

$\rightarrow$

NORTH MITTE AND PRENZLAUER BERG

North of Torstrasse, Mitte begins to morph into the quieter, more residential district of Prenzlauer Berg. Characterized by its leafy, cobbled streets and refurbished *Altbaus* (19th-century tenements), it's one of the most gentrified and laid-back parts of the city. Relatively low on major sights, it offers instead a stream of pleasant cafés and restaurants, independent boutiques and cosy bars. That said, the Berlin Wall Memorial along Bernauer Strasse is a must for all history fans and there are some interesting and unique museums scattered throughout the area.

Best for
Strolling, cafés, bars

Home to
Gedenkstätte Berliner Mauer, Hamburger Bahnhof, Neue Synagoge, Centrum Judaicum, Haus Schwarzenberg Museums, Museum für Naturkunde

Experience
The view from the area around the Wasserturm, part of a slightly elevated landscaped park that locals use for picnics and hanging out in the summer

PAGE 142

FRIEDRICHSHAIN

Once home to political anarchists, Friedrichshain has largely lost its radical left-wing image in favour of a more cosmopolitan air – especially around the central Boxhagener Platz, which is studded with buzzing cafés and restaurants, edgy bars and indie boutiques. The district is also popular for nightlife, and its Volkspark is one of the city's most popular recreational spots.

Best for
Restaurants, bars, nightlife

Home to
East Side Gallery, Karl-Marx-Allee, Volkspark Friedrichshain, Berghain, RAW Gelände

Experience
Urban art and nightlife in the RAW Gelände complex

PAGE 152

TIERGARTEN

At the heart of the city, Berlin's central park bursts to life with gardens, meadows and lakes threaded together with pleasant pathways. The wide boulevard Strasse des 17 Juni divides the park through the centre. Its southern fringe borders the bustling areas of Potsdamer Platz and the Kulturforum, while the northern edge runs parallel to important sights like the Reichstag and Regierungsviertel.

Best for
Strolling, museums, culture

Home to
Kunstgewerbemuseum, Gemäldegalerie, Potsdamer Platz, Reichstag, Siegessäule, Kulturforum, Haus der Kulturen der Welt

Experience
Rowing around the Neuer See in Tiergarten then a drink at one of its excellent beer gardens

→

PAGE 178

KREUZBERG

One of Berlin's most dynamic districts, Kreuzberg can be divided into several unofficial "zones". The northern section can be considered part of the tourist centre, with several significant sights and museums. The eastern section, sometimes referred to as SO36, is decidedly alternative, with a buzzy nightlife and a large concentration of Turkish and Middle Eastern immigrants. In contrast, Western Kreuzberg is more gentrified, characterised by pleasant cafés, tree-lined avenues and the historical Viktoriapark.

Best for
bars, clubs, cafés

Home to
Jüdisches Museum Berlin, Viktoriapark, Berlinische Galerie, Checkpoint Charlie, Deutsches Technikmuseum

Experience
the lively bars of East Kreuzberg

PAGE 196

AROUND KURFÜRSTENDAMM

Kurfürstendamm – usually abbreviated to the more manageable "Ku'damm" – is a 3.5-km- (2.2-mile-) long boulevard beginning at bustling Breitscheidplatz, close to the historical Zoological Garden and the distinctive Kaiser Wilhelm Memorial Church. It's lined on both sides with a non-stop mix of upscale fashion boutiques and high-street stores, and punctuated throughout with cafés, hotels, restaurants and cultural venues. Its side streets are also well worth exploring.

Best for
Shops, cafés, restaurants

Home to
Zoo Berlin, Kaiser Wilhelm Gedächtnis Kirche, KaDeWe, Bikinihaus Mall

Experience
Endless shopping opportunities, a vast array of dining options and plenty of culture – all along one famous boulevard

PAGE 208

AROUND SCHLOSS CHARLOTTENBURG

One of Berlin's premier royal sights, the Schloss Charlottenburg palace complex is almost a small village in itself. Its ensemble of extravagant Baroque buildings include former royal apartments, rooms brimming with antique porcelain and prestigious artworks and a mausoleum containing graves of the Hohenzollern family. The landscaped gardens are especially lovely in summer, and there are several other noteworthy museums and attractive buildings in the area.

Best for
Strolling, sightseeing

Home to
Schloss Charlottenburg, Museum Scharf-Gerstenberg, Museum Berggruen, Bröhan-Museum, Luisenkirche

Experience
A sunset walk around the manicured palace gardens

←

1 Rooftop of the Reichstag.

2 The Neues Museum.

3 Riverside park with a view of the Berliner Dom.

4 The goddess of victory atop the Brandenburger Tor.

It can be hard to know where to start in a city overflowing with famous sights and world-class museums. These itineraries pick out the highlights as well as some hidden gems, so you can make the most out of even a short trip to Berlin.

5 HOURS

Afternoon

Brimming with Neo-Classical architecture and artwork documenting the history of human creativity, Museumsinsel is a stately place to get a first impression of Berlin. For a taste of all the island has to offer, the Neues Museum (p86) has one of the most wide-ranging and exotic exhibitions and will provide plenty of motivation for a return visit. If you can pull yourself away from the treasures of the UNESCO-listed museums, wander over to Schlossplatz (p96) and past the recently erected Humboldt Forum, a replica of the former Royal Palace. After having lunch at the Heat (Karl-Liebknecht Strasse 3), take a walk along Unter den Linden (p72) and admire its multitude of restored historic buildings. Be sure to look into Schinkel's Neue Wache (p69) to see Käthe Kollwitz's poignant sculpture symbolising the suffering of the Berlin people during World War II, and at

Bebelplatz (p80) to see Micha Ullman's "Bibliotek", a memorial to the Nazi's 1933 book-burning. Continuing on down Unter den Linden you'll eventually end at the city's most famous icon, the Brandenburger Tor (p78) with your next stop – the Reichstag (p173) – just down the road.

Evening

Taking a tour (prebooking essential) of the magnificent Reichstag in the late afternoon means you can be on its famous domed rooftop for wonderful city views as the sun sets. The venue's Käfer restaurant offers traditional German cuisine, which you can walk off with a stroll south past the Tiergarten (p170) towards Potsdamer Platz (p162), making a stop at the impressive Holocaust Denkmal (p77).

$\rightarrow$

① Rotating restaurant in the Fernsehturm.

② Nikolaikirche, the oldest church in Berlin.

③ Marx and Engels.

④ DDR Museum.

1 DAY

Morning

Start with breakfast at Sphere, the rotating restaurant inside the iconic Fernsehturm *(p107)*, before heading to the viewing platform for panoramic vistas of the city. Back down at ground level, experience the everyday bustle of the city as locals crisscross Alexanderplatz, emerging from and disappearing into the various underground entrances of this transport hub, and streaming in and out of the many shops around the square. Much of the surrounding architecture, built in the 1960s by the GDR, is now heritage-listed; don't leave without admiring Walter Womacka's mosaic frieze on the Haus des Lehrers. For further insights into East German life, head to the engaging and highly interactive DDR Museum *(p110)*.

Afternoon

After the DDR Museum, walk along the riverbank past the famous statues of Marx and Engels *(p110)* towards the Nikolaiviertel *(p116)* which, despite its medieval history and character, was actually reconstructed by the GDR; look out for the tell-tale prefabricated buildings amidst the cobbled lanes and cute houses. As well as a gorgeous Rococo façade and original staircase, the Ephraim-Palais *(p113)* offers interesting exhibitions and a good restaurant for lunch. Other nearby sights and museums worth visiting include the 18th-century Knoblauchhaus *(p112)*, the Nikolaikirche – whose foundations date back to the 13th century – and the fantastic bronze statue of St George fighting the dragon.

Evening

After dropping into the Zille Museum *(p112)* to admire some of artist Heinrich Zille's collection of artworks and photographs, head to the Zille-Stube for hearty German fare, a beer and a welcoming atmosphere. If you still have some energy, enjoy an evening stroll around the romantic bridges, exquisite buildings and maritime atmosphere of the small but pretty Fischerinsel, one of the earliest settlement areas of Berlin.

←

1 Inside the Sony Center.

2 The Gemäldegalerie

3 The old belfry of Kaiser Wilhelm Gedächtnis Kirche.

4 Ending the evening at one of the city's traditional pubs.

2 DAYS

Day 1

Morning Start the day in style with breakfast and impressive views of the city at Panoramapunkt on the 25th floor of Kollhoff-Tower *(p164)*. From here you can explore the exciting area of Potsdamer Platz *(p162)* with its many museums, shops and fascinating sights, from modern art installations to original sections of the Berlin Wall outside the S-Bahn entrance – or if you have kids, enjoy a creative session at the LEGOLAND Discovery Centre *(p163)*. For a quick and healthy lunch, try Weiland's Wellness; for something grander, Trattoria la Strada.

Afternoon After lunch, walk across to the Kulturforum *(p176)*, West Berlin's answer to Museumsinsel. One of the most comprehensive museums is the Gemäldegalerie *(p158)*, which is well worth a couple of hours to explore. The adjacent Kunstgewerbemuseum *(p156)* has lots to interest design and fashion fans, while over on nearby Leipziger Platz *(p165)*, adults and kids alike can enjoy the multimedia Spy Museum.

Evening To experience the sophisticated side of Berlin, book dinner at the Michelin-starred FACIL before attending a concert at the Philharmonie *(p166)*. An evening stroll through the Tiergarten *(p170)* is a wonderful after-concert activity, or you can continue down Potsdamer Strasse *(p169)* for some classy cocktails at Victoria Bar.

Day 2

Morning Grab a casual breakfast at one of the hip cafés in the Bikinihaus Mall *(p202)*, after which you can browse local fashion and design boutiques. Cross the street to explore the interiors of the unique and moving Kaiser Wilhelm Gedächtnis Kirche *(p200)* before hitting the nearby Ku'damm boulevard *(p206)* for some serious shopping.

Afternoon Head down the elegant Fasanenstrasse *(p204)* to enjoy a classic villa-style lunch at the Café im Literaturhaus. The equally stunning villa next door hosts the beguiling Käthe-Kollwitz-Museum *(p216)*, which celebrates the life and work of this vital German artist. Next, catch a bus or underground train to the unmissable Charlottenburg Palace *(p212)*, leaving enough time to explore the gorgeous palace grounds; pause in between for a restorative coffee and cake at the Orangerie.

Evening If you have some time left, explore one or more of the palace's nearby museums, which include the Berggruen *(p217)*, the Scharf-Gerstenberg *(p216)* and the Schlossstrasse Villas. End your day the Berliner's way at the Brauhaus Lemke am Schloss *(p214)*, which offers a solid menu of traditional German dishes and beers.

Modern and Postmodern

One of the most famous collections of modern architecture can be found at Potsdamer Platz, which boasts skyscrapers by starchitects like Renzo Piano and Frank Gehry. Also worth seeking out is Daniel Libeskind's Jüdisches Museum Berlin, whose jagged, slashed façade and dramatic interior are intended to express notions of violence and absence.

→

Dramatic façade of the Jüdisches Museum Berlin

BERLIN'S INCREDIBLE
ARCHITECTURE

Berlin's history is brought to life by an eclectic mix of architecture on display across the city. With stunning buildings and gardens designed by some of the world's most famous architects, the city is overflowing with amazing structures and spaces which make Berlin feel like an open-air art gallery.

KARL FRIEDRICH SCHINKEL

Schinkel was one of the most renowned German architects; even today his work forms an essential element of the architectural landscape of Berlin. For many years Schinkel held a high-profile position in the Prussian Building Ministry. In Berlin and Potsdam he designed several dozen buildings, including palaces, civic buildings and churches, many of which still stand today. He also excelled at painting and even designed scenery for the opera house on Unter den Linden, among others.

Cold War Era

The former Eastern parts of the city are peppered with blocky GDR-era architecture. The most famous and impressive ensemble is around Alexanderplatz, whose iconic Fernsehturm - along with some of the surrounding prefabricated high-rises (such as the Haus des Lehrers) - was designed by prominent East German architect Hermann Henselmann.

→

GDR-era Haus des Lehrers on Alexanderplatz

Neo-Classical Designs

For decades, Neo-Classical architecture was all the rage in Berlin, and the city centre has many striking examples of this grand and elegant style. Many can be found on Museumsinsel and Unter den Linden, which feature several designs by the prolific Karl Friedrich Schinkel. Of special note are the Konzerthaus on the city's handsome Gendarmenmarkt, and the Neue Wache, designed as a guard house for the Kronprinzenpalais and now home to a World War II memorial.

← Neo-Classical columns decorating the Neue Wache

A Modern Medieval Quarter

The pretty Nikolaiviertel is the best place to get an idea of how the city used to look, although the area is not as old as it appears. Reconstructed during the 1980s by the GDR, it features cobbled streets and the 13th-century Nikolaikirche, as well as striking examples of Rococo at the Ephraim-Palais, and Baroque at the Knoblauchhaus.

↑ Pretty cobbled streets of Nikolaiviertel

For Romanticism

Visit the Alte Nationalgalerie *(p95)* to see Karl Friedrich Schinkel's *Gotischer Dom am Wasser* (1813). In the 19th century Romanticism turned away from religious themes and instead focused on the natural world and personal expression. This painting by Schinkel is a perfect example, cleaving to the themes of Romanticism with its stormy skies and gothic setting.

←

Karl Friedrich Schinkel's *Gotischer Dom am Wasser* (1813), Alte Nationalgalerie

BERLIN FOR
ART LOVERS

Alongside a slew of big-hitter institutions such as those on Museumsinsel, visitors to Berlin can find an endless constellation of independent galleries and private collections, showcasing the evolving history of artistic expression.

TOP 3 INDEPENDENT ART GALLERIES IN BERLIN

C/O Berlin
(p204)

Sammlung Boros
(p128)

König Gallery (St Agnes)
(p191)

For Die Brücke

Die Brücke (The Bridge) was an artistic movement founded by German Expressionists, who aimed to connect the Neo-Romantic and Expressionist movements. Despite the short existence of the group (1905-13), its members produced many distinctive works in various media. Head to the Brücke Museum in Dahlem to find out more *(p120)*.

Did You Know?

The Berlin Welcome Card includes unlimited public transport and discounts on many galleries.

For Street Art

The East Side Gallery *(p150)*, a 1.3-km- (0.8-mile-) long stretch of the Berlin Wall features dozens of political pieces, including Dmitri Vrubel's disturbing depiction of Brezhnev and Honecker kissing (1990). The gallery perfectly captures the nontraditional, often rebellious nature of modern street art.

↑ East Side Gallery, a graffiti-covered stretch of the Berlin Wall

For Renaissance

Religious themes were a popular source of inspiration in Renaissance art, which developed in the early 15th century. Donatello's intimate *Pazzi Madonna* (c 1425-30) was a pioneering piece in Renaissance marble relief artworks - make your way to the Bode-Museum *(p94)* on Museumsisel to see it for yourself.

←

Donatello's *Pazzi Madonna* at the Bode-Museum

For New Objectivity

Neue Sachlichkeit (New Objectivity) was a reaction to Expressionism, and aimed for as much realism as possible across a variety of disciplines from architecture to painting. Founded by the likes of Otto Dix and George Grosz, the movement originated in Germany in the 1920s. See great works by these artists at the Berlinisches Galerie *(Alte Jakobstrasse 124-128)*.

↑ Karl Schmidt-Rottluff exhibit at the Brücke Museum, Dahlem

→

Otto Dix's *The Poet Iwar von Lücken* (1926), Berlinisches Galerie

WAYS TO EXPLORE

There are many ways to explore Berlin for those who don't like heights or driving. Nordic walkers can be found in many of the city's parks, while boat trips along the Spree or on one of Berlin's lakes are a relaxing way to enjoy the city. For a pleasant day trip, take the train to Potsdam, which is full of castles and gardens.

BERLIN WITH A
DIFFERENCE

Berlin has all the usual big city attractions like museums, galleries and parks, but those who want to see the city in a different way will find plenty of more adventurous options. With its abundant natural features and unique structures, Berlin can feel like a playground for visitors of all ages.

Base Flying

One of the most popular base flying spots in the city, the plunge at Park Inn hotel in Alexanderplatz involves dropping off the top of the 125-m (410-ft) rooftop. Participants are secured by a special winch rappel system, the kind used by stuntmen, which reaches almost free fall speed.

↑ Base flying from the top of the Park Inn hotel on Alexanderplatz

Trabi Safari

Driving a Trabant – the boxy, toy-like car synonymous with the GDR – is a unique way to experience the city. It's possible to drive yourself and your group privately, take on a task-filled adventure or enjoy a leisurely tour where participants drive in a convoy, listening in to a guide via radio equipment. Tours last up to two hours.

← Trabi World, host of the Trabi Safari driving tour of Berlin

TOP 5 BERLIN TOUR COMPANIES

Fat Tire Bike Tours
W fattiretours.com

Reederei Riedel Boat Tours
W reederei-riedel.de

Bus Tours
W bex.de

Alternative Berlin (Walking Tours)
W alternativeberlin.com

Berliner Unterwelten (Underground History Tours)
W berliner-unter welten.de

→ Die Welt helium balloon and nearby tourist kiosks *(inset)*

Die Welt Balloon

The sight of the iconic Die Welt helium balloon – one of the world's biggest – hovering over central Berlin is familiar to most residents and visitors. For €23 you can float 152 m (500 ft) over Checkpoint Charlie and enjoy the panoramic views which span major sights like Potsdamer Platz, the Brandenburger Tor, the Tiergarten and Alexanderplatz. Rides usually take 15 minutes but longer options are available, as are helicopter flights from the same company.

Hands-on Museums

From chatting to robots and sending notes via pneumatic tubes at the Museum for Communication, to deciphering machines and negotiating the laser maze at the Spy Museum, Berlin has plenty of hands-on fun. Kids can even get interactive with German history by enjoying a (virtual) drive in a Trabi at the DDR Museum and make their own physics experiments at the Museum of Technology's Spectrum Centre.

←

Tin-can telephone at the Museum für Kommunikation

BERLIN FOR
FAMILIES

Berlin may be marketed as a youthful and entrepreneurial city, but it's also a fantastic destination for families. It offers a multitude of green spaces and waterways for relaxing between activities, inspiring and interactive museums and plenty of family-friendly restaurants and cafés.

Taking a Break

Wherever you're based in the city, you'll never be far away from one of Berlin's magnificent parks, whether it's the sprawling and central Tiergarten, neighbourhood parks like Volkspark Friedrichshain, or the historical and vast Tempelhofer Feld.

KINDERCAFÉS

Unique to Berlin, *Kindercafés* (children's cafés) were created with both children and parents in mind. They merge safe play areas with a seating area selling drinks and snacks. Many also have information boards on local events and some sell nappies and even second-hand toys and children's clothing.

↑ Christmas market ice
rink and a boat ride on
the Spree *(inset)*

Outdoor Fun

Whether winter or summer, there is always
something fun to do outdoors. In summer,
enjoy a boat ride along the Spree, a stroll or
picnic in one of the city's unique parks, or try
your hand at some karaoke in the Mauerpark.
In winter lace up your ice-skates and head
to one of the many lakes dotted in and around
the city, or make use of numerous sledging hills.

Family Favourites

Among the many
popular family
activities in Berlin
are two zoos (plus
an aquarium) and the
LEGOLAND Discovery
Centre. You can also
take the fast elevator
ride up the Fernseh-
turm for panoramic
views of the city and
a slice of cake in the
revolving restaurant.

→
Hippos at Zoo Berlin,
the oldest zoo in
Germany

↑ Family enjoying a stroll
through the Tiergarten
park in central Berlin

World Food

The city's dining scene reflects its increasingly international population, with a wave of cuisines from all around the globe. Nobody blinks any more at seeing Japanese sashimi, Korean kimchi or Peruvian ceviche. Many of these dishes can be found together at street food markets such as those at Markthalle IX and Prenzlauer Berg's Street Food auf Achse. There are also trendy, upscale options like Ryōtei 893, matching contemporary cuisine to swanky interiors.
Try: Cocolo Ramen, The Bird

→

Cheesecake at
Cocolo Ramen
in Kreuzberg

BERLIN FOR
FOODIES

While casual street vendors and unpretentious pubs are still very much a part of the city's foodscape, Berlin's modern dining scene reflects the city's cosmopolitan status with a varied and international selection of mid-range restaurants, as well as numerous Michelin-starred upscale options.

Fine Dining

In 2018, Berlin had some 21 Michelin stars, making it a true fine-dining destination. Although no restaurants have yet bagged the coveted three stars, no less than seven have two stars, and all of them offer serious culinary fireworks – including the recently starred (2018) vegetarian spot Cookies Cream, and the locavore-themed Nobelhart & Schmutzig, which focuses exclusively on ingredients from the Brandenburg region.
Try: Tim Raue, FACIL

←

Chic interior of
Asian-inspired
restaurant Tim Raue

TOP 5 FOOD SHOPS IN BERLIN

KaDeWe Food Hall
w kadewe.de/en/food-restaurants

Rogacki
w rogacki.de

Maitre Philippe
w maitrephilippe.de

Rises Delicacies
w facebook.com/RisesDelicacies

Heide's
w facebook.com/heidesdeli

Unique Street Food

A trip to Berlin just wouldn't be complete without sampling the city's original street food. Every neighbourhood has stalls and kiosks selling snacks like *Currywurst* (sausage mixed with ketchup and curry powder) and *Boulette* (meatballs).
Try: Konnopke, Curry36, Mustafa's

Grilled fish at the Sunday market in Mauerpark ↑

WEEKEND FOOD MARKETS

The Saturday food markets are a vital institution in Berlin, serving not only as places to buy fresh, organic produce, but also as meeting points and local hang-out spots. Each neighbourhood has at least one major market; some of the best are the ones at Kollwitzplatz, Boxhagener Platz and Wittenbergplatz.

Customers enjoying Berlin's oldest beer garden, Prater ↑

German Tradition

It may lack the abundant beer-halls of Bavaria, but Berlin certainly pulls its weight when it comes to serving up traditional German food. As well as standard pub-style restaurants (*Kneipen*), there are also high-end and fusion restaurants carrying German cuisine into new territory.
Try: Prater, Oderquelle, Zur letzten Instanz

Classic Beer Gardens

There's nothing quite like enjoying a frothy beer while watching the summer sun filter gently through the leaves of Berlin's copious chestnut and lime (linden) trees. Prenzlauer Berg's Prater is the city's oldest and simplest beer garden, while the Tiergarten's Café am Neuen See is one of the leafiest, with a lake you can row around, a restaurant, a self-service casual food area and a children's play area. Most beer gardens are open from late April until late September, and usually offer some kind of snacks or meals. They generally get lively between 6 and 10pm.

$\rightarrow$

Lakeside Café am Neuen See in the Tiergarten

BERLIN FOR
BEER LOVERS

Germany's beer culture is world famous, and these days its golden, frothy pilsners and tasty wheat and dark beers are joined by an array of craft beers made in local microbreweries, often using traditional techniques.

TOP 3 TOP GERMAN BEER TYPES

Hefeweizen
The traditional Bavarian Weizenbier ("wheat beer"). The sweetness of the malted wheat is offset by the high carbonation and low hop bitterness.

Berliner Weissbier
A local variation of the Weizenbier. Often served in a bowl-shaped glass with a lager mixer or sweet syrups to balance out the sour taste.

Bock
First brewed in the 14th century, this lager now has many variations. The traditional bock is dark in colour and tastes rich and sweet.

Craft Beer

Berlin's growing interest in the craft beer trend is perfectly captured in the cool aesthetic and international clientele of spots such as the Castle Pub in Mitte and Badfish in Prenzlauer Berg.

$\rightarrow$

Customers enjoying the cool atmosphere of Kreuzberg's riverbank bars

Breweries with Beer Gardens

A microbrewery with its own beer garden really takes your experience to the next level, allowing you to enjoy the brewery's home-produced beers at any time of year – whether inside on a cold winter day or out in the summer sun. Eschenbräu in Wedding has a tavern-like interior plus a fairly large outside terrace, and Brauhaus Südstern in Neukölln is a large pub-style space with a beer garden that backs onto a park.

←

Berliner Pilsners, made at the Berliner-Kindl-Schultheiss brewery

---

DRINK

Herman

This intimate bar has an impressive selection of beers, many from the owner's homeland of Belgium. Be warned: many of them are incredibly strong.

☎ 30 44312854
🏠 Schönhauser Allee 173

€€€€

Hops & Barley

A down-to-earth and friendly pub, with home-brewed beers, simple snacks like sausage for sustenance, and a friendly, mixed crowd.

🏠 Wühlischstrasse 22/23
🌐 hopsandbarley-berlin. de

€€€€

↑ Trendy gastropub Salt 'n' Bone in Prenzlauer Berg

Classic Kneipen

With all the hipster bars and cafés in the city, Berlin's *Kneipen* (traditional pubs) often get overlooked, which is a shame as there are some very fine establishments that combine an excellent beer selection with warm service and a friendly, local ambiance. Dating from 1913, Prenzlauer Berg's Metzer Eck is one of the oldest family-run spots in the city. Leuchtturm in Schöneberg is similarly atmospheric, attracting a mixed but mostly local clientele to its 19th-century interior: German filmmaker Wim Wenders is said to drop by from time to time.

Luxury Fashion

Kurfürstendamm is the boulevard to head to for Chanel, Louis Vuitton, Prada and Gucci. Intersecting Tauentzienstrasse has a swish Peek & Cloppenburg, several upscale stores such as Swarovski and Montblanc, and the renowned KaDeWe department store, which has a fabulous gourmet food area on the sixth floor. Friedrichstrasse's Galerie Lafayette also has a selection of upscale haute couture, including Dior and Miu Miu.

← KaDeWe, the second-largest department store in Europe

BERLIN FOR
SHOPPERS

Berlin has it all in terms of retail, from second-hand stores to Germany's best luxury malls. The city's shops are also strong on antiques, books, art, porcelain and records, and a visit to the city's historical market halls is not to be missed.

↓ Mauerpark flea market in northern Berlin

Local Markets

Most neighbourhoods offer a large market of some kind, usually food on Saturdays and a flea market on Sundays. The food markets at Kollwitzplatz (Prenzlauer Berg) and Boxhagener Platz (Friedrichshain) are especially popular, as are the Mauerpark flea market and Arkonaplatz antiques market.

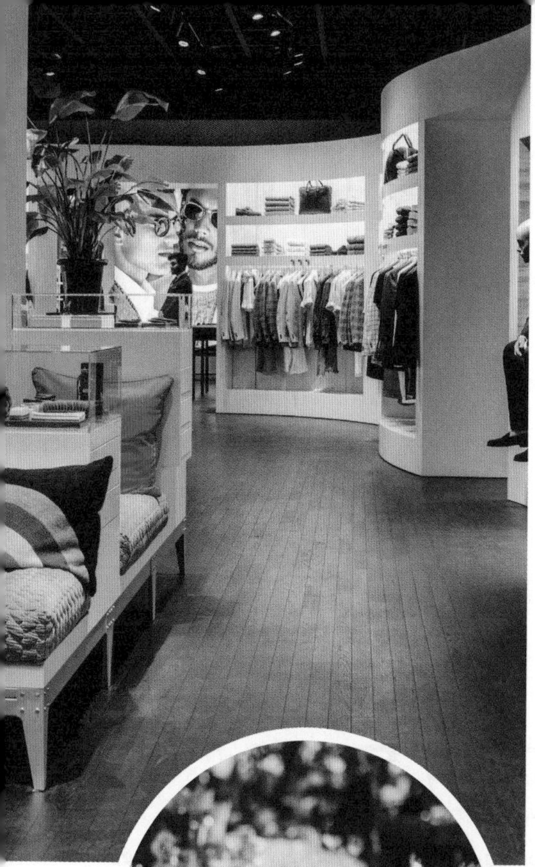

Mitte's High-End Boutiques

Mitte remains the home to Berlin's most cutting-edge designers. Knitwear veteran Claudia Skoda, jewellery designer Esther Perbandt and Wibke Deertz (A.D.Deertz) display their designs along the district's boutique-lined side streets.

← Suitsupply, a fashionable men's clothing store

CHRISTMAS MARKETS

Berlin fights the winter gloom with festive Christmas Markets. They're all slightly different, ranging from the intimate to the spectacular. All offer *Glühwein* (mulled wine), snacks and an assortment of gifts and entertainment.

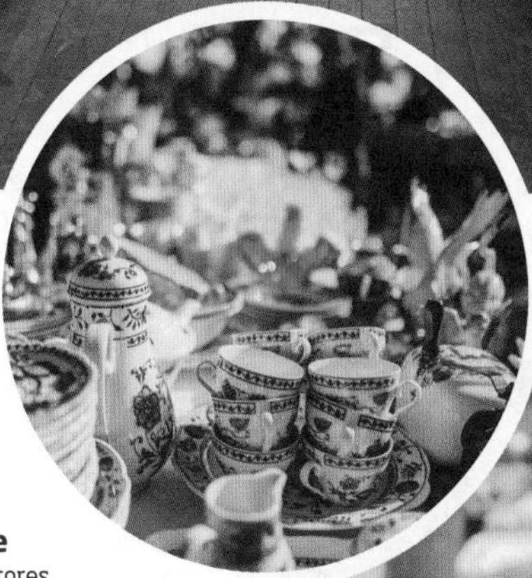

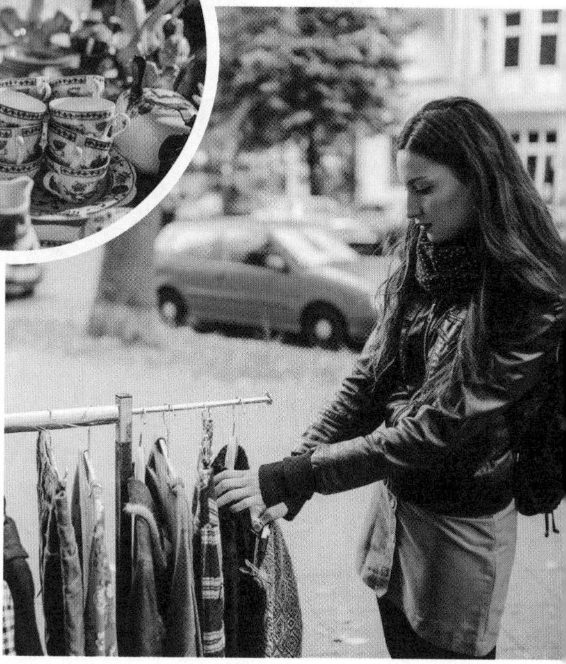

Vintage

Vintage stores are a staple in Berlin, and there's at least one great one in most neighbourhoods. The hugely popular PICKNWEIGHT chain - where you pay by weight - has stores in several areas, and also runs Mitte's Made in Berlin and Garage in Schöneberg. Friedrichshain's Humana Kaufhaus is a one-stop shop for all ages and styles.

→ Vintage tableware *(inset)* and clothes on sale in Berlin

Culture Lovers

Mainstream galleries such as the Daimler Contemporary and Akademie der Künste have regular free entry options, while many of the independent galleries – especially those around Auguststrasse – are usually free. For music lovers, the Philharmonie and Marienkirche have free weekly lunchtime concerts, and Marienkirche offers regular free organ recitals, while jazz fans can enjoy cost-free, high-quality jam sessions at Mitte's B-Flat club.

→

Last Night's Fortune Teller, an exhibition of Chinese art at the Daimler Contemporary

BERLIN ON A
SHOESTRING

Berlin is impressively affordable compared to many western European capitals, and food, beer, accommodation and cultural events can all be enjoyed on a modest budget – some even for free.

↑ Street food dish from Markthalle IX

Classic Berlin Dining

Berlin's farmer's markets offer traditional and cheap take-away options like grilled fish or falafel, as well as providing a great atmosphere where you can experience Berlin like a local. The city is also home to great street food markets – like those every Thursday at Markthalle IX.

> **INSIDER TIP**
> **Bus Routes**
>
> The 100 and 200 buses carry passengers past major city sights such as the Fernsehturm and Brandenburger Tor – all for the price of a bus ticket. Buy a day ticket to hop on and off.

TOP 5 BERLIN HOSTELS

Circus Hostel
North Mitte; Ⓦcircus-
berlin.de/hostel

Generator Hostel
Various; Ⓦgenerator
hostels.com

Ostel
Friedrichshain; Ⓦostel.eu

Grand Hostel
Kreuzberg; Ⓦgrand
hostel-berlin.de

EastSeven
Prenzlauer Berg; Ⓦeast
seven.de

Historical Insights

In Berlin, centuries of fascinating history is free to explore. Iconic sights like the Brandenburg Gate and the Reichstag cost nothing to visit; nor do major wartime and GDR-era sights such as the poignant Holocaust Memorial, the Topography of Terror, the Berlin Wall Memorial and the unmissable East Side Gallery.

← Sun peeking through
Brandenburger Tor on Pariser Platz

Park Secrets

Berlin's city parks offer not only open spaces for walks, picnics and sunbathing, but also insights into local history. Mauerpark contains some remnants of the Berlin Wall, while Tempelhofer Feld's former airport buildings have plenty of relics from the Third Reich and Cold War eras.

↑ Street entertainers
at Mauerpark

Local Parks

Every Berlin neighbourhood has its own *Volkspark* (people's park), which are much loved and well used by locals. Each has its own style and character: Volkspark Friedrichshain, for example, has volleyball and tennis courts, GDR-era memorials and a beautiful fountain covered in fairy-tale statues.

←

Märchenbrunnen, the fairy-tale fountain in Volkspark Friedrichshain

BERLIN'S
GREEN SPACES

Berlin has an unfair reputation for being industrial and grey, but in reality it's bursting with life and colour thanks to a variety of beautiful green spaces – not least the sprawling, sight-studded Grunewald forest in the south-east – as well as numerous waterways and abundant lakes.

BERLIN'S LAKES

Although they're not obvious to first- or even second-time visitors to Berlin, the city is sprinkled with a number of beautiful lakes where locals go to escape the crowds. Some, such as Wannsee in the west and Müggelsee in the east, have official lidos and charge a fee, but others are accessible for free. Two local favourites for their picturesque setting are the Tegeler See and Schlachtensee. There's also the 66 Lake Trail, a 416-km (258-mile) route for hiking or biking, connecting a series of stunning lakes in the state of Brandenburg.

Boats cruising along a peaceful stretch of the Spree river ↓

Vibrant Gardens

The city's gardens come into their own in spring, but can be enjoyed at any time of year. The Botanischer Garten in Dahlem is the big hitter, with a year-round schedule of events, and tropical greenhouses to enjoy in colder months. In the east, the Gärten der Welt offers an array of themed gardens and a Chinese tea pavilion.

→

Plants and colourful flowers *(inset)* in Dahlem's Botanischer Garten

Winding Waterways

Meandering through the city are Berlin's main rivers, the Spree and the Havel, and dotted throughout are a plethora of lakes as well as the Landwehr Canal. These natural spots are perfect for beaches in the summer and ice-skating in the winter, and they're a great place for a stroll all year round.

Pop Concerts

Most of the big pop and rock acts pass through Berlin on their European tours and there are several exciting venues where you can catch them. The most central is the Mercedes-Benz Arena in Friedrichshain, which hosts a mix of German and international stars, while the tent-shaped Tempodrom is one of the city's most popular and idiosyncratic venues.

←

Roger Waters of rock band Pink Floyd, playing at the Olympiastadion

BERLIN FOR
MUSIC LOVERS

Whether you enjoy an evening of classical music or prefer to spend the weekend on the dancefloor, Berlin has it covered. With everything from world-class venues and annual festivals to alternative clubs and infamous parties, you'll find every genre has a home in Berlin.

Inspiring Classical Music

For classical music connoisseurs, and anyone who wants to experience the best of Berlin, a concert at a grand, traditional venue such as the Konzerthaus (p74) will show you why Berlin is one of Europe's leading classical music destinations.

↑ The Berlin Philharmonic at Musikfest Berlin, a classical music festival

Indie Music

Berlin is a magnet for all forms of alternative culture, and music is no exception. Here you can find an array of local, national and global indie stars at cool clubs across the city, including punk favourite SO36 in Kreuzberg. There's also a collection of venues – Cassiopeia, Astra, Suicide Circus – at Friedrichshain's RAW Gelände complex *(p150)*.

←

Lido, a popular alternative music venue in Kreuzberg

CLUBBING IN BERLIN

Berlin and electronic music have gone hand in hand since the Berlin Wall fell to the bass-heavy sound of underground techno. House and techno still rule the roost, with clubs like Berghain, Watergate and Salon zur wilden Renate now legendary for hosting parties that can last for days.

Jazz

Berlin's jazz scene may not get much press, but locals can tell you it remains an integral part of the city's musical landscape. Long-standing traditional jazz venues such as A-Trane, Quasimodo and B-Flat are as popular as ever, thanks to their consistently high-quality line-ups of international and local players. There is also a slew of underground and alternative venues where musicians (both German and global) fuse jazz with soul, pop, rock and electronica. There are also jazz-themed events all year round, culminating in the city's long-running Jazz Festival each November.

↑ Jazz musicians performing at Quasimodo *(inset)* and Jazzfest Berlin

Stunning Views

There's something powerfully romantic about viewing a city from the top of the world. Several spots in Berlin make this possible, from the famous Fernsehturm, the Reichstag dome and Panoramapunkt to well-kept local secrets such as the top of Viktoriapark (Berlin's highest natural point), the Grunewaldturm in the vast Grunewald forest, and restaurants such as Hugos, NENI and the aptly named SkyKitchen.

$\rightarrow$

The tranquil palace grounds of Schloss Charlottenburg

BERLIN FOR
ROMANTICS

Berlin can deliver many moments of surprise, beauty and enchantment for couples on a romantic getaway. There are elegant buildings and gardens to admire during a leisurely city stroll and an endless number of cafés, bars and restaurants where you can stop for a romantic meal along the way.

Beautiful Bridges

Berlin has even more bridges than Venice, providing the perfect setting for a romantic walk where you can admire not only the city scenery but the bridges themselves. Some of the best are the Oberbaumbrücke in Friedrichshain, Schinkel's Schlossbrücke connecting Museumsinsel to Unter den Linden, and the Monbijoubrücke in north Mitte – all of which are decorated with detailed statues of historical or legendary figures. The riverbanks are another great place for a stroll, commanding great views of the cityscape.

$\leftarrow$

Outside bar terrace with a view of the Oberbaumbrücke

Romantic Dinners

Berlin's cafes and restaurants can be surprisingly romantic, thanks to their penchant for intimacy and candlelight. For a classically warm experience, head to one of Berlin's many elegant villa-restaurants, such as Schöneberg's Café Einstein or Café im Literaturhaus in Charlottenburg. Of course, you don't always need fine dining for a romantic meal – instead, enjoy a picnic by the Spree or in one of the city's parks or lakes. The grassy banks of Treptower Park and the secluded Insel der Jugend are especially charming.

← Outside dining on the Gendarmenmarkt

DAY TRIP TO POTSDAM

Potsdam's UNESCO-heritage complex of beautiful palaces and picturesque parks definitely deserves a full day of exploration. Located less than an hour from Berlin by car or train, Potsdam provides the perfect opportunity for a romantic mini-break away from Berlin's city centre.

Hidden Gems

If you're seeking somewhere quiet and secluded, Neukölln's Comenius Gardens are something of a hidden treasure, as is the exquisite fairy-tale Märchenbrunnen fountain in Volkspark Friedrichshain. Many of the parks also have open-air cinemas in summer, and you can rent rowing boats at lakes like the small but charming Neuer See in the Tiergarten.

↑ Couple enjoying a walk in Berlin's Tiergarten park

Berlin Story Bunker, a history museum in Kreuzberg ↓

The Story of Berlin

For an overview of the city's past, Berlin Story Bunker tells the history of the city through 30 multimedia stations featuring films, texts, photos and more. There's also an entire floor dedicated to recreating Hitler's bunker and his final days there in April 1945.

BERLIN'S
HIDDEN GEMS

Berlin's sprawling size, diverse history and idiosyncratic style mean it has plenty of surprises and rewards for those who want a unique experience of the city. Some are hidden in plain sight, while others require a bit of extra effort – exploring beyond the usual tourist areas.

Central Mitte Secrets

The artist-run Haus Schwarzenburg complex is tucked away in a courtyard in the middle of Hackesche Höfe. Inside you'll find a bar, an art-house cinema, a trio of insightful museums and a den of mechanical monsters.

→

Bar patrons enjoying an evening in a Hackesche Höfe courtyard

Stasi: The Secret Police

Berlin's Stasi-Museum is also the former headquarters of the GDR Ministry for State Security. Shortly after the Berlin Wall fell in 1989, the building was seized by demonstrators, who began the project to turn it into a museum. The office of the Stasi head, Erich Mielke, is preserved as part of the three-floor exhibition, which charts the Stasi's various illicit activities.

↓ Uniforms and military equipment on display at the Stasi-Museum

↑ The Olympiastadion in the western suburbs of Berlin

An Infamous Olympic Stadium

Berlin's Olympiastadion is one of the few remaining examples of Third Reich-era architecture, having been built for the 1936 Summer Olympics. Self-guided tours via 45 panels explain the building's usage and include a slew of war-era sights.

A Unique Museum

Blink and you'll miss Kreuzberg's Museum der Dinge (Museum of Things), which is tucked away in the third floor of a factory. Centred around the work of the Deutscher Werkbund (German Association of Craftsmen), it showcases a dizzying range of everyday items designed as a marriage of form and function, from snowglobes and toys to furniture and appliances.

→ Colourful display at Museum der Dinge

A YEAR IN
BERLIN

JANUARY

△ **Mercedes-Benz Fashion Week** *(mid-Jan)*.
Berlin's premier winter fashion event is held at
various locations throughout the city.

Days of Dance Berlin *(first two weeks in Jan)*.
At this contemporary dance festival, up-and-
coming choreographers and local dancers
perform at Sophiensaele, Sophienstrasse 18.

FEBRUARY

Transmediale *(first week in Feb)*. Festival for
media art and digital culture, held at Haus der
Kulturen der Welt.

△ **Berlinale** *(mid–end Feb)*. Various venues join
in the third-largest film festival in the world.

MAY

Re:publica *(first or second week in May)*.
One of the world's largest conferences on
digital culture is held at STATION Berlin.

△ **Carnival of Cultures** *(Whitsun weekend,
exact date varies)*. For three days, the streets
of Kreuzberg come alive with song and dance
displays celebrating multicultural Berlin.

JUNE

△ **Fête de la Musique** *(third Sun in Jun)*.
Local bands and visiting artists from across
Europe play at both indoor and outdoor
venues all over the city.

SEPTEMBER

Berlin Art Week *(mid–end Sep)*.
International and local artists of all styles
and media are exhibited in hundreds of
galleries across the city.

△ **BMW Berlin Marathon** *(third Sun in Sep)*.
This international event attracts thousands
of runners and brings the city's traffic to a
halt for several hours.

OCTOBER

Tag der Deutschen Einheit *(3 Oct)*. Berlin
celebrates the reunification of Germany with
a street festival at the Brandenburg Gate.

△ **Festival of Lights** *(early–mid-Oct)*. Dozens of
modern and historical buildings are illuminated
with magnificent light displays.

MARCH

△ **MaerzMusik** (*mid–end Mar*). A festival for contemporary music, held at Haus der Berliner Festspiele, Schaperstrasse 24.

Festtage (*last week in Mar*). A series of popular concerts and operas performed by world-class musicians at Staatsoper and Philharmonie.

APRIL

△ **Britzer Baumblüte** (*Apr–May*). A month-long spring festival organized in Britz, a suburb in the south of the city famous for its beautiful gardens.

JULY

△ **Classic Open Air** (*early–mid Jul*). Enjoy some outdoor classical music at the Konzerthaus Berlin.

Christopher Street Day (*third or fourth Sat of Jul*). Berlin's main gay pride event is celebrated with a parade around the Ku'damm and many other events across the city.

AUGUST

△ **Tanz im August** (*Aug–Sep*). Dance performances featuring companies and artists from all over the world are held across the city.

Lange Nacht der Museen (*third or fourth Sat in Aug*). Over 100 museums stay open until midnight or later.

NOVEMBER

△ **Jazzfest Berlin** (*first week in Nov*). Experience a world-renowned jazz festival at multiple venues across the city.

Interfilm (*mid–end Nov*). A festival for short films that attracts cinephiles from all over the world.

DECEMBER

△ **Weihnachtsmärkte** (*throughout Dec*). Fairs and festive Christmas gift stalls pop up all over the city to dispel the winter gloom.

Silvester (*31 Dec*). A massive, open-air New Year's Eve party on Strasse des 17 Juni.

1

A BRIEF
HISTORY

Over the course of seven centuries Berlin grew from fishing village to successful trading city and capital of Prussia. Having survived two world wars and over four decades of internal division, it is now the capital of one of the world's leading nations.

From Village to Prosperous Town

Berlin's written history began in the early 13th century, when the twin settlements of Berlin and Cölln grew up on opposite banks of the Spree river, around what is now the Nikolaiviertel (p116). Trading in fish, rye and timber, the towns formed an alliance in 1307, becoming Berlin-Cölln, a deal celebrated by the construction of a joint town hall.

The Hohenzollern Era

In 1411, Friedrich von Hohenzollern became the town's special protector, inaugurating what would become a 500-year rule for

1 A woodcut of the Stadtschloss palace.

2 Friedrich Wilhelm (the Great Elector), ruler of Brandenburg-Prussia from 1640 to 1688.

3 Friedrich II (Frederick the Great) King of Prussia from 1740 to 1786.

4 August Borsig's locomotive factory.

Timeline of events

1244
First written reference to the settlement of Berlin.

1307
Signing of the treaty between Cölln and Berlin.

1415
Friedrich von Hohenzollern appointed Elector of Brandenburg.

1432
Unification of Cölln and Berlin.

1618–48
Thirty Years' War between Habsburg states and other European countries.

the House of Hohenzollern. By 1443 Elector Friedrich II had begun construction of the town's first castle, the future Stadtschloss, which became the Elector's official residence in 1451. The city grew and thrived during the 15th and 16th centuries, but was also decimated by successive epidemics of the bubonic plague and the Thirty Years' War (1618–48), which turned the whole of the Holy Roman Empire into a bloody battlefield. Friedrich Wilhelm von Hohenzollern (later known as the Great Elector; *p215*) ascended the Brandenburg throne in 1640, ushering in a period of unprecedented growth.

Beginnings of the Modern City

Despite Napoleon's defeat of Prussia in 1806 and a subsequent two-year occupation of the city, Berlin grew exponentially throughout the 18th and 19th centuries. A slew of significant rulers, including the "Soldier-King" Friedrich Wilhelm I (1713–40) and Friedrich II (Frederick the Great, 1740–86), oversaw the city's transformation into a sophisticated cultural centre. By the early 19th century Prussia was industrialising rapidly, with August Borsig opening his locomotive factory in Berlin in 1837.

PEACE OF WESTPHALIA

After four years of negotiations, the German states, France and Sweden signed the Peace of Westphalia treaties. This resulted in major losses of territory for Germany, and a new political system emerged, with German princes enjoying complete political independence, under a weakened emperor and pope.

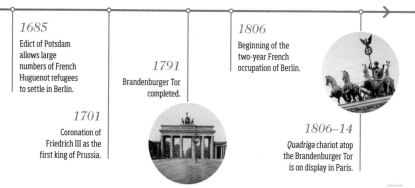

1685
Edict of Potsdam allows large numbers of French Huguenot refugees to settle in Berlin.

1701
Coronation of Friedrich III as the first king of Prussia.

1791
Brandenburger Tor completed.

1806
Beginning of the two-year French occupation of Berlin.

1806–14
Quadriga chariot atop the Brandenburger Tor is on display in Paris.

Building an Empire

Otto von Bismarck was appointed Chancellor under Wilhelm I, with a foreign policy to install Prussia in Austria's place at the head of all German-speaking states. Over the next six years, Prussia declared war on Denmark, Austria and France, acquiring and annexing various new territories. Bismarck's next move was the proclamation of a German Empire on 18 January 1871, with Berlin as its capital and King Wilhelm I as Kaiser (Emperor). Abolition of trade barriers and massive reparations paid by France after her defeat in the Franco-Prussian war (1870–71) led Berlin to enter another period of rapid industrial growth, accompanied by a population explosion (from 300,000 inhabitants in 1850 to 1.9 million by 1900).

Triumph and Disaster

The late 19th century saw an explosion of scientific invention in Berlin, including the completion of a new sewage system in 1876 which dramatically improved public health. By 1879 electric lamps lit the streets and in 1881 the first telephones were installed. A year later the first urban train line, the S-Bahn,

↑ The first German telephone, by Siemens & Halske (1878)

Timeline of events

1844
Opening of the Berlin Zoo (Zoologischer Garten).

1870–1
Franco-Prussian War. Annexation of French territories.

1871
Unification of Germany; Berlin becomes the capital of the German Empire.

1882
Opening of the S-Bahn, the first urban train line.

was opened. Berlin's booming cultural life was headed by such outstanding figures as writer Theodor Fontane and artists Max Liebermann (p245) and Käthe Kollwitz. As the city prospered, however, political developments throughout Europe were moving towards the stalemate of 1914. Initially, the outbreak of World War I had little effect on life in Berlin, but the subsequent famine, strikes and total German defeat led to the November Revolution in 1918, and the abdication of Kaiser Wilhelm II.

The Weimar Republic

A new constitution was signed in the town of Weimar in 1919, and throughout the subsequent "Weimar years" (1919–33) Germany struggled with political and economic instability. In Berlin, urban reform dramatically increased the size of the city, and the population swelled to 3.8 million. The city fell on hard times due to rising unemployment and hyperinflation, but despite this Berlin became the centre of a lively cultural scene. Leading figures included Max Reinhardt (p126) and Bertolt Brecht, and institutions like the Berlin Philharmonic (p166) and UFA film studio (p265) gained worldwide fame.

1 Otto von Bismarck, Prussian statesman and the first Chancellor of the German Empire.

2 *The Artist's Studio*, Max Liebermann, 1902.

3 Playwright and director Bertolt Brecht in his studio, with his colleague Elisabeth Hauptmann.

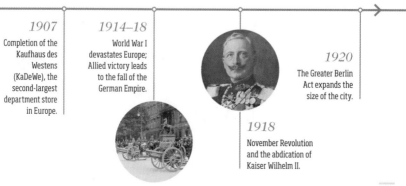

1907
Completion of the Kaufhaus des Westens (KaDeWe), the second-largest department store in Europe.

1914–18
World War I devastates Europe; Allied victory leads to the fall of the German Empire.

1920
The Greater Berlin Act expands the size of the city.

1918
November Revolution and the abdication of Kaiser Wilhelm II.

The Third Reich and World War II

The world stock-market crash of 1929 and the ensuing Depression put the German government under great pressure, paving the way for extremist politicians and the appointment of Adolf Hitler as Chancellor in 1933. The Reichstag fire in February of that year was used as a pretext to arrest Communist and liberal opponents, and, by March 1933, Hitler's Nazi (National Socialist German Workers) Party was in control. Hitler's invasion of Poland in 1939 signalled the start of World War II and in January 1942, the systematic extermination of all European Jews began. Finally, after years of bitter warfare, the tide began to turn against the Germans. In April 1945 more than 1.5 million Soviet soldiers invaded Berlin, where they found the populace starving and the city lying in ruins. Hitler committed suicide shortly after and Germany conceded defeat.

Divided City and Reunification

At the Potsdam Conference of 1945 (p262), Berlin was divided into four sectors, occupied by Soviet, US, British and French troops. This put the city at the centre of the Cold War (1947–91),

↑ An Allied soldier finds the head of a broken Hitler statue in the ruins of Berlin.

Timeline of events

1933

Hitler accedes to power.

1939–45

World War II; much of Berlin damaged or destroyed during air raids and the Battle of Berlin.

1961

Construction of the Berlin Wall begins, with the installation of barbed-wire fencing.

1963

US President John F Kennedy proclaims "*Ich bin ein Berliner*" ("I am a Berliner") in a speech in Schöneberg.

between the Soviet Union and the US and NATO. Tensions increased in 1949 with the birth of two German states: the Federal Republic of Germany in the west, and the German Democratic Republic (GDR) in the east. East Berlin became the capital of the GDR, and the isolated West Berlin remained a separate enclave of western Germany in the heart of the Communist eastern state. It was eventually enclosed by the Berlin Wall for 28 years, and GDR authorities shot at any refugees attempting to cross the border. The political changes that swept across Eastern Europe in 1989 led to the fall of the Wall, and on 3 October 1990 Germany was officially reunified.

Berlin Today

Berlin's cutting-edge cultural scene attracts visitors from all over the world. People are also drawn to the city's relatively affordable rents and burgeoning opportunities in the creative and start-up business sectors. With several LGBT+ districts and a large population of immigrants, the city's tolerant and inclusive atmosphere continues to make Berlin a model city for communities around the globe.

[1] Ruins of the Reichstag after the 1933 fire. ↑

[2] Adolf Hitler, Chancellor of Nazi Germany, saluting German troops.

[3] Fall of the Berlin Wall.

[4] A street in present-day Prenzlauer Berg.

Did You Know?

The Berlin Wall was about 155 km (96 miles) long and 3.6 m (11.8 ft) high.

1989

New border crossing regulations lead to the fall of the Berlin Wall on 9 November.

1990

Official reunification of Germany on 3 October, with the merging of the Federal Republic of Germany and the German Democratic Republic.

1991

Berlin becomes the capital of reunified Germany on 20 June.

2014

Germany wins the World Cup; celebration of the 25th anniversary of the fall of the Berlin Wall.

EXPERIENCE

DZ Bank building on Pariser Platz

Schiller's Monument and the Deutscher Dom

AROUND UNTER DEN LINDEN

The poetic name of central Mitte's grand boulevard Unter den Linden (Under the Linden Trees) comes from the trees that line part of this avenue between the Stadtschloss city palace and the Brandenburg Gate.

The area's development began in the Baroque period with the establishment of Dorotheenstadt to the north and Friedrichstadt to the south. From the early 18th century, prestigious buildings began to appear here, and over the following two centuries Unter den Linden became one of the city's most imposing avenues. World War II bombing took a heavy toll but, despite only partial reconstruction by the East German government, the area is still home to the highest concentration of historic buildings in Berlin.

AROUND UNTER DEN LINDEN

Must See
① Zeughaus (DHM)

Experience More
② Maxim Gorki Theater
③ Staatsbibliothek
④ Palais am Festungsgraben
⑤ Humboldt Universität
⑥ Neue Wache
⑦ Reiterdenkmal Friedrichs des Grossen
⑧ Altes Palais
⑨ Pierre Boulez Saal
⑩ Kronprinzenpalais
⑪ Staatsoper Unter den Linden
⑫ St-Hedwigs-Kathedrale
⑬ Alte Bibliothek
⑭ Unter den Linden
⑮ Komische Oper
⑯ Französischer Dom
⑰ Akademie der Künste
⑱ Konzerthaus
⑲ Friedrichstadtpassagen
⑳ Gendarmenmarkt
㉑ Deutscher Dom
㉒ Cold War Black Box
㉓ Ehemaliges Regierungsviertel
㉔ Holocaust Denkmal
㉕ Asisi Panorama Berlin
㉖ Museum für Kommunikation
㉗ Admiralspalast
㉘ Brandenburger Tor
㉙ Russische Botschaft
㉚ Bahnhof Friedrichstrasse
㉛ Pariser Platz

Eat
① Augustiner am Gendarmenmarkt

Stay
② Clipper City Home
③ Hotel Adlon

Shop
④ Galeries Lafayette
⑤ Quartier 206 Art & Fashion House

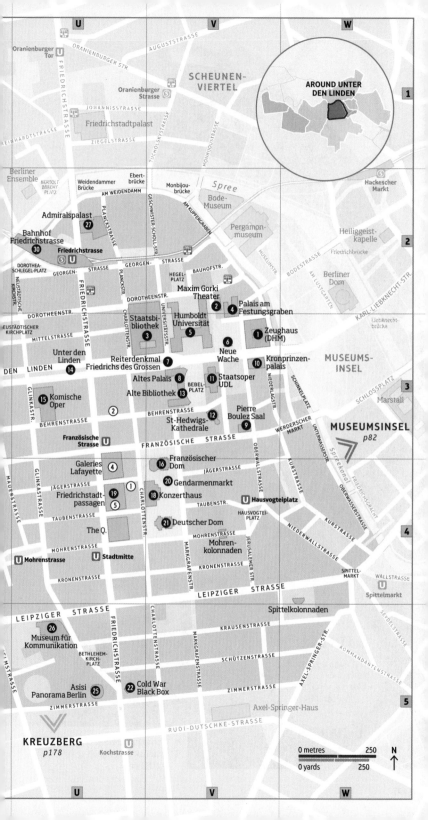

↑ The exhibition hall extension, designed by I M Pei

❶ ⊘ Ⓜ ▱ ♙

ZEUGHAUS (DHM)

⬙ V3 ⌂ Unter den Linden 2
Ⓢ & Ⓤ Friedrichstrasse Ⓢ Hackescher Markt
🚌 100, 200 🕙 10am–6pm daily 🌐 dhm.de

Housed in the oldest building on Unter den Linden, this museum explores the history of Germany through a fascinating collection of art, militaria, historical documents, film and crafts.

This former arsenal (*Zeughaus*) was built in the Baroque style in 1706. It is a magnificent structure; its wings surround an inner courtyard and the exterior is decorated with Schlüter's sculptures. Since 1952 it has housed the Deutsches Historisches Museum (German History Museum), which has a permanent exhibition that contains over one million objects about German history. In 2003, a strikingly curvaceous, glass-walled exhibition hall was added, designed by Walter Gropius student I M Pei. Its four different levels are used for temporary exhibitions about significant historical events.

↑ *Gloria Victis,* by Antonin Mercié, is a moving allegory inspired by the death of the artist's friend

↑ The outstanding Zeughaus building, one of the best examples of Baroque architecture in Berlin

↑ Portrait of Martin Luther, painted by Lucas Cranach the Elder in 1529

GALLERY GUIDE

The ground floor houses exhibits from 1918 to the present. The first floor contains collections dating from early civilizations and the Middle Ages right up to the beginning of the 20th century. A subterranean pathway links the Zeughaus to the temporary shows in the exhibition hall.

EXPERIENCE MORE

②

Maxim Gorki Theater

🚇 V2 🚌 Am Festungs-
graben 2 📞 20 22 11 15
Ⓢ & Ⓤ Friedrichstrasse
🚌 100, 200 🚊 M1

The Maxim Gorki theatre was once a singing school or *Sing-Akademie*. Berlin's oldest concert hall, it was built in 1827 by Carl Theodor Ottmer, who based his design on drawings by Karl Friedrich Schinkel *(p28)*. This modest Neo-Classical building, with its attractive façade resembling a Greco-Roman temple, was well known for the excellent acoustic qualities of its concert hall.

Many famous composer-musicians have performed here, including the violinist Niccolò Paganini and pianist Franz Liszt. In 1829, Felix Mendelssohn-Bartholdy conducted a performance of the *St Matthew Passion* by Johann Sebastian Bach here. It was the first time that the work had been performed in front of an audience since the composer's death in 1750. Following reconstruction after World War II, the building became a theatre.

③

Staatsbibliothek

🚇 U3 🚌 Unter den Linden 8
Ⓢ & Ⓤ Friedrichstrasse
🚌 100, 200 🕐 9am–9pm
Mon–Fri, 10am–5pm Sat
🌐 staatsbibliothek-berlin.de

The nucleus of the State Library collection was the library of the Great Elector, Friedrich Wilhelm *(p215)*, founded in 1661, first situated in the Stadtschloss and later moved to the Alte Bibliothek building. Its current home was designed by Ernst von Ihne and completed in 1914 on the site of the Academy of Science and the Academy of Fine Arts. This impressive building was severely damaged during World War II and underwent extensive restoration. The collection, of some three million books and periodicals, was scattered during the war. A collection of priceless music manuscripts ended up in the Jagiellonian Library in Krakow, Poland.

After the war only part of the collection was returned to the building in Unter den Linden, and the rest was held in West Berlin. Since reunification, both collections are once again under the same administration.

---

④

Palais am Festungsgraben

🚇 V2 🚌 Am Festungs-
graben 1 📞 618 14 60
Ⓢ Friedrichstrasse 🚌 100, 200 🚊 M1

The Festungsgraben Palace is one of the few structures in this part of town that retains its original interior décor. Built as a small Baroque palace in 1753, it owes its present form to major extension work, carried out in 1864 in the style of Karl Friedrich Schinkel, by Heinrich Bürde and Hermann von der Hude.

The late Neo-Classical style of the building is reminiscent of Schinkel's later designs. The interior includes a magnificent double-height marble hall in the Neo-Renaissance style which was modelled on the White Room in the former

WILHELM AND ALEXANDER VON HUMBOLDT

The Humboldt brothers rank among the most distinguished Berlin citizens. Wilhelm (1767–1835) was a lawyer and politician, occupying various government posts. It was on his initiative that the Berlin University (later renamed Humboldt University) was founded, and he conducted studies in comparative and historical linguistics there. Alexander, shown right (1769–1859), a professor at the university, researched natural science, including meteorology, oceanography and agricultural science.

↑ Neo-Classical façade of the Neue Wache

Stadtschloss *(p96)*. In 1934 one ground-floor room was turned into a music salon, and many musical instruments were brought here from the 19th-century house (now demolished) of wealthy merchant and manufacturer Johann Weydinger (1773–1837).

The palace is now used for private events.

---

❺

Humboldt Universität

📍 V3 🚇 Unter den Linden 6
📞 20930 Ⓢ & Ⓤ Friedrichstrasse 🚌 100, 200

The university building was constructed in 1753 for Prince Heinrich of Prussia, the brother of Frederick the Great. The university was founded in 1810 on the initiative of Wilhelm von Humboldt. It became the Berlin University but was renamed in von Humboldt's honour in 1949.

The overall design of the palace, with its main block and the courtyard enclosed within a pair of wings, has been extended many times. Two marble statues (1883) by Paul Otto stand at the entrance gate and represent Wilhelm von Humboldt (holding a book) and his brother Alexander, a famous explorer (sitting on a globe). The entrance gate leads to the courtyard, designed by Reinhold Begas.

Many famous scholars have worked at the university, including philosophers Fichte and Hegel, physicians Rudolf Virchow and Robert Koch, and physicists Max Planck and Albert Einstein. Among its graduates are Heinrich Heine, Karl Marx and Friedrich Engels.

After World War II, the university was in the Russian sector of the divided city and the difficulties encountered by the students of the western zone led to the establishment of a new university in 1948 – the Freie Universität *(p248)*.

---

❻

Neue Wache

📍 V3 🚇 Unter den Linden 4
Ⓢ Hackescher Markt
🚌 100, 200 🕐 10am–6pm daily

This war memorial, designed by Karl Friedrich Schinkel and built in the 1810s, is one of the finest examples of Neo-Classical architecture in Berlin. Its façade is dominated by a huge Doric portico with a frieze of bas-reliefs depicting goddesses of victory. On the triangular tympanum above the pediment are allegorical representations of Battle, Victory, Flight and Defeat.

EAT

Augustiner am Gendarmenmarkt
Hearty German fare (knuckle of pork, beef goulash) can be found at this Bavarian pub, which overlooks the Gendarmenmarkt, one of Berlin's most beautiful squares.

🚇 U4 🏠 Charlottenstrasse 55 📞 204 540 20

€€€

In the 1930s the building, originally a royal guardhouse, was turned into a monument to soldiers killed during World War I. In 1960, following its restoration, Neue Wache became the Memorial to the Victims of Fascism and Militarism. In 1993 it was again rededicated, this time to the memory of all victims of war and dictatorship.

Inside the building is a granite slab over the ashes of an unknown soldier, a resistance fighter and a concentration camp prisoner. Under the circular opening in the roof is a copy of the 20th-century sculpture *Mother with her Dead Son*, by Berlin artist Käthe Kollwitz, who lost her own son in World War I.

→ The modular design of the Pierre Boulez Saal

7

Reiterdenkmal Friedrichs des Grossen

V3 **Unter den Linden** **S & U Friedrichstrasse** **100, 200**

This equestrian statue of Frederick the Great is one of the most famous monuments in Berlin, featuring a massive bronze statue 5.6 m (18.5 ft) in height and standing on the centre lane of Unter den Linden. It was designed by Christian Daniel Rauch and completed in 1851. It depicts Frederick the Great on horseback, wearing a uniform and a royal cloak. The base of the high plinth is surrounded by statues of famous military leaders, politicians, scientists and artists. The top tier of the plinth is decorated with bas-relief scenes from the life of Frederick the Great. Out of line with GDR ideology, the monument was moved to Potsdam, where it stood by the Hippodrome in Park Sanssouci (p250) until its return in 1980.

8

Altes Palais

V3 **Unter den Linden 9** **S & U Friedrichstrasse** **100, 200**

The Neo-Classical Old Palace, near the former Opernplatz (Bebelplatz), was built for the heir to the throne – Prince Wilhelm (later Kaiser Wilhelm I). The Kaiser lived here all his life. He was able to watch the changing of the guards every day from the ground-floor window on the far left.

The palace, built in the 1830s, was designed by Carl Ferdinand Langhans. Its splendid furnishings were destroyed during World War II but the palace was subsequently restored and is now used by Humboldt Universität (p69).

← Frederick the Great astride his bronze steed

> The early Neo-Classical façade of the State Opera House is one of the most beautiful sights along Unter den Linden.

⑩

Kronprinzenpalais

🚩 V3 🏠 Unter den Linden 3
Ⓢ & Ⓤ Friedrichstrasse
🚌 100, 200, TXL

The striking, late Neo-Classical Crown Prince's Palace takes its name from its original inhabitants – the heirs to the royal, and later to the imperial, throne. Its form is the outcome of numerous changes made to what was originally a modest house dating from 1669. The first extensions, designed in the late Baroque style, were conducted by Philipp Gerlach in the 1730s. Between 1856 and 1857 Johann Heinrich Strack added the second floor. These extensions were rebuilt following World War II.

The palace served the royal family until the abolition of the monarchy. Under Communist rule it was renamed Palais Unter den Linden and reserved for official government guests. It was here, on 31 August 1990, that the pact was signed paving the way for reunification to begin.

Next to the palace, at Unter den Linden 1, is where the Kommandantur, the official quarters of the city's garrison commander, once stood. Totally destroyed during the last days of World War II, the original façade was rebuilt in 2003 by the giant German media company Bertelsmann, as part of their Berlin headquarters. Today, the building is mainly used for staging large exhibitions.

Joined to the main palace by an overhanging passageway is the smaller Prinzessinnenpalais (Princesses' Palace), built for the daughters of Friedrich Wilhelm III.

Today, behind the Baroque façade, a modern venue called PalaisPopulaire displays the Deutsche Bank's art collection. The ground-floor café, LePopulaire, offers traditional coffee and cake with stunning view of Berlin's landmarks.

⑪

Staatsoper Unter den Linden

🚩 V3 🏠 Unter den Linden 7
Ⓢ & Ⓤ Friedrichstrasse
🚌 100, 200, TXL
🕐 Opening times vary, see website for details
🌐 staatsoper-berlin.de

The early Neo-Classical façade of the State Opera House is one of the most beautiful sights along Unter den Linden. It was built by Georg Wenzeslaus von Knobelsdorff in 1741–3, but has been rebuilt and restored several times: in the 1840s after a fire, after World War II and after water damage in the GDR era. The latest works, completed in 2017, resulted in magical acoustics and much more comfortable seats.

The building is the home of the Berlin State Opera and has played host to stellar singers, musicians and artists; one of its directors and conductors was Richard Strauss. Audiences can expect Baroque opera as well as new productions.

> **€400,000,000**
> ———
> The cost of the refurbishment of the Staatsoper: almost double the original estimate.

---

⑨ Ⓜ️ 🖥️

Pierre Boulez Saal

🚩 V3 🏠 Französische Strasse 33D Ⓢ & Ⓤ Friedrichstrasse Ⓤ Hausvogteiplatz 🚌 100, 200, N2, TXL 🚋 M1, M12 🕐 Opening times vary, see website for details 🌐 boulezsaal.de

This concert hall opened in 2017 as part of the Barenboim-Said Akademie – an institution formed in continuation of Edward Said and Daniel Barenboim's West-Eastern Divan Orchestra to focus on music education in the humanistic tradition of the orchestra. American architect Frank Gehry has given the Pierre Boulez Saal impeccable acoustics and an intimate layout that ensures that no audience member is more than 14 m (50 ft) from the conductor. The hall hosts a diverse chamber music programme throughout the year, featuring both orchestras and soloists, with regular performances from the in-house Boulez Ensemble. There are also concerts for children.

→ Lime (linden) trees on Unter den Linden

12

St-Hedwigs-Kathedrale

📍V3 🏛Bebelplatz
Ⓢ&Ⓤ Hausvogteiplatz
🚌100, 200, TXL ⏰10am-5pm Mon-Wed, Fri & Sat; 11am-5pm Thu; 1-5pm Sun 🔒Closed for renovations 🌐hedwigs-kathedrale.de

The massive church of St Hedwig, set back from the road and crowned with a copper dome, is the Catholic Cathedral of the Roman Archdiocese of Berlin. It was built to serve the Catholics of Silesia (part of present-day Poland), which became part of the Kingdom of Prussia in 1742 following defeat in the Silesian Wars of 1740–63.

The initial design, by Georg Wenzeslaus von Knobelsdorff, was similar to the Roman Pantheon. Construction began in 1747 and the cathedral was consecrated in 1773, although work continued on and off until 1778. Its design was modified repeatedly. Later, additional work was carried out from 1886 to 1887. The cathedral was badly damaged during World War II, and rebuilt between 1952 and 1963.

The crypt holds the tombs of many bishops of Berlin. It is also the resting place of Bernhard Lichtenberg (1875–1943), a priest killed in a concentration camp and beatified as a martyr by Pope John Paul II.

13

Alte Bibliothek

📍V3 🏛Bebelplatz 1
📞20930 Ⓢ&Ⓤ Friedrichstrasse 🚌100, 200

The Old Library, known by locals as the *Kommode* or "chest of drawers" after its curved façade, is one of the city's most beautiful Baroque buildings. It was designed by Georg Christian Unger and built around 1775 to house the royal library collection. Unger based his design on an unrealized plan for an extension to the Hofburg complex in Vienna by Josef Emanuel Fischer von Erlach some 50 years earlier. The concave façade of the building is accentuated by the insertion of three breaks, surrounded at the top by a row of massive Corinthian pilasters. The building now houses the law faculty of Humboldt University.

14

Unter den Linden

📍U3 Ⓢ&Ⓤ Brandenburger Tor 🚌100, 200, TXL

One of the most famous streets in Berlin, Unter den Linden starts at Schlossplatz *(p96)* and runs down to the Brandenburg Gate *(p78)* and Pariser Platz. It was once the route to the royal hunting grounds that were later transformed into the Tiergarten *(p170)*. In the 17th century the street was planted with lime trees, to which it owes its name. The current trees were planted in the 1950s.

During the 18th century, Unter den Linden became the main street of the westward-growing city. It was gradually filled with prestigious buildings, many of which were restored after World War II. Today it also has several cafés and restaurants, as well as many smart shops. This street is also the venue for many interesting outdoor events; it is usually crowded with tourists and students browsing the bookstalls around the Humboldt Universität *(p69)* and the Staatsbibliothek.

Did You Know?

Many of the trees on Unter den Linden were chopped down for firewood during World War II.

⑮

Komische Oper

📍 U3 🏠 Behrenstrasse 55/57 ⑤ & Ⓤ Brandenburger Tor Ⓤ Französische Strasse 🚌 100, 147, 200 🌐 komische-oper-berlin.de

Looking at the modern façade of the Comic Opera theatre, it is hard to believe that it hides one of Berlin's most impressive interiors. Built in 1892, it has served as a variety theatre and as the German National Theatre, and has only housed the Komische Oper since World War II. The postwar reconstruction deprived the building of its former façades but the beautiful Viennese Neo-Baroque interior remained, full of stuccoes and gilded ornaments. Particularly interesting are the expressive, dynamically posed statues on the pilasters of the top balcony – the work of Theodor Friedel. The Komische Oper is one of Berlin's three leading opera companies, presenting extravagant and contemporary renditions musicals, operas and operettas.

⑯ ⌗

Französischer Dom

📍 V4 🏠 Gendarmenmarkt 6 Ⓤ Stadtmitte, Französische Strasse 🕐 Opening times vary, see website for details 🌐 franzoesischer-dom.de

The French Cathedral stands facing its German counterpart, the Deutscher Dom (p75), across the Gendarmenmarkt square. It was built for the French Huguenot community, who found refuge in Protestant Berlin following their expulsion from France after the revocation of the Edict of Nantes. The main building of the church, completed in 1705, was modelled on the Huguenot church in Charenton, France, which was destroyed in 1688. The entrance, on the west elevation (facing Charlottenstrasse), leads to an uncomplicated interior with a rectangular nave and semicircular sections on both sides. It features a late Baroque organ from 1754.

The structure is dominated by a massive, cylindrical tower which is encircled by Corinthian porticoes at its base. It was added around 1785, some 80 years after the church was built. It houses the Huguenot Museum, which details the history of the Huguenots in France and Brandenburg. Well-educated and highly skilled, they played a crucial part in Berlin's rise as a city of science, craft and commerce. The French language they brought with them survives to this day in many words used in the Berlin dialect.

⑰

Akademie der Künste

📍 T3 🏠 Pariser Platz 4 ⑤ & Ⓤ Brandenburger Tor 🚌 100, 200, TXL 🕐 10am–10pm daily 🌐 adk.de

The modern glass and steel façade of the Academy of Arts belies its historic and noble origins. Founded in 1696 by Prussian King Frederick I, it was one of Europe's first such institutions. Today its primary role is advising and supporting the German government in affairs of art and culture. It also houses a prestigious archive and hosts contemporary art exhibitions.

Main entrance of the Französischer Dom, built for the dispossessed French Huguenots ↓

18
Konzerthaus

🚇 V4 🅐 Gendarmenmarkt 2 Ⓤ Stadtmitte, Französische Strasse
🌐 konzerthaus.de

A late Neo-Classical jewel, the magnificent Concert Hall, formerly known as the Schauspielhaus, is one of the greatest achievements of Berlin's best-known architect, Karl Friedrich Schinkel *(p28)*.

It was built between 1818 and 1821 around the ruins of Carl Gotthard Langhans' National Theatre, which was destroyed by fire in 1817. The original portico columns were retained. Schinkel was responsible for the architectural structure and for the interior design, down to the door handles. Following bomb damage in World War II, it was reconstructed as a concert hall with a different interior layout. The exterior was restored to its former glory. The Konzerthaus is home to the Konzerthausorchester (formerly the Berlin Symphony Orchestra).

The theatre façade includes a huge Ionic portico with a set of stairs that was only used by the middle classes (the upper classes entered via a separate entrance where they could leave their horse-drawn carriages). The whole building is richly decorated with sculptures alluding to drama and music: statues of musical geniuses mounted on lions and panthers, as well as figures representing the Muses and a Bacchanal procession. The façade is crowned with the sculpture of Apollo riding a chariot pulled by griffins.

In front of the theatre stands a shining white marble statue of the poet and philosopher Friedrich Schiller.

It was sculpted by Reinhold Begas, and erected in 1869. Removed by the Nazis during the 1930s, the monument was finally returned to its rightful place in 1988. Schiller's head was copied by the sculptor from a bust of the poet created in 1794 by Johann Heinrich Dannecker. The statue is mounted on a high pedestal surrounded by allegorical figures representing Lyric Poetry, Drama, Philosophy and History.

19
Friedrichstadtpassagen

🚇 U4 🅐 Friedrichstrasse Quartier 205, 206, 207
Ⓤ Französische Strasse, Stadtmitte

This group of passages is part of a huge development of luxury shops, offices, restaurants and apartments built along Friedrichstrasse.

Quartier 207 is the famous Galeries Lafayette, a branch of the French department store occupying a charming building designed by Jean Nouvel and constructed almost entirely of glass. The building's axis is formed by an inner courtyard, which is defined by two glass cones with their bases facing each other. The highly reflective glass panes, together with the multicoloured stands that are clustered around the structure, make an extraordinary impression on the visitor.

The next passage, Quartier 206, has offices and smart luxury boutiques, and is the work of the American design team Pei Cobb Freed & Partners. The building owes its alluring, but somewhat nouveau-riche, appearance to the use of forms inspired by Art Deco architecture, including sophisticated details and expensive stone cladding.

The southernmost building in the complex, and the largest passage, is Quartier 205 – now called "The Q" – another complex of shops, designed by Oswald Mathias Ungers.

→
Quartier 206 in the Friedrichstadtpassagen

↑ The Deutscher Dom, overlooking the expansive Gendarmenmarkt

⑳

Gendarmenmarkt

🚩 V4 Ⓤ Stadtmitte, Französische Strasse

This is one of Berlin's most beautiful squares, created at the end of the 17th century as a marketplace for the newly established Friedrichstadt. It is named after the Regiment Gens d'Armes, who stabled their horses here. Two cathedrals with magnificent towers, the Deutscher Dom and the Französischer Dom (p73), stand on each side with the Konzerthaus (p74) in the middle.

㉑

Deutscher Dom

🚩 V4 🏠 Gendarmenmarkt 1 Ⓤ Stadtmitte, Französische Strasse 📞 22 73 04 31 🕐 May-Sep: 10am-7pm Tue-Sun; Oct-Apr: 10am-6pm Tue-Sun

The German Cathedral at the southern end of Gendarmenmarkt, to the left of the Konzerthaus, is an old German Protestant-Reformed church built in 1708 by Giovanni Simonetti. The design was based on a five-petal shape, and in 1785 it acquired a dome-covered tower identical to that of the French Cathedral across the square. Burned down in 1945, the church was finally rebuilt in 1993. Its exterior was painstakingly reconstructed, including its sculpted decorations. The interior is now modern and hosts an exhibition, *"Wege, Irrwege, Umwege"* ("Paths, Confusions, Detours"), about Germany's parliamentary democracy.

㉒

Cold War Black Box

🚩 U5 🏠 Friedrichstrasse 47 Ⓢ & Ⓤ Potsdamer Platz Ⓤ Stadtmitte, Kochstrasse 🚌 M29, M48 🕐 10am-6pm daily 🌐 bfgg.de

Located directly across from the always-packed Haus am Checkpoint Charlie (p191), the Cold War Black Box provides a quieter, more measured look at the Cold War years. Throughout its intimate, black-walled space, it tackles big-hitter topics such as nuclear war and espionage, as well as peace and democracy.

The exhibition comprises around 500 items, including GDR-era grenades once used for practice by school children, a machine to measure radioactivity and a Soviet photo gun used for reconnaissance missions. There are also several media stations with film excerpts, interviews, photos, and explorations of international connections with the Korean War and the Cuban missile crisis.

SHOP

Galeries Lafayette

This sleek Parisian import sells an array of French and international brands in its many departments, ranging from beauty products to clothing and gourmet delicacies.

🚩 U4 🏠 Französische Strasse 23 🕐 10am-8pm Mon-Sat 🌐 galerieslafayette.de

---

Quartier 206 Art & Fashion House

Next door to Galeries Lafayette is this Art Deco complex with even more fashion stores.

🚩 U4 🏠 Friedrichstrasse 71 🕐 10:30am-7:30pm Mon-Sat 🌐 q206berlin.de

23

Ehemaliges Regierungsviertel

◘ T5 ◙ Wilhelmstrasse, Leipziger Strasse, Voss Strasse Ⓤ Potsdamer Platz, Mohrenstrasse

The name means "former government district", because Wilhelmstrasse, and the area situated to the west of it up to Leipziger Platz (p165), was where the main government departments had offices from the mid-19th century until 1945. The building at Voss Strasse No. 77 was once the Reich's Chancellery and Otto von Bismarck's office, and from 1933 it served as the office of Adolf Hitler. It was from here that Hitler, his senior staff and his mistress Eva Braun withdrew to the Führerbunker, an elaborate underground complex that served as both command centre and residence.

In the spring of 1945 the square was the scene of such fierce fighting that after World War II most of the damaged buildings had to be torn down. Among those that survived are the former Prussian Landtag offices – the huge complex occupying the site between Leipziger and Niederkirchner Strasse. This building, designed in the Italian Renaissance style, was designed by Friedrich Schulze, and constructed between 1892 and 1904. It consists of two segments: the section on the side of Leipziger Strasse (No. 3–4) once housed the upper chamber of the National Assembly (the Herrenhaus) and is now used by the Bundesrat. The building on the side of Niederkirchner Strasse (No. 5) is the former seat of the Landtag's lower chamber, and is now the Berliner Abgeordnetenhaus (House of Representatives).

The other surviving complex is the former Ministry of Aviation, at Leipziger Strasse No. 5, built for Hermann Göring in 1936 by Ernst Sagebiel. This awesome building is typical of the architecture of the Third Reich.

FÜHRERBUNKER

The specific location of Hitler's bunker was kept a secret for many decades to deter neo-Nazi pilgrims. Destroyed and flooded after World War II, the area now hosts an aptly unimpressive car parking area and a huddle of GDR-era residential buildings. An information board installed by the nonprofit Berliner Unterwelten group (which runs fascinating tours of other bunkers and subterranean historic sites throughout the city) shows the layout of the structure.

← A small corner of the massive Holocaust Denkmal

STAY

Clipper City Home
The 59 smart apartments offered here range from compact studios to deluxe options. All feature kitchens with Nespresso machines and microwaves, refrigerators, desks, designer bathrooms and free Wi-Fi.

QU3 **A**Behren-strasse 47 **W**clipper-boardinghouses.de

€€€

Hotel Adlon
This glamorous hotel has a stellar historic guest list, from Greta Garbo to Barack Obama. It remains one of the best addresses in town thanks to sumptuous rooms, several high-end restaurants and a vast, two-storey spa.

QT3 **A**Unter den Linden 77 **W**hoteladlon. grandluxuryhotels.com

€€€

24

Holocaust Denkmal

QS/T4 **A**Ebertstrasse **C**28 04 59 60 **S**&**U**Bran-denburger Tor **=**100, 200 **Q**Apr-Sep: 10am-8pm Tue-Sun; Oct-Mar: 10am-7pm Tue-Sun **Q**Mon

The Holocaust Memorial for the Jews killed by the Nazis between 1933 and 1945 was inaugurated in 2005. It covers 19,000 sq m (205,000 sq ft) next to the Brandenburg Gate. Above ground, visitors walk through an undulating field of concrete slabs; below lies an information centre on the history of the genocide.

25

Asisi Panorama Berlin

QU5 **A**Friedrichstrasse 205 **S**&**U**Potsdamer Platz **U**Stadtmitte, Kochstrasse **=**M48, M29 **Q**10am-6pm daily **W**asisi.de

Turkish-German artist Yadegar Asisi paints enormous, highly detailed panoramas known

for their sense of realism. His Berlin panorama is 15 m (49 ft) high, 60 m (196 ft) wide and set inside a large cylindrical structure next to Checkpoint Charlie. It depicts a fictional day along a stretch of the Berlin Wall in the 1980s. On one side is Kreuzberg, complete with punks, run-down buildings and daily West Berlin life; on the other side, an eerily quiet Mitte, all border fortifications, no people and the TV tower looming in the distance. With a soundtrack by film composer Eric Babak, the experience is absorbing and unexpectedly moving.

26

Museum für Kommunikation

QU5 **A**Leipziger Strasse 16 **U**Stadtmitte, Mohren-strasse **=**200, 265, M48 **Q**9am-8pm Tue, 9am-5pm Wed-Fri, 10am-6pm Sat & Sun **W**mfk-berlin.de

Founded in 1872 as the Post Office Museum, the Museum of Communication is the

world's oldest establishment of its kind. Soon after it was founded, it moved into the corner of the huge building constructed for the main post office. The office wings, with their modest Neo-Renaissance elevations, contrast with the grand Neo-Baroque façade. Exhibits illustrate the history of postal and telecommun-ication services, including contemporary digital media.

↑ The Neo-Classical Russische Botschaft, built to impress in war-ravaged 1950s Berlin

birth of the Third Reich and Hitler's ascent to power. It was here, too, that the Russian flag was raised in May 1945, and on 17 June 1953 that 25 workers demonstrating for better conditions were killed.

The gate, in East Berlin, was restored during 1956–8, after it suffered extensive damage in World War II. Until 1989 it stood watch over the divided city. It was restored again between 2000 and 2002.

㉗ Admiralspalast

🚇 U2 🏛 Friedrichstrasse 101-102 📞 25 50 70 00 🚇&🚇 Friedrichstrasse

The Admiralspalast, built in 1911, was one of the Roaring Twenties' premier entertainment complexes in Berlin, and one of the many variety and vaudeville theatres that once lined Friedrichstrasse. Originally designed as an indoor swimming pool above a natural hot spring, it was later transformed into an ice-skating rink and, after heavy damage in World War II, an Operettentheater that staged light musical entertainment.

In 2006, following restoration work, the theatre reopened with a much-discussed production of Bertolt Brecht's *Die Dreigroschenoper* (*The Threepenny Opera*), and now once again serves as a vibrant entertainment complex, with a large stage, a café and a nightclub. Designed by Heinrich Schweitzer, the beautifully restored façade is punctuated by Doric half-columns and inlaid with slabs of Istrian marble. The façade on Planckstrasse, designed by Ernst Westphal, features exotic overlapping motifs.

㉘ Brandenburger Tor

🚇 S3 🏛 Pariser Platz 🚇&🚇 Brandenburger Tor 🚌 100, 200

The Brandenburg Gate is the quintessential symbol of Berlin. This magnificent Neo-Classical structure, completed in 1795, was designed by Carl Gotthard Langhans and modelled on the entrance to the Acropolis in Athens. A pair of pavilions, once used by guards and customs officers, frames its powerful Doric colonnade. The bas-reliefs depict scenes from Greek mythology, and the whole structure is crowned by the Quadriga sculpture designed by Johann Gottfried Schadow. The goddess of victory with her four-horsed chariot was originally regarded as a symbol of peace. In 1806, during the French occupation, the Quadriga was dismantled on Napoleon's orders and taken to Paris. On its return in 1814, it was declared a symbol of victory, and the goddess received the staff bearing the Prussian eagle and the iron cross adorned with a laurel wreath. The Brandenburg Gate has borne witness to many of Berlin's important events, from military parades to celebrations marking the

㉙ Russische Botschaft

🚇 T3 🏛 Unter den Linden 63/65 🚇&🚇 Brandenburger Tor 🚌 100, 200

The monumental white Russian Embassy building is an example of the Stalinist "wedding-cake" style, or *Zuckerbäckerstil*. Completed in 1953, it was the first postwar building erected on Unter den Linden. It is built on the site of a former palace that had

Brandenburger Tor dominating Pariser Platz ↓

housed the Russian (originally Tsarist) embassy from 1837.

The work of Russian architect Anatoli Strischewski, this structure, with its strictly symmetrical layout, resembles the old Berlin palaces of the Neo-Classical period. The sculptures that adorn it, however, belong to an altogether different era: the gods of ancient Greece and Rome have been replaced by working-class heroes.

30
Bahnhof Friedrichstrasse

U2 **Reichstagufer 17** **9am-7pm Tue-Fri, 10am-6pm Sat & Sun** **hdg.de**

One of the city's most famous urban railway stations, Bahnhof Friedrichstrasse used to be the border station between East and West Berlin during the Cold War years.

It was built in 1882 to a design by Johannes Vollmer.

1,000,000

The number of people who flock to Pariser Platz for Berlin's New Year's Eve party.

In 1925 a roof was added, covering the hall and the platforms. The original labyrinth of passages, staircases and checkpoints no longer exists but it is possible to see a model of the station at the Stasi-Museum (p231).

Now a museum itself, the only remaining structure from the original station is the special pavilion once used as a waiting room by those waiting for emigration clearance. It earned the nickname Tränenpalast, the "Palace of Tears", as it is here that Berliners from different sides of the city would say goodbye to each other after a visit.

31
Pariser Platz

T3 **S & U Brandenburger Tor** **100, 200**

This square, at the end of Unter den Linden, was created in 1734. Originally called Quarré, it was renamed Pariser Platz after 1814, when the Quadriga sculpture from the Brandenburg Gate was returned to Berlin from Paris.

The square, enclosed on the west by the Brandenburg Gate, saw most of its buildings destroyed in 1945. Following reunification, the square was redeveloped, and twin houses designed by Josef Paul Kleihues now flank the Brandenburg Gate. On the north side of the square are the Dresdner Bank building and the French Embassy. On the south are the US Embassy, the DZ Bank head office and the Academy of Fine Arts (p73). To the east is the rebuilt Hotel Adlon (p77), a legend in Berlin hospitality.

A SHORT WALK
AROUND BEBELPLATZ

Distance 1.5 km (1.1 mile) **Nearest tram station** Georgenstr./Am Kupfergraben
Time 15 minutes

The section of Unter den Linden between Schlossbrücke and Friedrichstrasse is the perfect place for a walk to get an introduction to the city. There are some magnificent Baroque and Neo-Classical buildings, many of which were designed by famous architects, as well as several restored palaces that are now used as public buildings. Of particular interest is the beautiful Baroque Zeughaus (the former Arsenal), which now houses the Deutsches Historisches Museum (German History Museum).

The impressive Reiterdenkmal Friedrichs des Grossen (Equestrian statue of Frederick the Great) dates from 1851 (p70).

Humboldt Universität's courtyard entrance is framed by two guardroom pavilions and crowned with the allegorical figures of Dawn and Dusk (p69).

The Neo-Baroque Staatsbibliothek (State Library) building was designed by Ernst von Ihne and completed in 1914. It houses a collection that dates from the 17th century (p68).

UNIVERSITÄTSSTRASSE

CHARLOTTENSTRASSE

UNTER DEN LINDEN

BEHRENSTRASSE

↑ I M Pei's modern exhibition hall at Zeughaus (DHM)

A sleek and stylish exhibition space shows off the brands of the Volkswagen Group. There's also a shop and several dining options.

The Neo-Classical Altes Palais (Old Palace) was built between 1834 and 1837 for the future Kaiser Wilhelm I. It was reconstructed after World War II (p70).

Since 1993, the Neue Wache (New Guard) monument has served as a memorial to all victims of war and dictatorship (p69).

A glass wing designed by I M Pei sits adjacent to the beautiful Baroque building of Zeughaus (DHM), the German Historical Museum. The Zeughaus pediment shows the Roman goddess of wisdom (p66).

Locator Map
For more detail see p64

The magnificent avenue of Unter den Linden was replanted with four rows of lime trees in 1946 (p72).

The rear elevation of Kronprinzenpalais (Crown Prince's Palace) features a magnificent portal from the dismantled Bauakademie building (p71).

● **START**

↑ Interior of the Friedrichswerdersche Kirche

● **FINISH**

The Neo-Gothic Friedrichswerdersche Kirche was designed by Karl Friedrich Schinkel, the architect of so many of Berlin's notable 19th-century buildings.

The Staatsoper (State Opera House) on Unter den Linden is Germany's oldest theatre building not attached to a palace residence (p71).

Designed in the 18th century as the Forum Fridericianum, Bebelplatz square was renamed in 1947 in honour of social activist August Bebel. The Nazis burned books here in 1933.

19th-century bas-reliefs by Theodor Wilhelm Achtermann adorn the supports of St-Hedwigs-Kathedrale (p72).

The west side of Bebelplatz features a Baroque library – the Alte Bibliothek – with an unusual concave façade, which locals have nicknamed the "chest of drawers" (p72).

0 metres 100
0 yards 100

N ↑

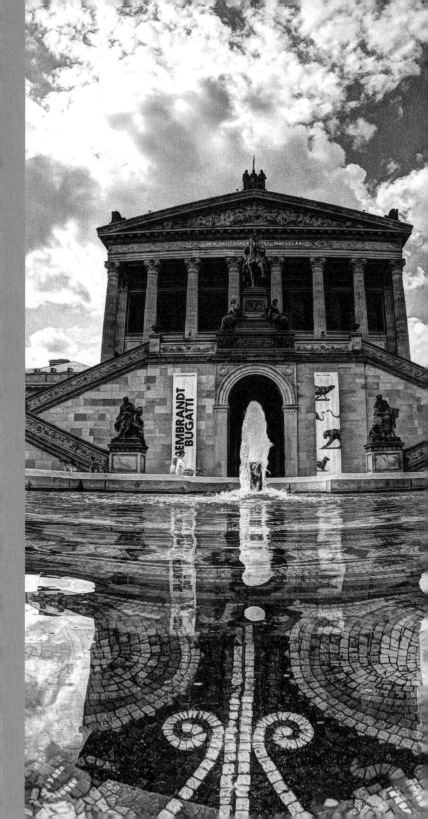

MUSEUMSINSEL

The long island nestled in the tributaries of the Spree river is the cradle of Berlin's history. It was here that the settlement of Cölln was established at the beginning of the 13th century, which grew up together with its twin settlement of Berlin on the opposite bank of the Spree.

Not a trace of Gothic and Renaissance Cölln is left now: the island's character was transformed by the construction of the Brandenburg Electors' palace, which served as their residence from 1470. Over the following centuries, the palace was converted first into a royal home and later into an imperial palace – the huge Stadtschloss. Although the palace was razed to the ground in 1950, several buildings on the island's north side have survived, including the huge Berliner Dom and the impressive collection of museums that give the island its name – Museumsinsel.

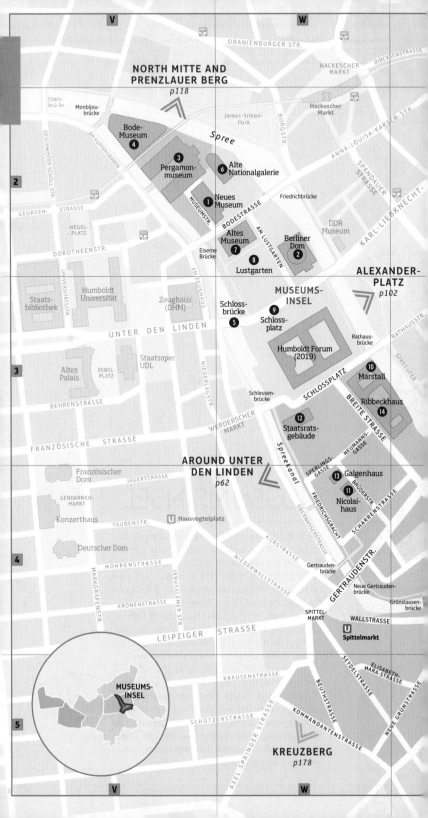

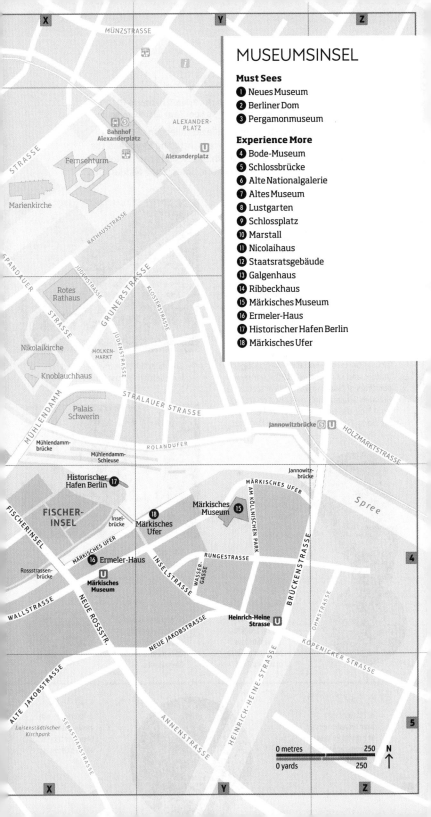

MUSEUMSINSEL

Must Sees
1. Neues Museum
2. Berliner Dom
3. Pergamonmuseum

Experience More
4. Bode-Museum
5. Schlossbrücke
6. Alte Nationalgalerie
7. Altes Museum
8. Lustgarten
9. Schlossplatz
10. Marstall
11. Nicolaihaus
12. Staatsratsgebäude
13. Galgenhaus
14. Ribbeckhaus
15. Märkisches Museum
16. Ermeler-Haus
17. Historischer Hafen Berlin
18. Märkisches Ufer

0 metres 250
0 yards 250

N

① ⊘ Ⓜ ⊡ ⌂

NEUES MUSEUM

📍V2 🏛Bodestrasse 1-3 🚇Hackescher Markt, Friedrichstrasse 🚌100, 200 🚋12, M1, M4, M5 🕐10am–6pm daily (to 8pm Thu) 🌐smb.museum

The New Museum is home to an unparalleled collection of Berlin's archaeological treasures from diverse areas including Egypt and the Middle East. Through its exceptional exhibits, visitors can explore human history and culture from prehistoric times to the Middle Ages.

The Neues Museum Today

The New Museum was built in the mid-19th century to relieve the overcrowded Altes Museum. In 1945 the building was badly damaged, but the reconstruction effort under British architect David Chipperfield – a skilful blend of conservation, restoration and creation of new spaces – was highly successful, and history remains palpable in every room.

The two main collections are the Egyptian Museum and Papyrus Collection and the Museum for Pre-history and Early History. The former showcases four millennia of ancient Egyptian and Nubian cultures, while the latter focuses on Europe and parts of Asia. Special themes and items include 19th-century wall paintings of Nordic mythological scenes, Heinrich Schliemann's collection of artifacts from Troy, the Neanderthal from Le Moustier, the Berlin Gold Hat and a bust of Nefertiti.

↑ The museum building, designed by Friedrich August Stüler

↑ The museum's architecture and décor were designed to complement the exhibits

The bust of Nefertiti is made of stucco-coated limestone

c 1184 BC
The "Treasure of Priam" artifacts are said to have belonged to a king of ancient Troy.

c 100–50 BC
▽ Very little is known about the beautifully crafted Egyptian bust known as the Berlin Green Head.

Highlights

c 1345 BC
▲ This bust may have served originally as a model for other portraits, and was not considered art itself.

c 200 AD
▲ Bronze bracelet attributed to a Germanic tribe of eastern Germany.

Did You Know?

The museum was closed
for 70 years, from
1939 to 2009.

Sarcophagi from the Egyptian ↑
Museum and Papyrus Collection

2

BERLINER DOM

🗺 W2 🚇 Am Lustgarten 🚆 Hackescher Markt 🚌 100, 200
🕐 9am-8pm daily (to 7pm in winter), noon-8pm Sun & public hols
🌐 berlinerdom.de

Standing on the east bank of the Spree, Berlin Cathedral is singled out from its neighbours on Museumsinsel, allowing visitors to fully take in this awe-inspiring city landmark.

History of the Cathedral

The original Berliner Dom was completed in 1750, based on a modest Baroque design by Johann Boumann. The present Neo-Baroque structure is the work of Julius Raschdorff and dates from 1894 to 1905. The central copper dome is some 98 m (321 ft) high. Following severe World War II damage, the cathedral has been restored in a simplified form but still contains some original features like the pulpit and altar.

Sauer's Organ contains some 7,200 pipes.

270

The number of steps up to the dome's walkway, with great views over Museumsinsel.

Hidden beneath the floor, the Imperial Hohenzollern family crypt contains 100 richly decorated sarcophagi.

GREAT VIEW
Light Show

For ten days in October, Berlin gets a kaleidoscopic remix during the annual Festival of Lights, when famous sights like the Berliner Dom become canvases for creative light shows.

↑ During the Festival of Lights, the façade of the cathedral is transformed by changing light and video projections

The mosaics inside the dome contain over half a million tiles each.

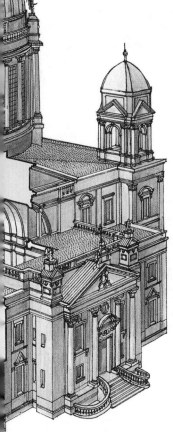

↑ The impressive Neo-Renaissance interior features some extravagant furnishings and impressive decorations

DOME MOSAICS

Look up at the interior of the dome to marvel at Anton von Werner's intricate mosaics. All but destroyed during World War II, von Werner's original designs were used by Tuscan company Ferrari & Bacci to reproduce the mosaics between 1975 and 2002.

↑ The Berliner Dom, a Neo-Baroque cathedral dating back to 1750

3 ⊘ Ⓜ ▭ 🛍

PERGAMONMUSEUM

📍V2 🏛Am Kupfergraben 5 Ⓢ Hackescher Markt, Friedrichstrasse
🚌100, 200 🚋12, M1 🕐10am–6pm daily (to 8pm Thu) ⓦ smb.museum

This unique museum is home to a magnificent collection of large architectural treasures excavated by German archaeologists in the late 19th century. The exhibits are as awe-inspiring for their fantastic designs as for their grand scale.

Built between 1910 and 1930 to a design by Alfred Messel and Ludwig Hoffmann, this museum houses one of Europe's most famous collections of antiquities. The three independent collections – the Collection of Classical Antiquities (Greek and Roman), the Museum of the Ancient Near East and the Museum of Islamic Art – are the result of intensive archaeological excavations by late 19th- and early 20th-century German expeditions to the Near and Middle East. Due to renovations, some areas of the museum – including the hall containing the Pergamon Altar – will remain closed until 2024. However, the south wing, housing highlights like the Ishtar Gate and the Processional Way, remains open.

↑ The Pergamonmuseum backs on to the river Spree

→ The museum's front entrance and courtyard

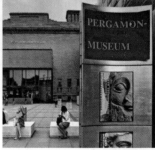

GALLERY GUIDE

The central section of the ground floor houses reconstructions of ancient monumental structures. The ground-floor wings containing the Collection of Classical Antiquities are closed for renovation until 2023. In the south wing, the ground floor is dedicated to the Museum of the Ancient Near East, and the first floor contains the Museum of Islamic Art.

↑ The Miletus Market Gate and a detail from the Pergamon Altar *(inset)*, from the Antikensammlung collection

MUSEUM OF THE ANCIENT NEAR EAST

The collection on display in the Vorderasiatisches Museum (Museum of the Ancient Near East) is one of the richest in the world, due to hugely successful excavations begun by German archaeologists in the 1880s. The collection features architecture, sculpture and jewellery from Babylon, Iran and Assyria, with pieces dating as far back as the 4th century BC.

One striking exhibit is the magnificent Ishtar Gate and the Processional Way that leads to it. These were both built during the reign of Nebuchadnezzar II (604–562 BC) in the ancient city of Babylon. The original avenue was about 180 m (590 ft) long. Many of the bricks used in its reconstruction are new, but the lions – sacred animals of the goddess Ishtar (mistress of the sky, goddess of love and patron of the army) – are all originals. Although impressive in size, the Ishtar Gate has in fact not been reconstructed in full, and a model of the whole structure shows the scale of the original complex. Only the inner gate, framed by two towers, is on display, decorated with dragons and bulls, emblems of the Babylonian gods Marduk, patron of the city, and Adad, god of storms.

INSIDER TIP
Pergamon Panorama

A 360-degree panorama of the ancient city of Pergamon will be on show until the famous Pergamon Altar is back on display. This jaw-dropping, ultra-realistic panorama was created by artist Yadegar Asisi, who has other work on display in Berlin (p77).

→

The magnificent Ishtar Gate (6th century BC)

COLLECTION OF CLASSICAL ANTIQUITIES

←

Marble statue of Athena Parthenos (Athena the Virgin)

Berlin's collection of Greek and Roman antiquities (Antikensammlung) came into existence during the 17th century. The centre-piece of the collection is the huge Pergamon Altar from the acropolis of the ancient city of Pergamon in Asia Minor, which is now Bergama, Turkey. It is thought to have been built to celebrate victory in war and to have been commissioned by King Eumenes in 170 BC. This artistic masterpiece was discovered in a decrepit state by German archaeologist Carl Humann, who, after long negotiations, was allowed to transport the surviving portions of the altar to Berlin.

Roman architecture is represented by the striking 2nd-century-AD market gate from the city of Miletus.

MUSEUM OF ISLAMIC ART

Must See

The history of the Museum für Islamische Kunst (Museum of Islamic Art) began in 1904, when Wilhelm von Bode launched the collection by donating his own extensive selection of carpets. He also brought to Berlin a 45-m- (150-ft-) long section of the façade of the Mshatta Palace, a Jordanian desert palace. The façade, covered with exquisitely carved limestone cladding, was presented to Kaiser Wilhelm II in 1903 by Sultan Abdul Hamid of Ottoman. The palace was part of a group of defence fortresses and residential buildings dating from the Omayyad period (AD 661–750), and probably built for the Caliph al-Walid II.

Another fascinating exhibit is a beautiful 13th-century *mihrab*, the niche in a mosque that shows the direction of Mecca. Made in the Iranian town of Kashan, renowned for its ceramics, the *mihrab* is covered in lustrous metallic glazes that make it sparkle as if studded with sapphires and gold. The collection's many vivid carpets come from as far afield as Iran, Asia Minor, Egypt and the Caucasus. Highlights include an early 15th-century carpet from Anatolia decorated with an unusual dragon and phoenix motif and, dating from the 14th century, one of the earliest Turkish carpets in existence.

Other rooms hold collections of miniature

↑ Islamic carpets on display at the Pergamonmuseum

paintings and various objects for daily use. An interesting example of provincial Ottoman architecture is an exquisitely panelled early 17th-century reception room, known as the Aleppo Zimmer, which was once part of a Christian merchant's house in the Syrian city of Aleppo.

Did You Know?

The museums of Museumsinsel have been undergoing renovations since 2013. Work is due to finish in 2026.

↑ Façade of the Mshatta Palace (AD 744)

↑ The wedge-shaped Bode-Museum on Museumsinsel

EXPERIENCE MORE

4

Bode-Museum

V2 **Monbijoubrücke (Bodestrasse 1-3)** **Hackescher Markt, Friedrichstrasse** 🚌 **100, 147, 200** 🚊 **12, M1, M4, M5, M6** 🕙 **10am–6pm Tue–Sun (to 8pm Thu)** **smb.museum**

The Bode-Museum building was designed in the 1890s by Ernst von Ihne to fit the wedge-shaped end of the island. The interior was designed with the help of an art historian, Wilhelm von Bode, who was the director

Did You Know?

Museumsinsel was designated a UNESCO World Heritage Site in 1999.

of the Berlin state museums at the time. The museum, which opened in 1904, displayed a rather mixed collection that included some Old Masters. Its original name, Kaiser Friedrich Museum, was changed after World War II. Following the reassembling of the Berlin collections, all of the paintings were put in the Gemäldegalerie (p158). The Egyptian art and the papyrus collection were moved to the Ägyptisches Museum (Egyptian Museum) at Charlottenburg. They are now housed at the Neues Museum (p86).

All the collections are back on display following major renovation work. Highlights include an outstanding collection of some of the world's oldest coins, from Athens in the 6th century BC, as well as Roman, medieval and 20th-century coins. There are also sculptures by Tilman Riemenschneider, Donatello, Bernini and Canova.

5

Schlossbrücke

W3 **Hackescher Markt** 🚌 **100, 200**

This is one of the city's most beautiful bridges, connecting Schlossplatz (p96) with Unter den Linden (p72). It was built in 1824 to a design by Karl Friedrich Schinkel (p28), who was one of Germany's most influential architects. Statues were added to the top of the bridge's sparkling granite pillars in 1853. These figures were also created by Schinkel and made of stunning white Carrara marble. The statues depict tableaux taken from Greek mythology, for instance Iris, Nike and Athena training and looking after their favourite young warriors.

Remember to take a close look at the wrought-iron balustrade, which is delightfully decorated with intertwined sea creatures.

Alte Nationalgalerie

W2 **Bodestrasse 1-3**
**Hackescher Markt,
Friedrichstrasse** 100,
200 12, M1, M4, M5
10am-6pm Tue-Sun (to
8pm Thu) smb.museum

The Old National Gallery was
completed in 1876 to a design
by Friedrich August Stüler,
who took into account the
sketches made by Friedrich
Wilhelm IV. The building is
situated on a high platform
reached via a double staircase.
On the top stands an
equestrian statue of Friedrich
Wilhelm IV, the work of
Alexander Calandrelli in 1886.
Details on the façade reflect
the building's purpose – the
tympanum features Germania
as patron of art, while the top
is crowned with a person-
ification of the arts.

Originally meant to house
modern art, the current
museum includes works of
masters such as Adolph von
Menzel, Wilhelm Leibl, Max
Liebermann (p245) and Arnold
Böcklin. There is no shortage
of sculptures either, with
works by Christian Daniel
Rauch, Johann Gottfried
Schadow, Antonio Canova and
Reinhold Begas. Another two
halls display paintings from
the German Romantic era,
including works by Caspar
David Friedrich, Karl Friedrich
Schinkel and Karl Blechen.

↑ An Adolph von Menzel
work at the Alte
Nationalgalerie

Altes Museum

W2 **Am Lustgarten
(Bodestrasse 1-3)**
Hackescher Markt
100, 200, TXL 10am-
6pm Tue-Sun (to 8pm Thu)
smb.museum

The Old Museum building,
designed by Karl Friedrich
Schinkel, is undoubtedly one
of the world's most beautiful
Neo-Classical structures, with
an impressive 87-m- (285-ft-)
high portico supported by 18
Ionic columns. Built in 1830
for the royal collection of art
and antiquities, it now houses
part of Berlin's Collection of
Classical Antiquities, with
permanent exhibitions on
the art and culture of ancient
Greece and on Roman and
Etruscan art and sculptures,
with temporary exhibition
space on the second floor.

Lustgarten

W2 **Hackescher Markt**
100, 200

The enchanting garden in
front of the Altes Museum
looks as though it has always
been there, but in its present
form it was established in
the late 1990s.

Used to grow vegetables
and herbs for the Stadtschloss
until the late 16th century,
it became a real *Lustgarten*
(pleasure garden) in the
reign of the Great Elector
(p215). However, its statues,
grottoes, fountains and exotic
vegetation were removed
when Friedrich Wilhelm I
(1688–1740), known for his
love of military pursuits,
turned the garden into an
army drill ground.

Following the construction
of the Altes Museum, the
ground became a park,
designed by Peter Joseph
Lenné in 1831 it was adorned
with a monolithic granite bowl
by Christian Gottlieb Cantian,
to a design by Schinkel. The
63-tonne (70-ton) bowl,
measuring nearly 7 m (23 ft)
in diameter, was intended for
the museum rotunda, but was
too heavy to carry inside.

After 1933, the Lustgarten
was paved over and turned
into a parade ground, remaining as such until 1989. Its
current restoration is based
on Lenné's original designs.

BERLIN'S BRIDGES

Despite wartime damage, Berlin's bridges
are still well worth seeing. The Spree river
and the city's canals have some exemplary
architecture on their banks, while many of
the bridges were designed and decorated
by famous architects and sculptors. There
are several particularly stunning bridges
as you head west from Museumsinsel.

Bridges of Museumsinsel
① Schleusenbrücke
② Jungfernbrücke
③ Gertraudenbrücke

→

The impressive Marstall overlooking the Spree

9 Schlossplatz

⊡ W3 **Ⓢ Hackescher Markt**
🚌 100, 200

This square was once the site of a gigantic residential complex known as the Stadtschloss (City Palace). Built first as a castle in 1451, it served as the main residence of the Brandenburg Electors. Rebuilt in the style of a three-storey palace in the 16th century, it became the main seat of the Hohenzollern family for almost 500 years until the end of the monarchy. The palace partly burned down during World War II, and in 1950–1, despite protests, the palace was demolished and the square was renamed Marx-Engels-Forum under the GDR. All that remains of the original palace is the triumphal-arch portal that once adorned the façade on the Lustgarten side.

In 1989 the square reverted to its original name, Schlossplatz, and in 1993 a full-scale model of the old palace was built out of cloth stretched over scaffolding. After a lengthy debate and an architectural competition won by Franco Stella, it was decided to rebuild the palace as a museum complex with three reconstructed historical façades and a modern one. Opening in 2020, the complex contains a reconstruction of the original Schlüterhof courtyard and a pedestrian passage through the building. As Berlin's newest cultural venue, the complex was named "the Humboldt Forum" after two of Berlin's most prominent intellectual figures:

Wilhelm and Alexander von Humboldt (p68).

10 Marstall

⊡ W3 **Ⓐ Schlossplatz/ Breite Strasse 36-37**
Ⓤ Spittelmarkt
🚌 147, 248, M48

The buildings of the former Royal Stables form a huge complex, occupying the area between the Spree and Breite Strasse, south of Schlossplatz. The wing on the side of Breite Strasse is a fragment of the old structure built in 1669. It was designed by Michael Matthias Smids and is the only surviving early Baroque building in Berlin. The wings running along Schlossplatz and the Spree river were built much later, in 1901, but are reminiscent of the Berlin Baroque style – probably because von Ihne modelled them on designs by Jean de Bodt from 1700.

Once the imperial home of more than 300 horses, together with a fleet of royal carriages and sleighs, the building now houses the Hanns Eisler Academy of Music and also hosts a branch of the Berlin City Library.

HOUSE OF ONE

Along with the museum renovations on the north end of Museumsinsel, the development of the ambitious and unique House Of One is taking place to the south. The project blends a synagogue, a church and a mosque to provide a place of worship for Jews, Christians and Muslims alike. Located at Petriplatz in the historic Cölln district, its various sections will be linked by a communal room that will serve as a meeting point for interested visitors and religious parties.

Nicolaihaus

W4 ⌂ **Brüderstrasse 13**
☎ **20 45 81 63** Ⓤ **Spittel-**
markt 🚌 **147, 265, M48**

Built around 1670, the
Nicolaihaus is a fine example
of Baroque architecture, with
its original, magnificent oak
staircase still in place. The
rear wing features another
fine staircase from the
Weydinger-Haus. The house
owes its fame, however, to
its time as the home and
bookshop of the publisher,
writer and critic Christoph
Friedrich Nicolai (1733–1811).
One of the outstanding
personalities of the Berlin
Enlightenment, Nicolai was
a supporter of such notable
cultural figures as the Jewish
philosopher Moses Mendelssohn *(p130)* and the playwright Gotthold Ephraim
Lessing. Other regular
artistic visitors included
Johann Gottfried Schadow,
Karl Wilhelm Ramler and
Daniel Chodowiecki, all
commemorated with a wall
plaque. Today, the building
houses the offices of the
German Association of
Protected Buildings, and
is open to the public only
by appointment.

⑫
Staatsratsgebäude

W3 ⌂ **Schlossplatz 1**
Ⓢ & Ⓤ **Alexanderplatz**
🚌 **100, 147, 200, M48**

The former Staatsrats-
gebäude, an administrative
building that was once the
seat of the highest state
government council of East
Germany, was constructed
in 1964. It now stands alone
on the southern side of the
square, as all the other former
Socialist state buildings that
once formed the government
centre in this area have long
been demolished. The Staatsratsgebäude features the
remaining original sculptures,
including the magnificent
atlantes by the famous
Dresden sculptor Balthasar
Permoser. Their inclusion,
however, was not due to their
artistic merit, but rather to
their propaganda value: it
was from the balcony of the
portal that Karl Liebknecht
proclaimed the birth of the
Socialist Republic.

⑬
Galgenhaus

W4 ⌂ **Brüderstrasse 10**
☎ **206 13 29 13** Ⓤ **Spittel-**
markt 🚌 **147, 265, M48**
⊘ **10am–6pm Mon–Sat**

The Gallows House, so named
for a local legend in which an
innocent woman was hanged,
was originally built as the
presbytery of the lost church
of St Peter. Redesigned in the
Neo-Classical style around
1805, the front portal and one
room on the ground floor are
all that remain of the original
Baroque structure. The new
building is, however, a delight:
perfectly symmetrical, it
resembles nothing so much as
a dolls' house made life-size.
    Today the building houses
the commercial Kewenig
Gallery, which acquired the
building in 2013. Before
opening it undertook a major

restoration of the building,
which shows off the surviving
original interior features.

⑭
Ribbeckhaus

W3 ⌂ **Breite Strasse 35**
Ⓤ **Spittelmarkt** 🚌 **147, 248,**
M48

Four identical, picturesque
gables crown central Berlin's
only surviving Renaissance
building, the Ribbeck House.
It was built around 1624 for
Hans Georg von Ribbeck, a
court counsellor, who soon
sold it to Anna Sophie of
Brunswick. After her death
in 1659, the house passed to
her nephew, Elector Friedrich
Wilhelm. As crown property,
it later housed various state
administrative offices.
    The façade has beautiful
wrought-iron grilles on the
ground-floor windows and
a late Renaissance portal,
bearing the date and coat
of arms of the von Ribbecks.
This was replaced in 1960 with
a copy, but apart from that,
the house is a remarkable
example of architectural
survival from the city's history.

↑ Renaissance portal
of the Ribbeckhaus

→ The Weapons Room in the Märkisches Museum

Did You Know?

The southern end of Museumsinsel, below Gertraudenstrasse, is known as Fischerinsel.

15 ♿

Märkisches Museum

📍 Y4 🏠 Am Köllnischen Park 5 🚇 & Ⓤ Jannowitz-brücke Ⓤ Märkisches Museum, Heinrich-Heine Strasse 🚌 147, 248, 265, M48 🕐 10am–6pm Tue–Sun 🌐 stadtmuseum.de

This architectural pastiche is a complex of red-brick buildings that most resembles a medieval monastery. It was built between 1901 and 1908 to house a collection relating to the history of Berlin and the Brandenburg region, from the time of the earliest settlers to the present. Inspired by the Brick Gothic style popular in the Branden-burg region, architect Ludwig Hoffmann included references to Wittstock Castle and to St Catherine's Church in the city of Brandenburg. In the entrance hall you'll find a statue of the hero Roland standing guard, which is a copy of the 15th-century monument in the city of Brandenburg. The main hall features the original Gothic portal from the Berlin residence of the Margraves of Brandenburg, demolished in 1931. Also featured is one of the original horse's heads from the Schadow Quadriga, which crowns the Brandenburg Gate (p78).

A further collection in the same building is devoted to the Berlin theatre during the period 1730 to 1933, including many posters, old programmes and stage sets. One of the galleries houses some charming old-time mechanical musical instruments, which are played by musicians once a week, at 5pm on Friday, in a special show.

The Märkisches Museum is a branch of the Stadtmuseum Berlin organization, and those who wish to find out more about the history of the city can visit other affiliated museums and monuments such as the Nikolaikirche (p112) and the Ephraim-Palais (p113). Surrounding the museum is the Köllnischer Park, which has a kennel built in 1928 to house brown bears kept as city mascots, and an unusual statue of Berlin artist Heinrich Zille (p112).

---

⑯ Ermeler-Haus

🚇 X4   🏛 Märkisches Ufer 10 Ⓤ Märkisches Museum, Heinrich-Heine Strasse 🚌 147, 248, 265, M48

With its harmonious Neo-Classical façade, the Ermeler House stands out as one of the most handsome villas in Berlin. This house was once the town residence of Wilhelm Ferdinand Ermeler, a wealthy merchant and shopkeeper who made his money trading in tobacco. It originally stood on Fischerinsel on the opposite bank of the river, at Breite Strasse No. 11, but in 1968 the house was dismantled and reconstructed on this new site. The house was remodelled in 1825 to Ermeler's specifications, with a decor that includes a frieze alluding to aspects of the tobacco business. Restorers have recreated much of the original façade. The Rococo furniture dates from about

1760 and the notable 18th-century staircase has also been rebuilt.

A modern hotel has been built to the rear of the house facing Wallstrasse, using Ermeler-Haus as its kitchens, while the first-floor rooms are used for special events.

---

⑰ Historischer Hafen Berlin

🚇 X4   🏛 Märkisches Ufer Ⓤ Märkisches Ufer, Heinrich-Heine Strasse 🚌 147, 248, 265 🕐 1–6pm Sat & Sun 🌐 historischer-hafen-berlin.de

Moored on the south shore of the island in an area called Fischerinsel, and opposite the Märkisches Ufer, are several examples of boats, barges and tugboats which operated on the Spree river at the end of the 19th century. These craft constitute an open-air

museum, the Historic Port of Berlin, which was once located in the Humboldt Port. One of the boats is now used as a café, while another, the *Renate Angelika*, houses a small exhibition on the history of inland waterway transport on the Spree and Havel.

---

⑱ Märkisches Ufer

🚇 Y4   Ⓤ Märkisches Museum, Heinrich-Heine Strasse 🚌 147, 248, 265, M48

Once called Neukölln am Wasser, this street, which runs alongside the Spree river, is one of the few corners of Berlin where it is still possible to see the town much as it must have looked in the 18th and 19th centuries. Eight pretty houses have been meticulously conserved here. Two Neo-Baroque houses at No. 16 and No. 18, known as Otto-Nagel-Haus, used to contain a small museum displaying paintings by Otto Nagel, a great favourite with the Communist authorities. The building now houses the photo archives for the state museums of Berlin.

A number of pretty garden cafés and fashionable restaurants make this attractive area very popular with tourists.

←

Boats moored at the Historischer Hafen Berlin

A SHORT WALK
MUSEUMSINSEL

Distance 1km (0.5 miles) **Nearest tram station** Georgenstr./Am Kupfergraben **Time** 10 minutes

A stroll around the northern end of this island will introduce you to some of Berlin's most famous sights, like the Lustgarten and the Berliner Dom (Berlin Cathedral). It is also where you will find some of the most important museums in the east of the city. These include the Bode-Museum, the Altes Museum and the splendid Pergamon-museum with its collection of antiquities

This railway bridge is also used by the S-Bahn.

START

The dome-covered rounded corner of the Bode-Museum provides a prominent landmark at the tip of the island (p94).

The Pergamonmuseum is famous for its reconstruction of fragments of ancient towns such as Miletus and Babylon, as well as the original friezes from the Pergamon Altar (p90).

AM KUPFER-GRABEN

0 metres 100
0 yards 100

N

↑ The current building of the Berliner Dom was completed in 1905

← The Lustgarten, originally used to grow food for the Stadschloss kitchens

Locator Map
For more detail see p84

The equestrian statue of King Friedrich Wilhelm IV in front of the Alte Nationalgalerie (Old National Gallery) is the work of Alexander Calandrelli (p95).

The Neues Museum (New Museum) houses the Egyptian Museum and Papyrus Collection plus parts of the Museum of Pre- and Early History, as well as items from the Collection of Classical Antiquities (p86).

The corners of the Altes Museum (Old Museum) building feature figures of Castor and Pollux, heroes of Greek myth (p95).

The Neo-Baroque interior of the Berliner Dom (Berlin Cathedral) features some extravagant 19th-century furnishings.

BODESTRASSE

BODESTRASSE

BODESTRASSE

LUSTGARTEN

The Lustgarten park has had several incarnations, including a kitchen garden and a military parade ground. In the 20th century it was often used for political rallies (p88).

SCHLOSSBRÜCKE

KARL–LIEBKNECHT STR.

● **FINISH**

The unusual Schlossbrücke (Palace bridge) features statues made of stunning white Carrara marble (p94).

Did You Know?

The museums here have been undergoing extensive renovations and updates since 1999.

ALEXANDERPLATZ

This area is the historical centre of the city, as it includes the site where the settlement of Berlin was first established in the 13th century. Traces of Berlin's earliest history can still be found here, including the city's oldest surviving church – Marienkirche, founded in 1280 – and the reconstructed old town around Nikolaiviertel. The area still offers cosy mews and alleys, which are surrounded by postwar high-rise blocks.

The legacy of East Berlin is also particularly strong in the architecture around Alexanderplatz. The GDR regime replaced the huge apartment buildings and department stores just to the north with a square, Marx-Engels-Forum and the Fernsehturm, which can be seen from almost anywhere in the city.

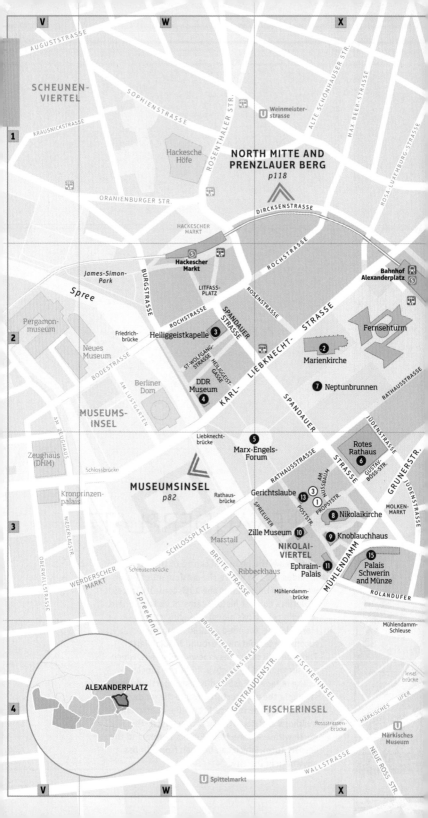

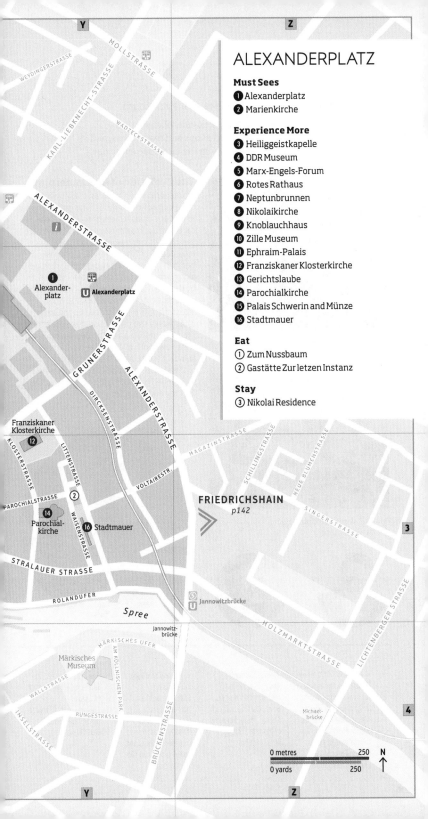

ALEXANDERPLATZ

Must Sees
1 Alexanderplatz
2 Marienkirche

Experience More
3 Heiliggeistkapelle
4 DDR Museum
5 Marx-Engels-Forum
6 Rotes Rathaus
7 Neptunbrunnen
8 Nikolaikirche
9 Knoblauchhaus
10 Zille Museum
11 Ephraim-Palais
12 Franziskaner Klosterkirche
13 Gerichtslaube
14 Parochialkirche
15 Palais Schwerin and Münze
16 Stadtmauer

Eat
1 Zum Nussbaum
2 Gastätte Zur letzten Instanz

Stay
3 Nikolai Residence

❶ ALEXANDERPLATZ

📍Y2 ⑤&Ⓤ Alexanderplatz 🚌100, 200, 248, M48 🚊M5, M6, M8

Despite its lack of pretty architecture, Alexanderplatz is still a bustling square well worth a visit for its shops and restaurants, and to get a taste of the dynamic side of Berlin the locals see every day.

↑ Walter Womacka's mural *Unser Leben* (*Our Life*) circling the Haus des Lehrers

↑ The World Clock, an iconic city landmark

The Evolution of Alexanderplatz

Alexanderplatz, or "Alex" as it is known locally, has a long history, although it is difficult now to find any visible traces of the past. Once called Ochsenmarkt (oxen market), it was the site of a cattle and wool market. It was later renamed after Tsar Alexander I, who visited Berlin in 1805. Houses and shops sprang up along with a market hall and train station, and by the early 20th century "Alex" had become one of the city's busiest spots. In 1929, attempts were made to develop the square, though only two office buildings were added – the Alexanderhaus and the Berolinahaus. These two, both by Peter Behrens, are still standing today. World War II erased most of the square's older buildings and it is now surrounded by 1960s edifices, including the Park Inn and the Fernsehturm.

Timeline

1928

△ Alfred Döblin's novel *Berlin Alexanderplatz*, set in working-class neighbourhoods near Alex during the 1920s, describes the trials and tribulations of petty criminal protagonist Franz Biberkopf.

1931

△ Döblin himself worked on Piel Jutzi's film adaptation of his book, starring Heinrich George, Maria Bard and Margarete Schlegel, among others.

1939

△ Richard Schneider-Edenkoben's *Silvesternacht am Alexanderplatz* (*New Year's Eve on Alexanderplatz*) is considered one of the better films from the Third Reich.

1967

The light-hearted *Ein Lord am Alexanderplatz* (*A Lord of Alexanderplatz*) depicts the square during its East German years.

Fernsehturm

📍X2 🏠Panoramastrasse 1A 🚇&ⓊAlexanderplatz 🚌100, 200, M48, TXL 🚋M2, M4, M5, M6 ⏰Mar-Oct: 9am-midnight daily; Nov-Feb: 10am-midnight daily 🌐tv-turm.de

The Television Tower, nicknamed Telespargel (toothpick) by locals, is the city's tallest structure, at 368 m (1,207 ft), and is one of the tallest structures in Europe. One of the attractions of the tower is the revolving restaurant: a full rotation takes about half an hour, so it is possible to get a bird's-eye view of the whole city while sipping a cup of coffee. On a clear day visibility can reach up to 40 km (25 miles).

↑ The Fernsehturm is visible from almost any point in Berlin. The viewing platform is 203 m (666 ft) above the ground, offering a full view of the city

THE FUTURE OF ALEXANDERPLATZ

The plan to breathe some contemporary life into Alexanderplatz goes back to 1993. A mix of factors has consistently thwarted those plans – as has the city's decision to protect some of the Soviet-style buildings as heritage-status structures. However, the Senate has given preliminary approval for three proposed buildings by prominent city architect Hans Kollhoff. Whether these plans become reality is yet to be seen, but it's the furthest the ideas have got in a quarter of a century.

1980
△ Director Rainer Werner Fassbinder's 15-½-hour television adaptation of *Berlin Alexanderplatz* flopped upon release, but is now considered his magnum opus.

2001
△ *Die Liebenden vom Alexanderplatz* (*The Lovers from Alexanderplatz*) by Detlef Rönfeldt involves a woman fleeing to New York during war time and returning after the war.

2004
△ The *Bourne Supremacy*, shot extensively in Berlin, features a scene where Bourne meets agent Nicky Parsons at Alex's World Clock.

2015
Ernst Haffner's 1932 "long-lost" novel *Blood Brothers*, republished in 2015, depicts the illicit underworld of late-Weimar Berlin, with much of the action taking place on and around Alexanderplatz.

❷ 🔁 Ⓜ 📁

MARIENKIRCHE

📍 X2 🏠 Karl-Liebknecht-Strasse 8 Ⓢ & Ⓤ Alexanderplatz
🚌 100, 200, 248, M48, TXL 🚊 M4, M5, M6 🕐 10am–6pm daily
🌐 marienkirche-berlin.de

The church of St Mary is a tranquil, medieval oasis in the heart of Berlin. The early Gothic hall design and the lavish Baroque touches make this one of the most interesting churches in the city.

Marienkirche was first established as a parish church in the second half of the 13th century and construction was completed early in the 14th century. The main building is a long, red-brick Gothic hall which still contains many beautiful decorations and features dating from the mid-15th to early 18th century, such as the baptismal font (1437) and the pulpit (1703). During reconstruction works in 1380 the church was altered slightly but its overall shape changed only in the 15th century, when it acquired the front tower. In 1790, the tower was crowned with a dome designed by Carl Gotthard Langhans. The church was once hemmed in by buildings, but today it stands alone in the shadow of the Fernsehturm (Television Tower; *p107*).

The dome that crowns the tower includes both Baroque and Neo-Gothic elements.

→

Marienkirche, a medieval parish church

The central part of the Gothic altar, known as the retable, dating from 1510, features three unknown monks.

Totentanz, meaning "dance of death", is the name of a 22-m- (72-ft-) long Gothic wall fresco, dating from 1485.

↑ The red main hall was built in the Brick Gothic style some time in the mid- to late 13th century

Main entrance

↑ The Baroque altar was designed by Andreas Krüger around 1762; *(inset)* sculpture detail from Andreas Schlüter's pulpit, completed in 1703

The Gothic baptismal font dates from 1437.

Main altar

Did You Know?

Home to the best organ music in the city, Marienkirche holds free concerts several times a week.

The Von Röbel Family Tomb is a richly decorated Mannerist-Baroque memorial.

Andreas Schlüter's pulpit is a masterpiece carved from alabaster.

↑ *Crucifixion* (1562), by Michael Rihenstein, depicts Christ flanked by Moses and St John the Baptist

EXPERIENCE MORE

3 Heiliggeistkapelle

W2 **Spandauer Strasse 1** **Hackescher Markt** **100, 200** **M4, M5, M6**

The Chapel of the Holy Spirit is the only surviving hospital chapel in Berlin. It was built as part of a hospital complex in the second half of the 13th century, and was rebuilt in the 15th century. The hospital was demolished in 1825, but the chapel was retained. In 1906, it was made into a newly erected College of Trade, designed by Cremer & Wolffenstein.

The chapel is a fine example of Gothic brick construction. Its modest interior features a 15th-century star-shaped vault. The supports under the vault are decorated with half-statues of prophets and saints.

4 DDR Museum

W2 **Karl-Liebknecht-Strasse 1** **Hackescher Markt** **100, 200** **10am-8pm daily (to 10pm Sat)** **ddr-museum.de**

This hands-on museum on the Spree embankment opposite the Berliner Dom (p88) gives an insight into the daily lives of East Germans during the era of the DDR and demonstrates how the secret police kept a watchful eye on the city's people. Exhibits include a replica of a typical living room and a gleaming example of the iconic Trabant car.

5 Marx-Engels-Forum

W3 **Hackescher Markt, Alexanderplatz** **100, 200, 248, M48**

This vast square, which stretches from the Neptune fountain to the Spree river in the west, was given the inappropriate name Marx-Engels-Forum (it is not really a forum). Devoid of any surroundings, the only features in this square are the statues of Karl Marx and Friedrich Engels. The statues, added in 1986, are by Ludwig Engelhart. Due to the ongoing extension of an underground line, the statues were moved into a corner.

The square's fate after the work is completed is still being discussed. Some prefer that the area be built up with small-scale developments, while others wish it to be recreated as a public forum.

> **Did You Know?**
>
> If you plan to visit Rotes Rathaus, don't forget your passport – you can't get in without photo ID.

← The larger-than-life-size statues of Marx (seated) and Engels at the Marx-Engels-Forum

←

The tiered clock tower
of the Rotes Rathaus

7

Neptunbrunnen

Q X2 **A** Spandauer Strasse
(Rathausvorplatz)
S & **U** Alexanderplatz
S Hackescher Markt
🚌 100, 200

The magnificent, Neo-Baroque
style Neptune Fountain is a
splendid feature on the main,
axis of the Rotes Rathaus.
It was moved here from the
former Stadtschloss (Berlin
Castle) in 1969, and will return
there when rebuilding of the
castle is complete.

The statue of Neptune in
a dynamic pose at the centre
of the fountain is surrounded
by four figures representing
Germany's greatest rivers: the
Rhine, the Vistula, the Oder
and the Elbe. The naturalism
of the composition and the
detail, such as the beautiful
bronze fishes, crayfish and
fishing nets, are noteworthy.

6

Rotes Rathaus

Q X3 **A** Rathausstrasse
15 **C** 90 26 0
S & **U** Alexanderplatz
U Klosterstrasse
🚌 100, 200, 248, M48
O 9am-6pm Mon-Fri

This impressive structure
is Berlin's main town hall; its
name means simply "Red
Town Hall". Its predecessor
was a much more modest
building and by the end of
the 19th century it was
insufficient to meet the needs
of the growing metropolis.

The present building was
designed by Hermann
Friedrich Waesemann, and its
construction was completed
in 1869. The architect took his
main inspiration from Italian
Renaissance municipal
buildings, but the tower is
reminiscent of Laon cathedral
in France. The walls are made
from red brick and it was

this, rather than the political
orientation of the mayors,
that gave the town hall its
name. The building has a
continuous frieze known as
the "stone chronicle", which
was added in 1879. It features
scenes and figures from
the city's history and the
development of its economy
and science.

The Rotes Rathaus was
badly damaged during
World War II and, following
its reconstruction (1951–58),
it became the seat of the
East Berlin authorities. The
West Berlin magistrate was
housed in the Schöneberg
town hall (p241). After the
reunification of Germany, the
Rotes Rathaus became the
centre of authority, housing
the offices of the mayor, the
magistrates' offices and
state rooms. The forecourt
sculptures were added in
1958. These are by Fritz
Cremer and depict Berliners
helping to rebuild the city.

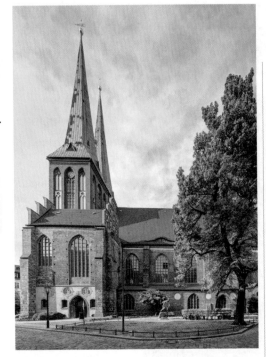

←

The copper-clad double
spires of the Nikolaikirche

Baroque building in Nikolaiviertel that escaped damage
during World War II. It was
built in 1759 for the Knoblauch
family, which includes the
famous architect, Eduard
Knoblauch. His works include,
among others, the Neue
Synagoge (p130).

The current appearance of
the building is the result of
work carried out in 1835, when
the façade was given a Neo-
Classical look. The ground
floor houses a popular wine
bar, while the upper floors
belong to a museum. On
the first floor it is possible
to see the interior of an early
19th-century middle-class
home, including a beautiful
Biedermeier-style room.

10

Zille Museum

🚇X3 📍Propststrasse 11
🚇Klosterstrasse
🚌100, 147, 200, 248, M48
🕙11am-6pm Mon-Sat,
1-6pm Sun 🌐zillemuseum-
berlin.de

Artist, illustrator and
photographer Heinrich
Zille (1858–1929) was one
of Berlin's best-known
personalities. Renowned for
his caricatures of everyday
working-class life in the
city, Zille was partly
responsible for Berlin's image

8

Nikolaikirche

🚇X3 📍Nikolaikirchplatz
Ⓢ&Ⓤ Alexanderplatz
ⓊKlosterstrasse
🚌100, 200, 248, M48
🕙10am-6pm daily
🌐stadtmuseum.de

The Nikolaikirche is the oldest
sacred building of historic
Berlin. The original structure
erected on this site was
started probably around 1230
when the town was granted
its municipal rights. What
remains now of this stone
building is the massive base
of the two-tower façade of the
present church, which dates
from c 1300. The presbytery
was completed around 1402,
but the construction of the
main building went on until
the mid-15th century. The
result was a magnificent
Gothic brick hall-church,
featuring a chancel with an
ambulatory and a row of low
chapels. In 1877 Hermann

Blankenstein, who conducted
the church restoration works,
removed most of its Baroque
modifications and recon-
structed the front towers.

Destroyed by bombing in
1945, the Nikolaikirche was
eventually rebuilt in 1987 and
shows a permanent exhibit
on Berlin's history. The west
wall of the southern nave
contains Andreas Schlüter's
monument to the goldsmith
Daniel Männlich and his wife,
which features a gilded relief
portrait of the couple above
a mock doorway.

9

Knoblauchhaus

🚇X3 📍Poststrasse 23
Ⓢ&Ⓤ Alexanderplatz
ⓊKlosterstrasse 🚌248,
M48 🕙10am-6pm Tue-Sun
🌐stadtmuseum.de

A small townhouse situated
on elegant Poststrasse, the
Knoblauchhaus is the only

> **INSIDER TIP**
> **Free Concerts**
>
> The Nikolaikirche hosts
> free 30-minute classical
> concerts every Friday at
> 5pm. Under the motto
> "Listen - Relax - Reflect"
> they span works from
> major composers as well
> as chamber music, and
> often employ the
> church's own organ.

as a loud, rebellious, snarky, poor, proud and sometimes downright unsavoury capital.

Zille's collection of sketches, drawings, lithographs, photographs and cartoons can now be found in this small but charming three-room museum, along with a film and some family pictures. It has only minimal information in English, but the gist of the artist's work is easy to appreciate. His scabrously funny portrayals of beggars, urchins, labourers and prostitutes, finding in them a zest for life that transcended the poverty of their existence, made him immensely popular with Berlin's underclass.

Nearby you can find a reconstructed (and relocated) version of one of Zille's favourite watering holes, Zum Nussbaum (p115), whose characters and stories often informed his work.

---

11 ⟨⟩

Ephraim-Palais

🔲X3 **🅰Poststrasse 16**
🆂&🆄Alexanderplatz
🆄Klosterstrasse **🚌248,**
M48 **🕙10am-6pm Tue &**
Thu-Sun, noon-8pm Wed
🆆stadtmuseum.de

The corner entrance of the Ephraim-Palais, standing at the junction of Poststrasse and Mühlendamm, used to be called *"die schönste Ecke Berlins"*, meaning "Berlin's most beautiful corner". This Baroque palace was built by Friedrich Wilhelm Diterichs in 1766 for Nathan Veitel Heinrich Ephraim, Frederick the Great's Mint master and court jeweller.

During the widening of the Mühlendamm bridge in 1935 the palace was demolished, which may have been due in some part to the Jewish origin of its owner. Parts of the façade, saved from demolition, were stored in a warehouse in the western part of the city. In 1983 they were sent to East Berlin and used in the reconstruction of the palace, which was erected a few metres from its original site. One of the first-floor rooms features a restored Baroque ceiling, designed by Andreas Schlüter. The ceiling previously adorned Palais Wartenberg, which was dismantled in 1889.

Currently the Ephraim-Palais houses a branch of the Stadtmuseum Berlin (Berlin City Museum). It hosts a series of temporary exhibitions and events focused on Berlin's local artistic and cultural history.

> **Zille was partly responsible for Berlin's image as a loud, rebellious, snarky, poor, proud and sometimes downright unsavoury capital.**

→
Visitors on the spiral staircase at the Ephraim-Palais

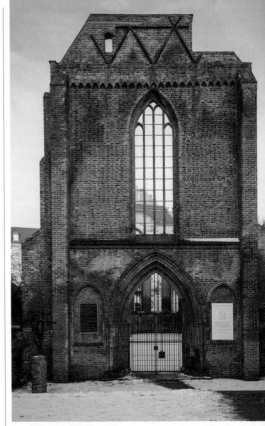

⑫

Franziskaner Klosterkirche

📍Y2 🏛Klosterstrasse 74
Ⓤ Klosterstrasse
🚌 248

These picturesque ruins surrounded by greenery are the remains of the early Gothic Franciscan Friary Church. The Franciscan friars settled in Berlin in the early 13th century. Between 1250 and 1265 they built a church and a friary, which survived almost unchanged until 1945. The church was a triple-nave basilica with an elongated presbytery, widening into a heptagonal section that was added to the structure in around 1300.

Protestants took over the church after the Reformation and the friary became a famous grammar school, whose graduates included Prussian Chancellor Otto von Bismarck.

The friary was so damaged in World War II that it was subsequently demolished, while the church was partially reconstructed in 2003–4 and is now a venue for concerts and exhibitions. The giant Corinthian capitals, emerging from the grass near the church ruins, are from a portal from the Stadtschloss (City Palace) (p96).

---

⑬

Gerichtslaube

📍X3 🏛Poststrasse 28
📞241 56 97
Ⓢ & Ⓤ Alexanderplatz
Ⓤ Klosterstrasse 🚌100, 200, 248, M48, TXL

This small building, with its sharply angled arcades, has had a turbulent history. It was built around 1280 as part of Berlin's old town hall in Spandauer Strasse. The original building was a single-storey arcaded construction with vaults supported by a

↑ Ruins of the Franziskaner Klosterkirche

central pillar. It was open on three sides and adjoined the shorter wall of the town hall. A further storey was added in 1485 to provide a hall, to which the magnificent lattice vaults were added several decades later, in 1555.

In 1692, Johann Arnold Nering refurbished the town hall in a Baroque style but left the arcades unaltered. Then, in 1868, the whole structure was dismantled to provide space for the new town hall, the Rotes Rathaus (p111). The Baroque part was lost forever, but the Gothic arcades and the first-floor hall were moved to the palace gardens in Babelsberg, where they were reassembled as a building in their own right. When the Nikolaiviertel (p116) was undergoing renovation it was decided to restore the court of justice as well. The present building in Poststrasse is a copy of a part of the former town hall, erected on a different site from the original one. Inside it is a restaurant serving local cuisine.

1621

The year the original gin mill opened on the site of Berlin's oldest pub: Gaststätte Zur letzten Instanz.

14

Parochialkirche

Q Y3 **A** Klosterstrasse 67
C 24 75 95 10
U Klosterstrasse **=** 248
O 9am–3:30pm Mon–Fri

The Parish Church was, at one time, one of the most beautiful Baroque churches in Berlin. Johann Arnold Nering prepared the initial design, with four chapels framing a central tower. Unfortunately, Nering died as construction started in 1695. The work was continued by Martin Grünberg, but the collapse of the nearly completed vaults forced a change in the design. Instead of the intended tower over the main structure, a vestibule with a front tower was built. The church was completed in 1703, but then, in 1714, its tower was enlarged to accommodate a carillon.

World War II had a devastating effect on the Parochialkirche. The interior was completely destroyed, and the tower collapsed. Following stabilization of the main structure, the façade was restored, with reproduced historic elements set within a plain interior. In 2016, a replica of the former tower top was mounted. It bears a new carillon with 52 bells.

EAT

Zum Nussbaum

A reconstruction of a 16th-century pub, serving traditional Berlin cuisine including rollmops, meatballs and vegetable pancakes, as well as local beers.

Q X3 **A** Am Nussbaum 3
O noon–10pm daily
C 242 30 95

€€€

Gaststätte Zur letzten Instanz

The oldest pub in Berlin has served everyone from Beethoven to Angela Merkel. The menu offers classic German fare, including pork knuckle and *Rinderroulade* (beef olive) in a classic wood-panelled room.

Q Y3 **A** Waisenstrasse 14–16 **O** noon–1am Tue–Sat (to 10pm Sun) **C** Mon
W zurletzteninstanz.com

€€€

15

Palais Schwerin and Münze

Q X3 **A** Molkenmarkt 1–3
S & **U** Alexanderplatz
U Klosterstrasse
= 248, M48

These two adjoining houses have quite different histories. The older one, at Molkenmarkt No. 2, is Palais Schwerin, which was built by Jean de Bodt in 1704 for a government minister, Otto von Schwerin. Despite subsequent remodelling, the palace kept its beautiful sculpted window cornices, the interior wooden staircase and the magnificent cartouche featuring the von Schwerin family crest.

The adjoining house is the Münze, or Mint, built in 1936. Its façade is decorated with a copy of the frieze that once adorned the previous Neo-Classical Mint building in Werderscher Markt. The antique style of the frieze was designed by Friedrich Gilly and produced in the workshop of J G Schadow.

16

Stadtmauer

Q Y3 **A** Waisenstrasse
S & **U** Alexanderplatz
U Klosterstrasse **=** 248

The Town Wall that once surrounded the settlements of Berlin and Cölln was erected in the second half of the 13th century. The ring of fortifications, built from brick and fieldstone, was made taller in the 14th century. Having finally lost its military significance by the 17th century, the wall was almost entirely dismantled, though some small sections survive around Waisenstrasse, having been incorporated into other buildings.

↓ Gaststätte Zur letzten Instanz by the Stadtmauer

A SHORT WALK
NIKOLAIVIERTEL

Distance 1 km (0.5 miles)
Nearest U-Bahn station Märkisches
Museum **Time** 10 minutes

St Nicholas' Quarter, or the Nikolaiviertel, owes
its name to the parish church whose spires rise
above the small buildings in this part of town.
The Nikolaiviertel is full of narrow alleys crammed
with popular restaurants, tiny souvenir shops and
small museums. The district retains the features
of long-destroyed Alt-Berlin (Old Berlin) and is
usually filled with tourists looking for a place to
rest after an exhausting day of sightseeing –
particularly in the summer. Almost every other
house is occupied by a restaurant, inn, pub or
café, so the area is quite lively until late at night.

Did You Know?

The reconstructed
buildings were not
rebuilt in their
original locations.

*The Nikolaikirche
is now a museum,
with its original
furnishings
incorporated into
the exhibition
(p112).*

*The replica arcades and
medieval courthouse of
Gerichtslaube now contain
popular restaurants (p114).*

0 metres   75   N
0 yards   75   ↑

*This statue of St George
Slaying the Dragon once
graced a courtyard of
the Stadtschloss.*

POSTSTRASSE

SPREEUFER

*A Biedermeier-style
room can be found on
the first floor of the
Knoblauchhaus building,
which is one of the few to
escape World War II
damage (p112).*

START

*One noteworthy feature
of the Ephraim-Palais is its
elegant façade. Inside
there is also an impressive
spiral staircase and
balustrade (p113).*

↑ A bear, the symbol of
Berlin, inside a fountain
in front of Nikolaikirche

The historic core of Alt-Berlin was reconstructed under the GDR

Locator Map
For more detail see p104

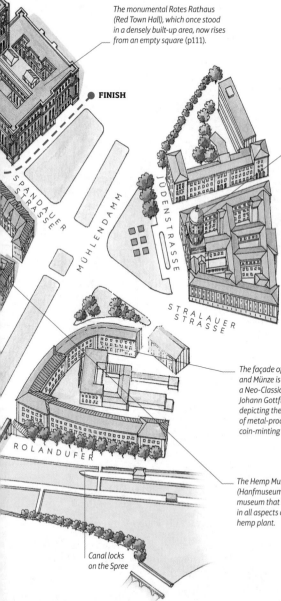

The monumental Rotes Rathaus (Red Town Hall), which once stood in a densely built-up area, now rises from an empty square (p111).

FINISH

The Stadthaus, built in 1911 by Ludwig Hoffmann, now houses several departments of the Town Hall.

SPANDAUER STRASSE

MÜHLENDAMM

JÜDENSTRASSE

STRALAUER STRASSE

The façade of Palais Schwerin and Münze is decorated with a Neo-Classical frieze by Johann Gottfried Schadow, depicting the development of metal-processing and coin-minting (p115).

ROLANDUFER

The Hemp Museum (Hanfmuseum) is a small museum that specializes in all aspects of the hemp plant.

Canal locks on the Spree

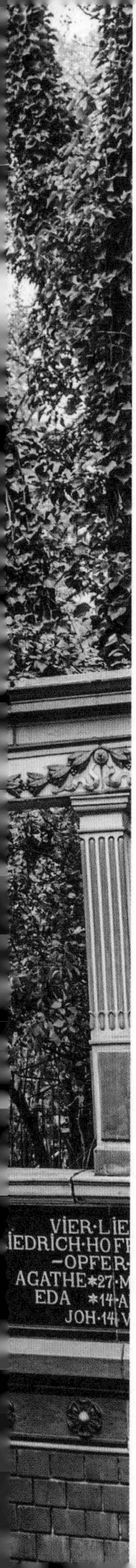

VIER·LIE
IEDRICH·HOF
-OPFER
AGATHE✱27·M
EDA ✱14·A
JOH·14·V

Tomb in Dorotheenstädtischer Friedhof

NORTH MITTE AND PRENZLAUER BERG

The area northwest of Alexanderplatz, formerly called Spandauer Vorstadt, is a historic district established in the Middle Ages. Some 18th-century buildings still stand here, though the area has mainly developed into a lively neighbourhood of buzzing bars, cafés and designer shops.

The southeastern part of the area is known as Scheunenviertel (Barn Quarter). In 1672, the Great Elector moved the hay barns – a fire hazard – out of the city limits. From that time it became a refuge for Jews fleeing Russia and Eastern Europe, and the Spandauer Vorstadt later developed into Berlin's affluent Jewish Quarter. To the north is Prenzlauer Berg, a bohemian hub in the 1990s and now, after gentrification, a beautiful and pleasant place to live and visit.

NORTH MITTE AND PRENZLAUER BERG

Must Sees
1 Gedenkstätte Berliner Mauer
2 Hamburger Bahnhof

Experience More
3 Museum für Naturkunde
4 Volksbühne
5 Deutsches Theater
6 Brecht-Weigel-Gedenkstätte
7 Dorotheenstädtischer Friedhof
8 Friedrichstadtpalast
9 Sammlung Boros
10 Oranienburger Strasse
11 Berliner Ensemble
12 Neue Synagoge and Centrum Judaicum
13 Hackesche Höfe
14 Monbijoupark
15 Kollwitzplatz
16 Jüdischer Friedhof
17 Sophienkirche
18 Gedenkstätte Grosse Hamburger Strasse
19 Haus Schwarzenberg Museums
20 Torstrasse
21 Sophienstrasse
22 Zionskirche
23 Alte and Neue Schönhauser Strasse
24 Prater
25 Alter Jüdischer Friedhof
26 Synagoge Rykestrasse
27 Wasserturm
28 Kulturbrauerei

Eat
① Yam Yam
② Nola's am Weinberg
③ Rutz
④ Metzer Eck

Drink
⑤ Buck & Breck
⑥ Becketts Kopf

Stay
⑦ Circus Hotel
⑧ Ackselhaus and Blue Home

Shop
⑨ Goldhahn und Sampson
⑩ Thatchers
⑪ Saint George's English Bookshop

L

BERNAUER STR.
STRELITZER STR.

1 Gedenkstätte Berliner Mauer

ACKER STR.
ANKLA

Sophien-Friedhof

BERGSTRASSE

Nordbahnhof

ZINNOWITZER-STRASSE

HABERSAATHSTRASSE

INVALIDENSTRASSE

GARTENSTRASSE

BERGSTRASSE

U Naturkundemuseum

SCHWARZER WEG

Museum für Naturkunde **3**

MESSISCHE STR.

SCHLEGEL-STRASSE

NOVALISSTRASSE

CHAUSSEESTRASSE

Brecht-Weigel-Gedenkstätte **6**

STRASSE

Dorotheenstädtischer Friedhof **7**

TIECK STR.

③

TORSTRASSE

TUCHOLSKYSTR.

Hamburger Bahnhof **2**

INVALIDENSTRASSE

Sandkrug-brücke

ROBERT-KOCH-PLATZ

HANNOVERSCHE STRASSE

LINIENSTR.

AUGUSTS

Hauptbahnhof
S U R

WASHINGTON-PLATZ

Charité Universitätsmedizin Berlin

LUISENSTRASSE

Stadtkanal

Humboldt Universität

FRIEDRICHSTR.

U Oranienburger Tor

Oranienburger Strasse **10**

Neue Synago and Centrur Judaicum **12**

ORANIENBURG

KAPELLE-UFER

UNTERBAUMSTR.

KARLPLATZ

REINHARDTSTR.

SCHUMANNSTR.

Deutsches Theater **5**

Sammlung Boros **9**

Oranienburger Str.

JOHANNISSTR.

8

ZIEGELSTR.

TUCHOLSKYSTR.

SCHEUNE VIERTEL

Friedrichstadt-palast

Monbijou-brücke

TIERGARTEN
p152

REINHARDTSTR.

MARIENSTRASSE

Berliner Ensemble **11**

ALBRECHT-STRASSE

BERTOLT-BRECHT-PLATZ

Bundestag U

SCHIFFBAUERDAMM

LUISENSTR.

SCHIFFBAUERDAMM

Spree

S U Friedrich-strasse

AROUND UNTER DEN LINDEN
p62

Marschallbrücke

REICHSTAGUFER

I J K L

1 2 3 4

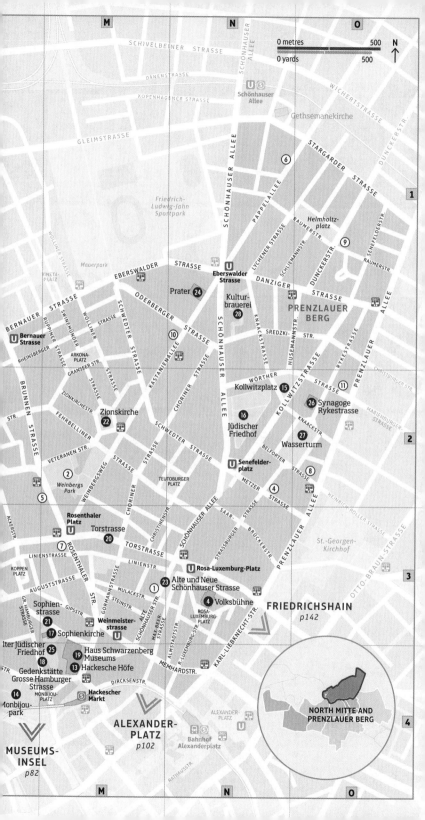

↑ The Window of Memorial shows those who died trying to cross the Wall

❶ ⓜ 🏛

GEDENKSTÄTTE BERLINER MAUER

📍 L2 🏛 Bernauer Strasse 119 Ⓢ Nordbahnhof Ⓤ Bernauer Strasse
🚌 M8, M10 🚌 245, 247 🕐 Opening times vary, see website for details
🌐 berliner-mauer-gedenkstaette.de

The Berlin Wall Memorial on Bernauer Strasse is dedicated to the people who were killed by the Eastern border guards while attempting to escape into West Berlin.

Bernauer Strasse

Only small fragments of the Berlin Wall have survived. One of these, along Bernauer Strasse, is now an official place of remembrance. The location of the memorial here is poignant as the street was cut in two, resulting in people jumping to the West side from upper-floor buildings that stood right on the dividing line, while border guards were bricking up doors and windows facing west. Today, the memorial is a grim reminder of the hardship the division inflicted on the city. It includes a museum and various installations along 2 km (1 mile) of the former border.

Structure of the Berlin Wall

Initially the Berlin Wall consisted simply of rolls of barbed wire. However, these were eventually replaced by a 4-m (13-ft) wall, safeguarded by a second wall made from reinforced concrete. This second wall was topped with a thick pipe to prevent people from reaching the top of the Wall with their fingers. Along the Wall ran what was known as a "death zone", an area controlled by guards with dogs. Where the border passed close to houses, the inhabitants were relocated. Along the entire length of the 55-km (96-mile) wall there were 293 watchtowers, along with 57 bunkers and, later on, alarms.

↑ The *Mauerspringer* (wall jumper) sculpture, added to the site in 2003

28

The number of years that the Berlin Wall split the city in two.

GHOST STATIONS

Hidden inside Nordbahnhof station is a fascinating public exhibition about "ghost stations": stations where trains passed through East Germany but passengers were not able to leave the train until it reached West Berlin again. These stations were dimly lit places patrolled by armed East German border guards and occasionally used for daring escapes.

HAMBURGER BAHNHOF

📍 J3 🏠 Invalidenstrasse 50/51 Ⓢ&Ⓤ Hauptbahnhof 🚌 120, 130, 147, 240, 245, TXL, M41, M85 🕐 10am–6pm Tue–Sun (to 8pm Thu) 🌐 smb.museum

At the Museum of Contemporary Art, multimedia exhibits sit alongside exemplary pieces of modern art to help visitors understand the development of styles such as Pop Art and Expressionism.

An Ever-Changing Museum

This art museum is situated in a specially adapted Neo-Classical building that was built in 1847 as a railway station. Following extensive refurbishment by Josef Paul Kleihues, it was opened to the public in 1996. At night, the façade is lit up by a neon installation by Dan Flavin. The museum has an ever-changing rotation of artworks by modern masters, including Beuys and Warhol, and more recent artists such as Kippenberger, Polke and Nauman. It also hosts a selection from the world-renowned Friedrich Christian Flick Collection of Art from the second half of the 20th century. Now film, video, music and design sit alongside painting and sculpture, resulting in one of the best modern and contemporary art museums in Europe.

↑ The museum's impressive Neo-Classical façade

Mao (1972), a well-known portrait by Andy Warhol that ↓ elevated the Chinese Communist leader to the rank of pop icon

↑ *Volk Ding Zero* (2009), a 3-m- (9-ft-) high bronze sculpture by Georg Baselitz, was inspired by African, German and Polish folk art

GALLERY GUIDE

All works on display at the Hamburger Bahnhof are temporary and exhibits shown here may not necessarily be on display. The Rieckhallen shows selected works from the Friedrich Christian Flick Collection in rotation. The main hall is used for unusual installations and occasional fashion shows.

EXPERIENCE MORE

3

Museum für Naturkunde

📍 J3 🏛 Invalidenstrasse 43
Ⓤ Naturkundemuseum
🚌 147, 245 🕐 9:30am-6pm
Tue-Fri, 10am-6pm Sat,
Sun & public hols ❌ Mon
🌐 museumfuer
naturkunde.berlin

Berlin's Natural History Museum is one of the biggest in the world, its collection numbering over 30 million exhibits. Occupying a purpose-built Neo-Renaissance building completed in 1889, the museum has been operating for over a century, and despite several periods of renovation has maintained its old-fashioned atmosphere.

The highlights of the museum are Europe's best-preserved *Tyrannosaurus rex* skeleton and the world's largest original dinosaur skeleton, which is housed in the glass-roofed courtyard. The colossal 23-m- (75-ft-) long and 12-m- (39-ft-) high *Brachiosaurus brancai* was discovered in Tanzania in 1909 by a German fossil-hunting expedition. Six other smaller reconstructed dinosaur skeletons and a replica of the fossilized remains of an *Archaeopteryx lithographica*, thought to be the prehistoric link between reptiles and birds, complete this fascinating display. The adjacent rooms feature countless colourful shells and butterflies, as well as taxidermy. Particularly popular are the dioramas – scenes of mounted animals set against the background of their natural habitat. A favourite is Bobby the Gorilla,

↓ The Dinosaur Hall at the
Museum für Naturkunde

MAX REINHARDT (1873-1943)

This actor and director became famous as one of the 20th century's greatest theatre reformers. He worked in Berlin, first as an actor in the Deutsches Theater, and then from 1905 as its director. As well as setting up the Kammerspiele, he produced plays for the Neues Theater am Schiffbauerdamm (renamed the Berliner Ensemble) and the Schumann Circus (later to become the Friedrich-stadtpalast). His experimental productions of classic and modern works brought him worldwide fame. Forced to emigrate because of his Jewish origins, he left Germany in 1933 for the United States, where he died in 1943.

who was brought to Berlin Zoo in 1928 as a 2-year-old and lived there until 1935. There is also a fine collection of minerals and meteorites.

4
Volksbühne

☉ N3 ⌂ Rosa-Luxemburg-Platz 📞 24 06 55 Ⓤ Rosa-Luxemburg-Platz 🚌 100, 200 🚋 M8

Founded during the early years of the 20th century, the People's Theatre owes its existence to the efforts of the 100,000 members of the Freie Volksbühne (Free People's Theatre Society). The original theatre was built in 1913, a time when the Scheunen-viertel district was undergoing rapid redevelopment. During the 1920s the theatre became famous thanks to the director Erwin Piscator (1893–1966), who later achieved great acclaim at the Metropol-Theater on Nollendorfplatz.

Destroyed during World War II, the theatre was rebuilt in the early 1950s to a design by Hans Richter. Now one of the city's most important cultural spots, it often stages controversial performances.

5
Deutsches Theater

☉ K4 ⌂ Schumannstrasse 13A 📞 28 44 10 Ⓢ&Ⓤ Fried-richstrasse Ⓤ Oranien-burger Tor 🚌 147 🚋 12, M1

This theatre building first opened in 1850 as the Friedrich-Wilhelm Städtisches Theater, and in 1883, following reconstruction, it was renamed Deutsches Theater. It was here that Max Reinhardt began his career as an actor, before becoming director from 1905 until 1933.

Another famous figure associated with the theatre was Bertolt Brecht who, until 1933, wrote plays for it; after

World War II he became the director of the Berliner Ensemble (p129), whose first venue was here at the Deutsches Theater.

6
Brecht-Weigel-Gedenkstätte

☉ K3 ⌂ Chausseestrasse 125 📞 200 57 18 44 Ⓤ Naturkundemuseum, Oranienburger Tor 🚌 147, 245 🚋 12, M6 ⏰ 10am-3:30pm Tue & Sat, 10-11am Wed & Fri, 10am-6:30pm Thu, 11am-6pm Sun

The house where Bertolt Brecht and his wife, the actress Helene Weigel, lived and worked is now a memorial. Brecht, one of the greatest playwrights of the 20th century, was associated with Berlin from 1920, but emigrated in 1933. After the war, his left-wing views made him an attractive potential resident of the newly created German Socialist state. Lured by the promise of his own theatre, he returned to Berlin in 1948 with Weigel. He directed the Berliner Ensemble until his death, focusing mainly on productions of his own plays.

He lived in the first-floor apartment here from 1953 until he died in 1956. Weigel lived in the second-floor

↑ Dorotheenstädtischer Friedhof memorial to Johann Gottlieb Fichte

apartment, and after Brecht's death moved to the ground floor. She also founded an archive of Brecht's works, which is located on the second floor of the building.

7
Dorotheenstädtischer Friedhof

☉ K3 ⌂ Chausseestrasse 126 📞 461 72 79 Ⓤ Naturkundemuseum, Oranienburger Tor 🚌 142, 245, 247 🚋 12, M6, M8, ⏰ 8am-sunset daily

This small cemetery, established in 1763, is the final resting place of many famous Berlin citizens, including Bertolt Brecht and Helene Weigel. Many of the monuments are outstanding works of art, coming from the workshops of prominent Berlin architects, including Karl Friedrich Schinkel (p28) and Johann Gottfried Schadow, who are both buried here. A tranquil, tree-filled oasis, the cemetery is reached via a narrow path, leading from the street between the wall of the French Cemetery and the Brecht-Weigel-Gedenkstätte.

DRINK

Buck & Breck

This hipster bar is cunningly disguised as an art gallery. If you can find it, and if there's room, you'll be rewarded with impeccable drinks.

📍M2 🏛Brunnenstrasse 177 ⏰Opening times vary, see website for details 🌐buckandbreck.com

---

Becketts Kopf

Find the wrinkled visage of Mr Beckett staring from a dark window, ring the bell and enter Prenzlauer Berg's best cocktail spot.

📍N1 🏛Pappelallee 64 ⏰7pm–2am Mon–Thu & Sun (to 4am Fri & Sat) 🌐becketts-kopf.de

---

8

Friedrichstadtpalast

📍K4 🏛Friedrichstrasse 107 Ⓢ Oranienburger Strasse, Friedrichstrasse Ⓤ Oranienburger Tor 🚌147 🚊12, M1 🌐palast.berlin

Multicoloured glass tiles and a pink, plume-shaped neon sign make up the gaudy but eye-catching façade of the Friedrichstadt Palace. Built in the early 1980s, this massive theatre complex specializes in spectacular, Vegas-style shows involving gigantic casts and expensive special effects. Nearly 2,000 seats are arranged around a huge podium, used by turns as a circus arena, a swimming pool and an ice rink. A further huge stage is equipped with every technical facility. There is also a small cabaret theatre with seats for 240 spectators.

The original and much-loved Friedrichstadtpalast suffered bomb damage during World War II and was replaced with the existing version. Built as a market hall, the earlier building was later used as a circus ring. In 1918 it became the Grosse Schauspielhaus, or Grand Playhouse, opening in 1919 with a memorable production of Aeschylus's *The Oresteia*, directed by Max Reinhardt (*p126*). The old building was extraordinary, its central dome supported by a forest of columns and topped with Expressionist, stalactite-like decoration. An equally fantastical interior provided seating for 5,000 spectators.

9

Sammlung Boros

📍K4 🏛Reinhardtstrasse 20 Ⓢ&Ⓤ Oranienburger Tor 🚌147 🚊M1, M12 ⏰3–8pm Thu, 10am–8pm Fri–Sun 🌐sammlung-boros.de

This former air-raid bunker, built by architect Karl Bonatz, is an intriguing gallery location. The bunker has a chequered history; once used as a POW prison by the Red Army, it later became a warehouse, then in the 1990s

← Michel Majerus on show at the Sammlung Boros

As you stroll around the district it is worth looking out for a number of interesting buildings, such as the one at Oranienburger Strasse No. 71–2, built by Christian Friedrich Becherer in 1789 for Germany's Great National Masonic Lodge.

🅫 Did You Know?

The bunker that houses Sammlung Boros used to be an underground venue for live concerts and techno parties.

---

it was a popular club. In 2003 art collector Christian Boros bought the building and converted it into a gallery space. It houses the Boros Collection of modern art. No more than 12 guests can visit at one time and advance online registration is required.

---

⑩ Oranienburger Strasse

📍 K3 **Ⓢ Oranienburger Strasse, Hackescher Markt** **Ⓤ Oranienburger Tor** **🚋 12, M1, M4, M5, M6**

Oranienburger Strasse is home to many of Berlin's most popular nightspots. People of all ages flock here, spending pleasant hours in the area's numerous cafés, restaurants and bars. The district has traditionally been a centre for alternative culture, and home to the famous state-sponsored Tacheles centre for the arts, previously occupied by artist squatters. The Tacheles centre has closed, but many good art galleries remain in this area.

---

⑪ Berliner Ensemble

📍 K4 **🏠 Bertolt-Brecht-Platz 1** **📞 28 40 81 55** **Ⓢ & Ⓤ Friedrichstrasse** **🚌 147** **🚋 12, M1**

Designed by Heinrich Seeling and completed in 1892, this theatre has seen many changes in Berlin's cultural life. First known as the Neues Theater am Schiffbauerdamm, it soon became famous for staging important premieres and for its memorable productions by Max Reinhardt. These included Shakespeare's *A Midsummer Night's Dream* in 1905, which, for the first time, used a revolving stage and real trees as part of the set. In 1928 the theatre presented the world premiere of Bertolt Brecht's *The Threepenny Opera*. The building was destroyed during World War II and subsequently restored with a much simpler exterior, but its Neo-Baroque interior survived intact.

The theatre returned to prominence in 1954 with the arrival of the Berliner Ensemble under the directorship of Brecht and his wife, actress Helene Weigel. The move from its former home, the Deutsches Theater *(p127)*, to the new venue was celebrated by staging the world premiere of Brecht's *The Caucasian Chalk Circle*. After Brecht's death, Weigel took over the running of the theatre, maintaining its innovative tradition.

Samuel Beckett's *Endgame*, staged by ↓ the Berliner Ensemble

Neue Synagoge and Centrum Judaicum

Q L3 **A** Oranienburger Strasse 28–30 **S** Oranienburger Strasse **M1, M5** **C** Apr–Sep: 10am–6pm Mon–Fri, 10am–7pm Sun); Oct–Mar: 10am–6pm Sun–Thu, 10am–3pm Fri) **Q** Jewish hols **W** centrumjudaicum.de

The building of the New Synagogue, by architect Eduard Knoblauch, was completed in 1866. The design, a highly sophisticated response to the asymmetrical shape of the plot of land, used a narrow façade flanked by a pair of towers and crowned with a dome containing a round vestibule. Small rooms opened off the vestibule, including an anteroom and two prayer rooms – one large and one small. The two towers opened onto a staircase leading to the galleries, and the main hall had space for around 3,000 worshippers. An innovative use of iron in the construction of the roof and galleries put the synagogue at the forefront of 19th-century civil engineering. This fascinating structure

was Berlin's largest synagogue until the night of 9–10 November 1938, when it was partially destroyed in the course of the infamous Kristallnacht (Night of Broken Glass), when thousands of synagogues, cemeteries, Jewish homes and shops were looted and burned by soldiers and Nazi supporters. The building was damaged further by Allied bombing in 1943 and was finally demolished in 1958 by government authorities. Reconstruction began in 1988 and the stunning new building was completed with due ceremony in 1995.

Adjoining the New Synagoge, the Centrum Judaicum (Jewish Centre) occupies the former premises of the Jewish community council, and contains a library, archives and a research centre devoted to the history and cultural heritage of the Jews of Berlin. The Centre also uses restored rooms of the Neue Synagoge to exhibit various materials relating to the local Jewish community, which included one of the greatest of all Jewish thinkers and social activists, Moses Mendelssohn.

Be aware that security is strict at both the Synagoge and the Centrum Judaicum.

↑ Triple domes of the Neue Synagoge

Hackesche Höfe

Q M4 **A** Rosenthaler Strasse 40–41 **S** Hackescher Markt **U** Weinmeisterstrasse **M1, M4, M5, M6**

Running from Oranienburger Strasse and Rosenthaler up as far as Sophienstrasse, the Hackesche Höfe (Höfe means "courtyard") is a huge, early 20th-century complex. It is made up of an intricate series of nine interconnecting courtyards surrounded by tall and beautifully proportioned buildings. The development dates from 1906, and was designed by Kurt Berendt and August Endell, both of whom were

---

MOSES MENDELSSOHN (1729–86)

One of the greatest German philosophers of the 18th century, Moses Mendelssohn arrived in Berlin in 1743 and was a central figure in the Jewish struggle for citizenship rights. About 50 years later the first Jewish family was granted full civic rights; however, it was not until the Emancipation Edict of 1812 that Jewish men finally became full citizens. The grandfather of composer Felix Mendelssohn-Bartholdy, he is immortalized in the drama Nathan der Weise (Nathan the Wise) by his friend Gotthold Ephraim Lessing.

outstanding exponents of the German Secession style.

Damaged during World War II, Hackesche Höfe has been restored to its original splendour. The first courtyard is especially attractive, featuring glazed facings with geometric designs decorated in fabulous colours. A whole range of restaurants, bars, art galleries, shops and restaurants can be found here, as well as offices and apartments on the upper floors. The complex also has a small theatre, the Chamäleon, specializing in contemporary circus shows. For many Berliners the Hackesche Höfe has become something of a cult spot, and for visitors it is definitely a sight not to be missed.

14

Monbijoupark

◨ L4 **◮ Oranienburger Strasse** **◎ Oranienburger Strasse, Hackescher Markt** **▦ M1, M4, M5, M6**

Little Monbijou ("My Jewel") Park, between Oranienburger Strasse (p129) and the Spree river, was once the grounds of the Monbijou Palace. Damaged by bombing during World War II, the ruined palace was dismantled in 1960.

A rare green space in this part of the city, the well-kept park is a pleasant place to relax. It features a marble bust of the poet Adelbert von Chamisso, and there is also an open-air swimming pool for children.

> For many Berliners the Hackesche Höfe has become something of a cult spot, and for visitors it is definitely a sight not to be missed.

STAY

Circus Hotel

This eco-friendly hotel offers comfortable rooms, a decent in-house bar and restaurant and friendly service, all right on buzzy Rosenthaler Platz.

◨ M3 **◮ Rosenthaler Strasse 1** **ⓦ circus-berlin.de**

€€€

Ackselhaus and Blue Home

This discreet hotel is set inside a beautifully restored 19th-century property, and has individually designed rooms and suites, plus a pleasant garden.

◨ O2 **◮ Belforter Strasse 21** **ⓦ ackselhaus.de**

€€€

HIDDEN GEM
Käthe Kollwitz

Famed German artist Käthe Kollwitz lived at Kollwitzstrasse 56 with her husband for many years. She was evacuated in 1943, and the house was bombed later that year, destroying many prints and drawings. A plaque marks the new house.

⑮ Kollwitzplatz

📍N2 Ⓤ Senefelderplatz

This green square is named after the German artist Käthe Kollwitz (1867–1945), who once lived nearby. It was here that the socially engaged painter and sculptor observed and painted the daily hardships of the working-class people living in overcrowded tenements. One of her sculptures stands on the square, now the social hub of the district, with a Thursday organic farmers' market, cool bars, restaurants and shops that extend into the surrounding streets. Käthe Kollwitz's work can be seen at the Käthe-Kollwitz-Museum (p216).

⑯ Jüdischer Friedhof

📍N2 Ⓐ Schönhauser Allee 22-25 🕿 441 98 24 Ⓤ Senefelderplatz 🕐 8am-4pm Mon-Thu, 7:30am-1pm Fri 🚫 Sat, Sun & public hols

This small Jewish Cemetery is hidden behind thick walls on Schönhauser Allee, but the serene atmosphere, with tall trees and thick undergrowth, is a welcome oasis. The cemetery was laid out in 1827, though the oldest gravestone dates back to the 14th century. It was Berlin's second-largest Jewish

The Baroque tower of the Sophienkirche ↓

Did You Know?

Spandauer Vorstadt is an area north of the Spree river. It's known for great shopping and nightlife.

cemetery after the Jüdischer Friedhof Weissensee (p235).

Among the many prominent Berliners resting here are the painter Max Liebermann (p245); Giacomo Meyerbeer, the composer and musical director of the Staatsoper Unter den Linden; and the author David Friedländer (1750–1834). The lapidarium, built in 2005, displays rescued gravestones from this and other historic Jewish cemeteries in Berlin.

⑰ Sophienkirche

📍M3 Ⓐ Grosse Hamburger Strasse 31 🕿 308 79 20 Ⓢ Hackescher Markt Ⓤ Weinmeisterstrasse 🚋 M1, M4, M5, M6 🕐 1-6pm Mon-Sat

A narrow passageway and a picturesque gate take you through to this small Baroque church. Founded in 1712 by Queen Sophia Luisa, the wife of Frederick I of Prussia, this was the first parish church of the newly developed Spandauer Vorstadt area, which had been growing steadily since the

during World War II, served as a detention centre for many thousands of Berlin Jews who were condemned to death in the camps at Auschwitz and Theresienstadt.

Until the years leading up to World War II, Grosse Hamburger Strasse was one of the main streets of Berlin's Jewish quarter. It was home to several Jewish schools, the old-people's home and the city's oldest Jewish cemetery, established in 1672.

At No. 27 stands a Jewish school founded in 1778 by Moses Mendelssohn (p130). Rebuilt in 1906, the building was reopened as a Jewish secondary school in 1993. The empty space once occupied by house No. 15–16, destroyed by World War II bombing, is now an installation, *The Missing House* by Christian Boltanski, with plaques recording the names and professions of the former inhabitants of the house.

Middle Ages. Johann Friedrich Grael designed the tower, which was built between 1729 and 1735. In 1892 the building was extended to include a presbytery, though the church still retains its original Baroque character.

A modest, rectangular structure, Sophienkirche is typical of its period, with the tower adjoining the narrower side elevation. The interior still contains a number of its original 18th-century furnishings, including the pulpit and the font.

Several gravestones dating from the 18th century, have survived in the small grave-yard surrounding the church.

18

Gedenkstätte Grosse Hamburger Strasse

◉ M4 ◭ Grosse Hamburger Strasse ⬠ Hackescher Markt 🚊 12, M1, M4, M5, M6

An otherworldly group of figures in bronze stands on Grosse Hamburger Strasse, bearing witness to the extermination of the street's Jewish community. On this spot once stood a Jewish home for the elderly which,

→

Haunting figure from the Jewish memorial

 SHOPPING AREAS IN DOWNTOWN MITTE

Hackescher Höfe
Renovated Art Nouveau shopping complex.

Alte Schönhauser Strasse
Extension of Schönhauser Allee.

Neue Schönhauser Strasse
Small street packed with boutiques, cafés and eateries.

Mulackstrasse
Elegant side street, home to many local design stores.

Steinstrasse
Parallel to Mulackstrasse, with many shops and cafés.

19 🚲 Ⓜ 🛍️

Haus Schwarzenberg Museums

📍M4 🏠Rosenthaler Strasse 39 ⓈHackesher Markt ⓊWeinmeisterstrasse 🚌N2, N5, N42 🚊M1, M5 🌐hausschwarzenberg.org

The Haus Schwarzenberg complex is a cool and grungy hangover from the early 1990s. Its crumbling, postwar façades are splattered with colourful street art – some by famous local artists like El Bocho and Miss Van. Its courtyard consciously eschews high-end boutiques and cafés in favour of an edgy bar, a street-art shop and gallery and the **Monsterkabinett**: a collection of moving mechanical monsters built by the owners, a nonprofit artist collective. The complex also hosts a trio of notable, small museums that explore local resistance to the Nazis. The **Gedenkstätte Stille Helden** (Silent Heroes Memorial Centre) commemorates people who risked their lives to hide or rescue persecuted Jews. One such man was Otto Weidt, a German entrepreneur who saved a number of his blind, Jewish employees at his workshop, which is now the **Museum Blindenwerkstatt Otto Weidt** (Museum Otto Weidt's Workshop for the Blind). It displays photographs and back-stories of Weidt, his family and his workers, and visitors can still see the room where Jewish families were hidden. The third museum, the **Anne-Frank-Zentrum**, offers an engaging and eclectic look at the famous teenager's life.

Monsterkabinett
⊛ 🕐 Times vary, see website for details
🌐monsterkabinett.de

Gedenkstätte Stille Helden
⊛ 🕐 10am–8pm daily
🌐gedenkstaette-stillehelden.de

←

Café Cinema, a legendary bohemian meeting place in Haus Schwarzenburg

it is a busy, noisy and sometimes polluted street, Torstrasse has its charms and has been almost completely transformed from a largely working-class bohemian area into a more appealing location, particularly for young urbanites. The 19th-century residential buildings lining the street have been gentrified to make way for cool bars, trendy cafés, gourmet restaurants, art galleries and fashion shops. "Soto", the area south of Torstrasse, has the highest concentration of independent designers and brand outfitters in the city.

Museum Blindenwerk-statt Otto Weidt

◈ ⏰ 10am–8pm daily
🖥 museum-blindenwerk statt.de

Anne-Frank-Zentrum

◈ ⏰ 10am–6pm Tue–Sun
🖥 annefrank.de

20

Torstrasse

📍 M3 Ⓤ Oranienburger Tor, Rosenthaler Platz, Rosa-Luxemburg-Platz
🚌 142 🚊 M1, M8

Formerly a customs road and Berlin's northern border around 1800, Torstrasse is now a main thoroughfare connecting Prenzlauer Allee and Friedrichstrasse. Although

21 ⊛

Sophienstrasse

📍 M3 Ⓢ Hackescher Markt Ⓤ Weinmeisterstrasse
🚊 M1, M4, M5, M6

The area around Sophien-strasse and Gipsstrasse was first settled at the end of the 17th century. In fact, Sophien-strasse was once the main street of Spandauer Vorstadt (p119). The area underwent extensive restoration during the 1980s that was designed to preserve its small-town character. Today, the narrow lanes and three-storey buildings are reminiscent of Prague's Old Town. It was one of the first parts of East Berlin in which renovation was chosen in preference to large-scale demolition and redevelop-ment. Now these modest but charming 18th-century Neo-Classical buildings are home

1852

The year the Craftsman Association House at Sophienstrasse No. 18 was constructed.

to a number of different arts and crafts workshops, cosy bars, unusual boutiques, a puppet theatre and interesting art galleries.

One building with a particularly eventful history is Sophienstrasse No. 18. The house was erected in 1852, although its striking and picturesque terracotta double doorway dates from the time of its extensive restoration, undertaken in 1904 by Joseph Franckel and Theodor Kampfmeyer on behalf of the Crafts Society. Founded in 1844, the Crafts Society moved its headquarters to Sophienstrasse in 1905. On 14 November 1918 the very same house was used as the venue for the first meeting of the Spartacus League, later to become the Communist Party of Germany.

The main door of Sophien-strasse No. 21 leads into a row of interior courtyards running up as far as Gipsstrasse.

↑ Colourful residential buildings on Torstrasse

> "Soto", the area south of Torstrasse, has the highest concentration of independent designers and brand outfitters in the city.

↑ Soaring tower of the Neo-Romantic Zionskirche

22

Zionskirche

M2 **Zionskirchplatz** **44 92 19 1** **Senefelder-platz, Rosenthaler Platz** **12, M1** **Opening times vary, call ahead**

Located in the square named after it, Zionskirchplatz, this Protestant church was built between 1866 and 1873 – a tranquil oasis in the middle of this lively district. Both the square and the church have always been centres of political opposition. During the Third Reich, resistance groups against the Nazi regime congregated at the church, and when the Communists were in power in East Germany, the alternative "environment library" (an information and documentation centre) was established here. Church and other opposition groups active here played a decisive role in the transformation of East Germany in 1989–90.

23

Alte and Neue Schönhauser Strasse

N3 **Hackescher Markt** **Weinmeisterstrasse** **M1**

Alte Schönhauser Strasse is one of the oldest streets in the Spandauer Vorstadt district, running from the centre of Berlin to Pankow and Schönhausen. In the 18th and 19th centuries this was a popular residential area among wealthy merchants. During World War II, however, its proximity to the neighbouring Jewish district of Scheunenviertel (p140), devastated by the Nazis, decreased its popularity considerably.

For a long time, bars, small factories, workshops and retail shops were the hallmark of this neighbourhood. Small private shops survived longer

↑ Outside dining at Nola's am Weinberg

here than in most parts of Berlin, and the largely original houses maintained much of their pre-1939 atmosphere. Much has changed, however, since the fall of the Berlin Wall. Some of the houses have been restored, and many old businesses have been replaced by fashionable shops, restaurants and bars, making it one of the most expensive retail areas in the city. Throughout the district, the old and the new now stand side by side. One poignant example is at Neue Schönhauser Strasse No. 14. This interesting old house in the German Neo-Renaissance style was built in 1891 to a design by Alfred Messel. The first-floor rooms were home to the first public reading room in Berlin, while on the ground floor was a *Volkskaffeehaus*, a soup kitchen, with separate rooms for men and women. Here the poor of the neighbourhood could get a free bowl of soup and a cup of ersatz (imitation) coffee.

EAT

Yam Yam
Popular with local fashionistas, this canteen-style restaurant uses organic Korean vegetables and hot spices for owner Sumi Ha's *cha chang myun* and *bibimbap*.

🗺 M3 🏠 Alte Schönhauser Strasse 6 🕐 Noon-11pm Mon-Thu (to midnight Fri & Sat), 1pm-11pm Sun 🌐 yamyam-berlin.de

€€€

Nola's am Weinberg
This Swiss-themed restaurant serves fondue as well as risotto dishes and excellent brunches. It has a lovely summer terrace overlooking the pretty am Weinberg park.

🗺 M2 🏠 Veteranen Strasse 9 🕐 10am-1am daily 🌐 nola.de

€€€

Rutz
A star in Berlin's gourmet scene, Rutz is a Michelin-starred venue offering dishes based on local recipes served with a creative twist.

🗺 K3 🏠 Chausseestrasse 8 🕐 Opening times vary, see website for details 🌐 rutz-restaurant.de

€€€

Metzer Eck
In its heyday, this traditional eatery was a meeting point for Prenzlauer Berg's GDR bohemian luminaries. It still has oodles of character and serves cheap, simple dishes like meatballs and *Bockwurst*.

🗺 N2 🏠 Metzer Strasse 33 🕐 4pm-1am Mon-Fri, 6pm-1am Sat 🌐 metzer-eck.de

€€€

24
Prater

📍N1 🏠Kastanienallee 7-9
📞448 56 88 Ⓤ Eberswalder Strasse 🚋12, M1

Prater has been one of Berlin's best-known entertainment institutions for more than a century. The building, along with its quiet courtyard, was constructed in the 1840s and later became the city's oldest and largest beer garden. It now houses a restaurant, serving Berlin specialities, and stages a variety of pop, rock and folk concerts and theatre shows.

Did You Know?

Mendelssohn's rabbi and mentor, David Hirschel Fraenkel, is also buried at Alter Jüdischer Friedhof.

25
Alter Jüdischer Friedhof

📍M4 🏠Grosse Hamburger Strasse Ⓢ Hackescher Markt 🚋M1

The Old Jewish Cemetery was established in 1672 and, until 1827 when it was finally declared full, it provided the resting place for over 12,000 Berliners. After this date Jews were buried in cemeteries in Schönhauser Allee (p132) and in Herbert-Baum-Strasse. The Alter Jüdischer Friedhof was destroyed by the Nazis in 1943, and in 1945 the site was turned into a park. Embedded in the original cemetery wall, a handful of Baroque *masebas* (or tombstones) continue to recall the past. A *maseba* stands on the

grave of the philosopher Moses Mendelssohn (p130), erected in 1990 by members of the Jewish community.

26
Synagoge Rykestrasse

📍O2 🏠Rykestrasse 53
📞88 02 81 47 Ⓤ Senefelderplatz

This synagogue is one of the few reminders of old Jewish life in Berlin, and one of the few in Germany left almost intact during the Nazi regime. Built in 1904, the red-brick synagogue has a basilica-like nave with three aisles and certain Moorish features. Due to its location inside a huge tenement area, Nazi SA troops did not set it on fire during

> **This synagogue is one of the few reminders of old Jewish life in Berlin, and one of the few in Germany left almost intact during the Nazi regime.**

the Kristallnacht pogrom on 9 November 1938, when hundreds of other synagogues were razed to the ground. The synagogue welcomes visitors to its public services.

㉗

Wasserturm

🇵 O2 🅰 Knaackstrasse/ Belforter Strasse
🆄 Senefelderplatz

The unofficial symbol of this district is a 30-m- (100-ft-) high water tower, standing high on the former mill hill in the heart of Prenzlauer Berg. It was here that some of the windmills, once typical in Prenzlauer Berg, produced flour for the city's population. The distinctive brick water tower was built in 1874 by Wilhelm Vollhering and served as a reservoir for the country's first running water system. In the 1930s, the basement served as a make-shift jail, where Nazi SA troops held and tortured Communist opponents. This dark period is marked by a plaque.

㉘

Kulturbrauerei

🇵 N1 🅰 Schönhauser Allee 36–39 🆄 Eberswalder Strasse 🚋 12, M1, M10
🕙 10am–6pm Tue–Sun (to 8pm Thu) 🌐 hdg.de

This vast Neo-Gothic, industrial red-and-yellow-brick building was once Berlin's most famous brewery, Schultheiss, built by architect Franz Schwechten in 1889–92. Now housing the Kulturbrauerei (culture brewery), the huge complex with several courtyards has been revived as a cultural and entertainment centre, with concert venues, restaurants and cafés, and a cinema, as well as artists' ateliers. A popular Christmas market is also held here in December.

Inside the Kulturbrauerei, the Museum Alltagsgeschichte der DDR (Museum of Everyday Life in the GDR) features both permanent and temporary exhibitions on the former East Germany. Don't miss the reconstructed flat, or the "Trabi-Tent", a typically ingenious East German solution to a caravan holiday with no caravan.

↑ The Wasserturm, with its brickwork cladding

↑ Leafy avenue in the Alter Jüdischer Friedhof

A SHORT WALK
SCHEUNENVIERTEL

Distance 1.5 km (1 mile) **Nearest S-Bahn station** Oranienburger Strasse **Time** 15 minutes

From the 17th century to World War II, Scheunenviertel lay at the heart of Berlin's large Jewish district. During the 19th century the community flourished, its prosperity reflected in grand buildings such as the Neue Synagoge, which opened in 1866. Left to crumble for nearly 50 years after the double devastations of the Nazis and Allied bombing, the district enjoyed a huge revival after the fall of the Berlin Wall, and a walk in this area will reveal cafés and bars that are home to some of the city's liveliest nightlife.

START

The Postfuhramt was used originally as stables for the horses that delivered the post. Its ceramic-clad façade resembles a palace more than a post office and there are plans to turn it into a hotel.

Today the lavishly restored yards of Heckmann-Höfe are the most elegant in Berlin, and attract visitors with a restaurant and fashionable clothes shops.

Sparkling with gold, the restored Neue Synagoge is used for services (p130).

Next to the Neue Synagoge, the Centrum Judaicum (Jewish Centre) houses documents relating to the history and cultural heritage of the Berlin Jews (p130).

TUCHOLSKY STRASSE

ORANIENBURGER STRASSE

S-Bahn line

← The glittering golden domes of the Neue Synagoge

↑ Alter Jüdischer Friedhof, the city's oldest Jewish cemetery

Locator Map
For more detail see p120

NORTH MITTE AND PRENZLAUER BERG

Did You Know?

Alter Jüdischer Friedhof closed in 1794 after the introduction of new hygiene laws in Prussia.

FINISH

GROSSE HAMBURGER STRASSE

HACKESCHER MARKT

Sophienkirche is a small Protestant church founded by its namesake, Queen Sophie Luisa, in 1712 (p132).

The Gedenkstätte Grosse Hamburger Strasse memorial to the Berlin Jews stands on the site of the city's first Jewish old-people's home (p133).

Hackesche Höfe is an attractive series of interconnected court-yards, home to many popular entertainment venues (p130).

The city's oldest Jewish cemetery, Alter Jüdischer Friedhof, is now a tree-filled park after being destroyed by the Gestapo in 1943 (p138).

Once the grounds of a royal palace, the small Monbijoupark (p131) contains a marble bust of the poet Adelbert von Chamisso.

| 0 metres | 100 |
| 0 yards | 100 |

N ↑

FRIEDRICHSHAIN

This famous district was created in 1920 when several outlying villages were absorbed into the city as part of the Greater Berlin Act. The area was bombed heavily during World War II because of its many factories and, due to the damage, the district's residential buildings were left largely unattended during the GDR – which focused on constructing Soviet showstreet Karl-Marx-Allee and erecting their trademark *Plattenbauten* (prefab tower blocks) wherever it could.

After the Berlin Wall fell, the area became a magnet for left-wingers and squatters. Vague traces of the area's dissident culture remain, but most have been driven out by the same gentrifying process that has affected the rest of Berlin's inner-city areas.

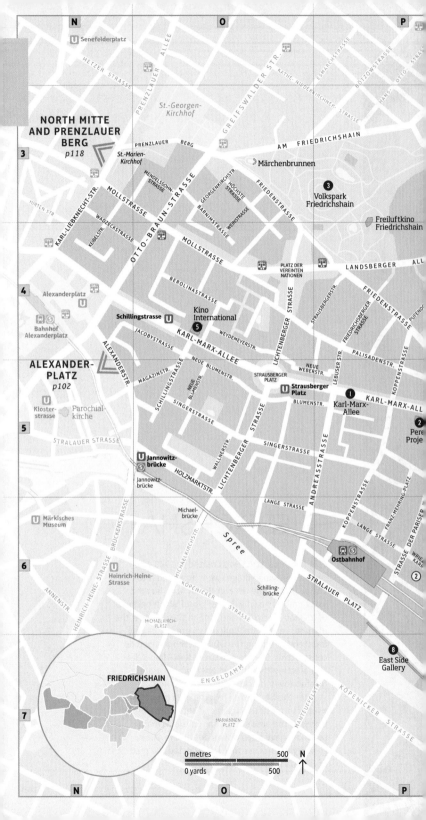

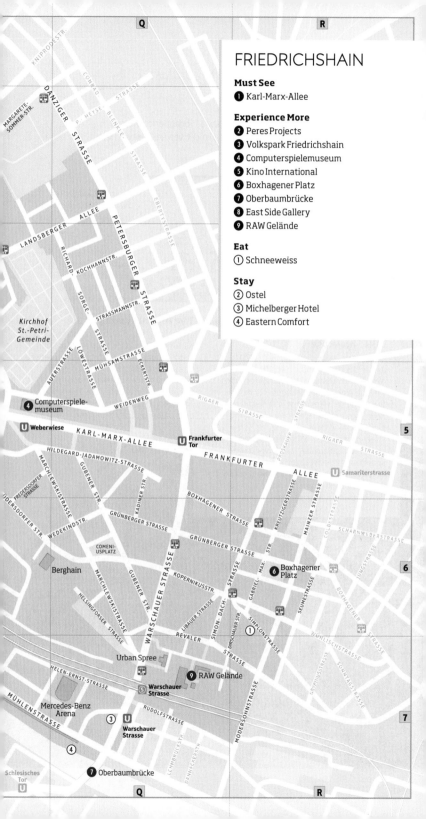

FRIEDRICHSHAIN

Must See
1. Karl-Marx-Allee

Experience More
2. Peres Projects
3. Volkspark Friedrichshain
4. Computerspielemuseum
5. Kino International
6. Boxhagener Platz
7. Oberbaumbrücke
8. East Side Gallery
9. RAW Gelände

Eat
1. Schneeweiss

Stay
2. Ostel
3. Michelberger Hotel
4. Eastern Comfort

❶
KARL-MARX-ALLEE

⚐ P5

The area around this wide boulevard has a vibrant and relaxed atmosphere. Most residents are in their mid-twenties, drawn here by the alternative cafés and cool bars.

The route leading east to Poland and Moscow was initially called Frankfurter Strasse, and then renamed Stalinallee in 1949. Having suffered severe damage during World War II, the street was chosen as the site for the construction showpiece of the new German Democratic Republic, featuring spacious and luxurious apartments for workers, as well as commercial infrastructure.

← A typical Socialist-era residential block, now in high demand for Berliners

taken from famous Berlin architects Schinkel (p28) and Gontard, as well as from the renowned Meissen porcelain.

GDR Showcase

The avenue was widened to 90 m (300 ft) and, in the course of the next 10 years, huge residential tower blocks and a row of shops were built on it. The first houses to be built on the street were Modernist in style and quickly denounced as "too Western". They were hidden behind trees while the rest of the street proceeded in a more aptly Socialist style. The next architects followed a style known in the Soviet Union as "pastry chef", which was "nationalistic in form, but socialist in content", and linked the whole work to Berlin's own traditions. Hence there are motifs

The Avenue Today

The buildings on this street, renamed Karl-Marx-Allee in 1961, are now considered historic monuments, and the section between Strausberger Platz and Frankfurter Tor is effectively a huge open-air museum of Socialist Realist architecture. The buildings have been cleaned up and the crumbling details are gradually being restored.

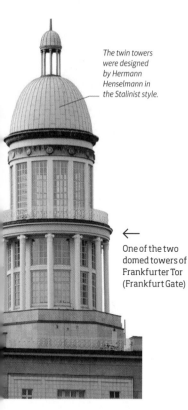

The twin towers were designed by Hermann Henselmann in the Stalinist style.

← One of the two domed towers of Frankfurter Tor (Frankfurt Gate)

WORKER UPRISING

In 1953, Karl-Marx-Allee was the site of a mass worker uprising. Increasing food costs and work quotas led people to begin peaceful protests, which were followed by strikes and marches as their calls fell on deaf ears. The situation escalated, with the uprising spreading across East Germany. The uprising ended on 17 June, when Soviet tanks were called in to help the police suppress a protest in East Berlin. Over 50 workers were killed and many more injured in the revolt.

↑ The 2-km (1-mile) boulevard stretches from Frankfurter Tor to Strausberger Platz

EXPERIENCE MORE

❷
Peres Projects

📍 P5 🏛 Karl-Marx-Allee 82
Ⓤ Weberwiese, Strauss-
berger Platz 🚌 142, N5
🕐 11am–6pm Mon–Fri
🌐 peresprojects.com

This well-known art gallery
is the latest of a series
of venues – a typically box-
shaped room with concrete
columns, large, street-facing
windows and pristine white-
painted walls. Known for
championing artists early in
their careers as well as the
occasional established name,
it shows consistently
innovative works from international contemporary
figures ranging from North
American artists like James
Franco and Brent Wadden
to locals such as the German
painter David Ostrowski.

❸
Volkspark Friedrichshain

📍 P3 🏛 Am Friedrichshain/
Friedenstrasse 🚌 142, 200
🚊 M5, M6, M8, M10

The extensive park complex
of Friedrichshain, with its
picturesque nooks and
crannies, was one of Berlin's
first public parks. It was laid
out in the 1840s on the basis
of a design by landscape
architect Peter Joseph Lenné,
with the idea of creating an
alternative Tiergarten for the
eastern districts of the city.
The greatest attraction here is
the Fountain of Fairy Tales (or
Märchenbrunnen) by Ludwig
Hoffmann, built in 1902–13.
It is a spectacular feature in
a Neo-Baroque style, its
fountain pools decorated with
small statues of turtles and
other animals. The fountain
is surrounded by well-known
characters from the fairy tales
by the Brothers Grimm.
There's a sports and games
area as well as plenty of room
for leisurely strolls. For the
adventurous, there is a challenging outdoor climbing wall.

❹ 🚳 Ⓜ
Computerspiele-museum

📍 P5 🏛 Karl-Marx-Allee 93a
Ⓤ Weberwiese, Strauss-
berger Platz 🚌 347, N5
🕐 10am–8pm daily
🌐 computerspiele
museum.de

The Computer Games Museum
is Europe's first museum for
video and computer games. It

↑ Bust of Frederick the
Great in Volkspark
Friedrichshain

displays over 300 items from a
life-size Lara Croft to a Wall of
Hardware with vintage games
and toys. Here also is pretty
much every arcade machine
and games console ever
made, including the immense
but pioneering Nimrod from
1951, and the Brown Box from
1959, developed by Ralph H
Baer – the inventor of video
games for home use. There's
also a small penny arcade (no
payment required) with
vintage slot machine games
like Donkey Kong, Asteroids
and Space Invaders, and more
contemporary game systems
like the 3D PlayStation
monitor from Sony.

← Group exhibition, The Second
Self, by artists regularly shown
at the Peres Projects gallery

Goods for sale *(inset)* at
Boxhagener Platz's
weekend market

5

Kino International

04 Karl-Marx-Allee 33
S & U Alexanderplatz
U Schillingstrasse N5
kino-international.com

One of the most eye-catching
buildings on the Karl-Marx-
Allee, this large, blocky and
historic cinema was a landmark
in the GDR and remains so
today – not least for its cameo
role in the classic movie
Goodbye Lenin and, since 1995,
its UNESCO-heritage status.
Used for hosting premieres
until the fall of the Wall, it still
operates as a cinema, with
state-of-the-art facilities and
a good rotation of commercial
and arthouse movies. It's
worth taking a moment to
inspect the sandstone reliefs
on the outside as well as the
distinctly retro-looking foyer.

EAT

Schneeweiss
One of Friedrichshain's
few upmarket
restaurants, "Snow
White" combines a
minimalist aesthetic
with an Alpine menu
that straddles Italian,
Austrian and south
German dishes: think
Wiener schnitzel and
Bavarian pasta.

R6 Simplonstrasse
16 6pm-1am Mon-Fri,
10am-1am Sat & Sun
schneeweiss-
berlin.de

€€€

6

Boxhagener Platz

R6 S & U Frankfurter
Allee U Frankfurter Tor
240, N40 M5, M10,
M13, 21

The most famous square in
Friedrichshain, Boxhagener
Platz ("Boxi" to its friends)
serves as both a historical
centre point for the area and
a social hub. Named after the
former nearby manor farm
and hamlet of Boxhagen,
these days it's surrounded
by shops, bars, galleries and
restaurants that draw a mix
of students, families, tourists
and the odd group of
harmless punks. At weekends
Boxi is especially popular due
to its excellent markets. The
Saturday food market has
been held here since 1903 and
offers an array of fruit and
vegetables, but also food
stalls selling everything from
falafel to grilled fish. And at
the Sunday flea market you
can find a variety of items
such as jewellery and vinyl
and second-hand clothes.

The streets leading off from
the square – Grünberger
Strasse, Krossener Strasse,
Gärtnerstrasse and Gabriel-
Max-Strasse – are also worth
exploring for their cafés,
boutiques, restaurants and
bars, while nearby Simon-
Dach-Strasse and RAW
Gelände *(p150)* are well
known for their upbeat
weekend nightlife.

**The extensive
park complex of
Friedrichshain, with
its picturesque nooks
and crannies, was
one of Berlin's first
public parks.**

STAY

Ostel

Set in a nondescript apartment block, this playful hostel recreates the atmosphere of East Germany with its 1970s vintage decor and photos of Erich Honecker.

Q P6 **A** Wriezener Karree 5 **W** ostel.eu

€€€

Michelberger Hotel

This alternative hotel is one of Friedrichshain's funkiest, with quirky rooms, a great lounge and restaurant, plus live music in the courtyard.

Q Q7 **A** Warschauer Strasse 39/40 **W** michelbergerhotel.com

€€€

Eastern Comfort

This floating hostel on a solar-powered boat on the Spree is a perennial backpacker favourite.

Q Q7 **A** Mühlenstrasse 73 **W** eastern-comfort.com

€€€

7 Oberbaumbrücke

Q Q7 **S** & **U** Warschauer Strasse **U** Schlesisches Tor **□** 347 **□** M10

This pretty bridge crossing the Spree river was built in 1896 to a design by Otto Stahn. It is made from reinforced concrete, but the arches are faced with red brick. The central arch is marked by a pair of crenellated Neo-Gothic towers. The most decorative element of the bridge, a Neo-Gothic arcade, supports a line of the U-Bahn.

Prior to reunification, the bridge linked districts from opposing sides of the Wall, and only pedestrians with the correct papers were able to cross. It is now open to traffic.

8 East Side Gallery

Q P7 **A** Mühlenstrasse **S** & **U** Warschauer Strasse **S** Ostbahnhof **□** 24, 140 **□** M10 **W** eastsidegallery-berlin.com

Since 1990, the 1,300-m (1-mile) stretch of the Berlin Wall along Mühlenstrasse between Ostbahnhof and Oberbaumbrücke has been known as the East Side Gallery. A huge collection of graffiti is on display here, the work of 118 different artists. It

also includes the Wall Museum, housed in a former warehouse near the Oberbaumbrücke. The museum features some 100 screens offering an audio-visual history of the Wall, with documentary footage and moving personal testimonies.

9 RAW Gelände

Q Q7 **A** Revaler Strasse 99 **S** & **U** Warschauer Strasse **□** 347 **□** M5, M10, M13

Formerly a 19th-century repair yard owned by the national railway (its official name was "Reichsbahn-Ausbesserungs-Werk", hence RAW), this sprawling complex

←

Street food stalls and a tattoo parlour at Urban Spree in the RAW Gelände complex

← The graffiti-covered East Side Gallery, bringing back memories of the Wall era

of graffiti-spattered warehouses and buildings today represents one of the most prominent alternative cultural spaces in the city. It's fun to stroll around any time of day, especially if you're a street-art fan, though it really comes alive in the evenings at weekends. The 70,000-sq-m (17.5-acre) site incorporates a slew of clubs and bars (Suicide Circus, Astra, Cassiopeia, Crack Bellmar), a couple of shack-like eateries, an indoor skate hall and a climbing wall that was once a World War II bunker. Haubentaucher is a trendy event and concert venue with an outdoor pool and beer garden for the warmer months.

One of the most exciting enterprises here is **Urban Spree**, a masterpiece in post-apocalyptic urban styling. The 1,700-sq-m (18,000-sq-ft) space is devoted to the promotion of "urban cultures", most notably street and graphic art, via a rotating procession of exhibitions, artist residencies, workshops and concerts. Its monthly changing art shows mostly involve high-profile local and international street artists (Low Bros, 1UP Crew, Jim Avignon) who usually paint the entire compound, including all 15 m (50 ft) of its 8-m- (25-ft-) high flagship "Artist Wall".

The gallery shop offers a well-curated range of books, as well as locally designed screen-printed T-shirts. On weekend evenings, the large beer garden draws the crowds with live music, from electronica to punk rock; a convenient starting point if you're planning a night out in one of the nearby clubs.

BERGHAIN

Often voted the best techno club in the world, this former power station features a cavernous main room, the smaller Panorama Bar upstairs and an experimental music area on the ground floor. Its minimal, industrial design aesthetic is as uncompromising as the notorious door policy – but if you can get in, expect some of the best DJs playing all through the weekend. Tip: weekday concerts tend to be ticket-only and much easier to get into. (Upcoming events and tickets: berghain.de)

Urban Spree
🄯🄯🄯 noon–midnight
Tue–Sun (to 3am Fri & Sat)
🅦 urbanspree.com

TIERGARTEN

Once a royal hunting estate, the Tiergarten became a park in the 18th century. In the 19th century a series of buildings – mostly department stores and banks – was erected at Potsdamer Platz. Many of these buildings were destroyed during World War II, and the division of Berlin into East and West changed the character of the area even further. The Tiergarten ended up on the west side of the Wall, and later regained its glory with the creation of the Kulturforum and the Hansaviertel. The area around Potsdamer Platz, however, fell in East Berlin and became a wasteland.

Following reunification, this area witnessed exciting development. Together with the government offices near the Reichstag, this ensures that the Tiergarten area is at the centre of Berlin's political and financial district.

TIERGARTEN

Must Sees

1. Kunstgewerbemuseum
2. Gemäldegalerie
3. Potsdamer Platz

Experience More

4. Philharmonie und Kammermusiksaal
5. Musikinstrumenten-Museum
6. Kupferstichkabinett
7. Kunstbibliothek
8. St-Matthäus-Kirche
9. Neue Nationalgalerie
10. Urban Nation
11. Potsdamer Strasse
12. Staatsbibliothek
13. Shell-Haus
14. Diplomatenviertel
15. Tiergarten
16. Villa von der Heydt
17. Grosser Stern
18. Haus der Kulturen der Welt
19. Sowjetisches Ehrenmal
20. Schloss Bellevue
21. Reichstag
22. Regierungsviertel
23. Bauhaus-Archiv
24. Siegessäule
25. Bendlerblock
26. Hansaviertel

Eat

1. Café am Neuen See
2. Lindenbräu
3. Vox
4. Ristorante essenza
5. Teehaus im Englischen Garten
6. Oh Panama
7. Joseph Roth Diele
8. Facil

Drink

9. Kumpelnest 3000
10. Victoria Bar
11. Tiger Bar

Stay

12. Das Stue
13. Ritz Carlton

Shop

14. Andreas Murkudis

0 metres 500
0 yards 500

N

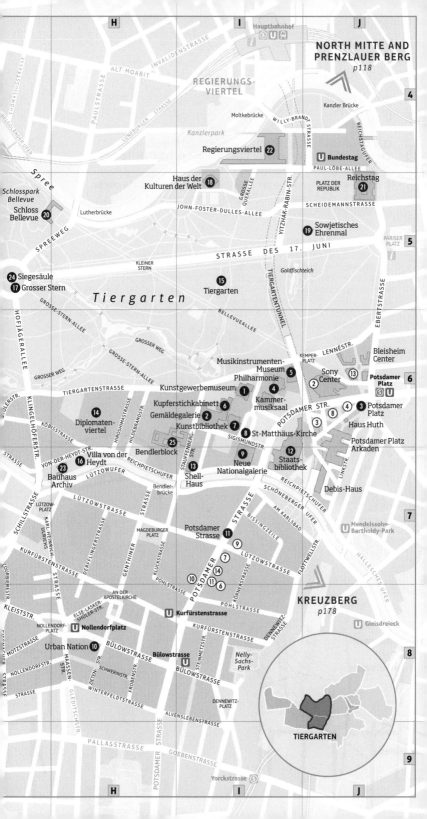

1 KUNSTGEWERBE MUSEUM

I6 🏛 Matthäikirchplatz Ⓢ & Ⓤ Potsdamer Platz Ⓤ Mendelssohn-Bartholdy-Park 🚌 200, M29, M48 🕐 10am–6pm Tue-Fri, 11am–6pm Sat & Sun 🌐 smb.museum

The Museum of Decorative Arts is home to unique artwork in media that visitors don't usually find in other museums: from tapestries and wedding dresses to clocks and furniture.

Treasures of Art and Design

The museum embraces many genres of craft and decorative art, from the early Middle Ages to the modern day. Goldwork is especially well represented, and among the most valuable exhibits is a collection of medieval goldwork from the church treasuries of Enger, near Herford, and the Guelph treasury from Brunswick. The museum also takes great pride in its collection of late Gothic and Renaissance silver from the town of Lüneburg's civic treasury. There are fine examples of Italian majolica, and 18th- and 19th-century German, French and Italian glass, porcelain and furniture.

Exhibits also include fashion, Jugendstil and Art Deco glassware and furniture, and Bauhaus and contemporary design.

Did You Know?

The fashion gallery offers 150 years of fashion history.

> There are fine examples of Italian majolica, and 18th- and 19th-century German, French and Italian glass, porcelain and furniture.

↑ The museum was designed by Rolf Gutbrod and completed in 1985

→ The boxy façade hides a spacious and open interior

GALLERY GUIDE

Visitors enter on the first floor, where there is a fashion gallery. On the ground floor are exhibits from the Middle Ages and the Renaissance, and on the second floor are handicrafts from the Renaissance through to Art Nouveau. The basement is devoted to exploring contemporary and Postmodern industrial design.

← A collection of contemporary furniture, one of the many unique exhibits at this museum

GEMÄLDEGALERIE

📍 I6 🏛 Matthäikirchplatz 4-6 ⓢ&ⓤ Potsdamer Platz ⓤ Mendelssohn-Bartholdy-Park 🚌 200, M29, M41, M48, M85 ⏰ 10am-6pm Tue-Sun (to 8pm Thu) 🌐 smb.museum

The Picture Gallery is the central attraction of the Kulturforum complex. Circling a striking inner courtyard, the gallery contains many of the world's finest 13th- to 18th-century European paintings.

The paintings in the Picture Gallery collection have been carefully chosen by specialists who, from the beginning of the 19th century, systematically acquired pictures to ensure that all the major European schools of painting were represented. After the division of the city in 1945, the collection was split over several sites in East and West Berlin. Following reunification, with the building of a new home as part of the Kulturforum development, this unique set of paintings was united again. The building was designed by Heinz Hilmer and Christoph Sattler and its exhibition space offers a superb environment in which to view the paintings. The pictures are gently lit by the diffused daylight that streams in from above, while the walls are covered in light-absorbing fabric. The vast hall that occupies the centre of the building allows the visitor to take a break from sightseeing at any time. The hall, with a futuristic sculpture by Walter de Maria set in a water-filled pool, provides an ideal place for moments of quiet contemplation and rest.

> **GALLERY GUIDE**
>
> The main gallery contains about 1,000 masterpieces grouped according to their country of origin and period. The educational gallery on the lower floor houses about 400 13th- to 18th-century European paintings and a digital gallery.

→

The sloped approach to the Kulturforum obscures the building within

c 1489

Saint John on Patmos, an oil on oak painting by Dutch artist Hieronymus Bosch.

1641

▽ Double portrait of the Mennonite preacher Cornelis Claesz Anslo and his wife Aeltje Gerritsdr Schouten, Rembrandt.

c 1480

△ *Virgin and Child Enthroned with Saints*, by Italian Renaissance artist Carlo Crivelli.

1559

△ Pieter Bruegel managed to illustrate more than 100 proverbs in his painting *Dutch Proverbs*.

c 1636

Landscape with Juno and Argus, Nicolas Poussin.

Did You Know?
—
The Kulturforum complex
includes art galleries,
concert halls
and theatres.

High ceilings and natural ↑
light help show off the
gallery's masterpieces

↑ *Portrait of a young man* (c 1490-1500) by Davide Ghirlandaio

Italian Painting

The collection of Italian paintings contains exemplary works by 14th- and 15th-century masters, including later works by Raphael, such as the *Madonna di Terranuova*, painted after Raphael's arrival in Florence around 1505.

The Venetian school is also well represented: *Portrait of a Young Man* by Giorgione is a vibrant and colourful study; there is also Titian's *Venus and the Organ Player* and Tintoretto's *Virgin and the Child Adored by Saints Mark and Luke*. It is worth comparing Caravaggio's *Cupid Victorious*, whose provocative and distinctly human sexuality contrasts with the spiritual orthodoxy of *Heavenly and Earthly Love*, by Giovanni Baglione. Similar in style, the two paintings convey opposing ideologies.

Works by Old Masters such as Giovanni Battista Tiepolo, Francesco Guardi and Antonio Canaletto represent the art of 18th-century Venice.

> All the most famous Dutch painters are represented but the works of Jan Vermeer and Rembrandt attract the greatest amount of interest.

Dutch and Flemish Painting

Within the large collection of excellent Flemish paintings, you can marvel at the Baroque vitality and texture evident in the canvases of friends and sometime collaborators Peter Paul Rubens, Jacob Jordaens, Jan Brueghel the Elder and Frans Snyders. The exceptional portraits of Anthony van Dyck are indicative of the artist at the height of his powers.

The gallery of 17th-century Dutch paintings probably holds the richest collection in the museum. Included among these are portraits by Frans Hals that perfectly illustrate his enormous artistic talents.

All the most famous Dutch painters are represented, but the works of Jan Vermeer and Rembrandt attract the greatest amount of interest. Rembrandt's works include the paintings *Samson and Delilah*, *Susanna and the Two Elders* and *Joseph and the Wife of Potiphar*. It is also worth taking time to view the *Man in the Golden Helmet*, a sad yet noble painting originally attributed to Rembrandt, which carbon-dating has shown to be the work of members of his studio. It is a magnificent tribute to his skill as a teacher.

INSIDER TIP
Dutch Proverbs

This work by Pieter Bruegel the Elder is one of the most outstanding pieces in the Dutch collection. To fully appreciate the mastery and humour in this work, make sure you read the accompanying information board.

French, English and Spanish Painting

The collection of French art includes highlights such as *The Madonna with Child* (c 1410), one of the oldest preserved works of art painted on a canvas. Nicolas Poussin, the mainspring of the French Classical tradition, and Claude Lorrain, famous for his idealized landscapes, showcase 17th-century French painting. The 18th century is represented by Jean-Antoine Watteau, Jean-Baptiste Siméon Chardin and François Boucher.

The smaller Spanish collection contains a portrait by Diego Velázquez, while the English collection includes good portraits by rivals Sir Joshua Reynolds and Thomas Gainsborough.

↑ *Jupiter as a child nourished by the goat Amalthea* (1639) by Nicolas Poussin

↑ Hans Multscher's 15th-century *Wurzach Altar*

German Painting

The German collection comprises works from the 13th to 18th centuries. It includes a fine body of religious art – notably the side panels of the 15th-century *Wurzacher Altar*, ascribed to Hans Multscher.

A real rarity is the *Nativity* by Martin Schongauer. Often thought of primarily as an engraver, he was one of the most significant painters of the late 15th century but few of his paintings have survived. Another artist known for both his engravings and paintings, Albrecht Dürer was a major figure in Renaissance art in northern Europe. His works here include *Madonna with the Siskin* and two portraits of Nürnberg patriarchs.

The 17th and 18th centuries are represented by the works of notable artists such as Adam Elsheimer and Johann Heinrich Tischbein.

EAT

Café am Neuen See
For a picturesque, lakeside break between museums, take a stroll to this Tiergarten beer garden.

📍 J6
🏠 Lichtensteinallee 2
🌐 cafeamneuensee.de

€€€

Lindenbräu
This popular watering hole serves Bavarian specialties and home-brewed fruit-flavoured wheat beer.

📍 J6
🏠 Bellevue-strasse 3-5
🌐 bier-genuss.berlin

€€€

Vox
This elegant hotel restaurant serves a modern fusion of Asian and international dishes.

📍 J6
🏠 Marlene-Dietrich-Platz 2
🌐 vox-restaurant.de

€€€

Ristorante essenza
Enjoy top-notch, creative Italian fare at this pleasant restaurant. The menu is matched with an extensive list of wines and champagnes.

📍 J6
🏠 Potsdamer Strasse 3
🌐 ristorante-essenza.de

€€€

❸

POTSDAMER PLATZ

📍 J6 🚇 & Ⓤ Potsdamer Platz 🚌 200, M41, M48, M85, N2
🌐 potsdamerplatz.de

To experience the vibrant energy of Berlin, there is no better place to visit than Potsdamer Platz, where there is so much to see and do that visitors will feel spoilt for choice.

Originally a green park in 1831, this square evolved into a major traffic hub thanks to the construction of a railway station, where the city's first ever train made its maiden journey. During the Roaring Twenties it was Europe's busiest plaza and a bustling entertainment centre, frequented by famous artists and authors. The square was almost destroyed during World War II and was left as a derelict wasteland for several decades. Redevelopment began in 1992, and Potsdamer Platz became Europe's largest construction site, where a total of $25 billion has been invested. Now the city's old hub is once again a dynamic centre, boasting an array of entertainment, shopping and dining opportunities in splendid modern buildings designed by architects such as Renzo Piano, Helmut Jahn and Arata Isozaki.

→
⑤
Leipziger Platz

📷 PICTURE PERFECT
Light Festival

Potsdamer Platz plays a leading role in Berlin's annual Festival of Lights in October. The illuminated installations and light displays are different every year, and are always unforgettable.

→ The best time to visit the Sony Center is in the evening, when the piazza is lit up

① Sony Center

◨ J6 ☐ Potsdamer Strasse 4 ◷ Open 24 hours daily 🅦 sonycenter.de

The Sony Center is one of Berlin's most exciting architectural complexes, a glitzy steel-and-glass construction covering a breathtaking 4,013 sq m (43,195 sq ft). The piazza at the heart of the Center has become one of Berlin's most popular attractions. Set under a soaring tent-like roof, it is dominated by a pool with constantly changing fountains. The light and airy piazza is surrounded by the offices of Sony's European headquarters, as well as apartment complexes, restaurants, cafés and shops. There is also a huge multiplex cinema and an integrated IMAX cinema showing nature and science films on imposing 360-degree screens.

One of the main attractions in the Sony Center is the **Museum für Film und Fernsehen** (Museum of Film and Television), which gives visitors a backstage glimpse

> The Sony Center is one of Berlin's most exciting architectural complexes, a glitzy steel-and-glass construction covering a breathtaking 4,013 sq m (43,195 sq ft).

of Hollywood and the historic UFA (Universum Film AG) film studios. The museum chronicles the development of cinema from the first silent movie hits to the latest science-fiction productions. However, the main focus is on German films from the glorious UFA days in the 1920s, when Germany's leading film company produced one smash hit after another at the Babelsberg studios *(p265)*. Films such as *The Cabinet of Dr Caligari*, directed by Robert Wiene, and *Metropolis*, by Fritz Lang, are presented with costumes, set sketches, original scripts, models and photos. Exhibits also explore the use of film during the Nazi era, when filmmaking became part of the propaganda machine. In addition, the museum documents the life and work of the actor Kurt Gerron, who died in Auschwitz. The

museum also features a range of other exhibitions with changing themes and special film programmes.

Just outside the Sony Center you'll find the **LEGOLAND® Discovery Centre**. It provides a wonderland of indoor adventure for young visitors, including rides and a 4D cinema, as well as hands-on activities like model-building workshops. There's also a LEGO® factory tour.

Museum für Film und Fernsehen

⌾⌾⌾⌾ ☐ Potsdamer Strasse 4 ◷ 10am–6pm Tue, Wed & Fri–Sun (to 8pm Thu) 🅦 deutsche-kinemathek.de

LEGOLAND® Discovery Centre

⌾⌾⌾ ☐ Potsdamer Strasse 4 ◷ 10am–7pm daily 🅦 legolanddiscoverycentre. de/berlin

↑ The Sony Center is a popular weekend hang-out for Berliners

② Daimler Quartier

🔲 J6

This vast complex comprises 19 modern buildings, all designed in different styles according to an overall plan by architects Renzo Piano and Christoph Kohlbecker. The buildings form a long column of magnificent modern architecture leading from Potsdamer Platz all the way down to the Landwehr Canal. The green traffic-light tower marking the beginning of the Daimler Quartier is a replica of the first automatic traffic light in Europe, which was erected on this very spot in 1924.

One of the highlights of this avenue is the Kollhof Tower skyscraper, which is topped by a 96-m- (315-ft-) high observation platform called **Panoramapunkt** (Panorama Point). It offers a breathtaking view and can be reached via Europe's fastest elevator.

The Daimler Quartier also contains the only historic building on Potsdamer Platz to escape destruction in World War II: the grey limestone building of Haus Huth, built for the wine dealer Christian Huth in 1912. The best view of the building is from its south side where a tiny park with trees offers a place to rest.

Today the offices of the famous car manufacturers

→ The buildings of the Daimler Quartier are considered a jewel of modern architecture

Daimler are located here, along with a restaurant, a small café and an upmarket wine shop. Haus Huth is also home to **Daimler Contemporary**, a small exhibition featuring key works and new additions to the corporation's collection of 20th-century art.

Panoramapunkt

🎫🚇 🏠 Potsdamer Platz 1 ⏱ Opening times vary, see website for details 🌐 panoramapunkt.de

Daimler Contemporary

🎫🕐 🏠 Alte Potsdamer Strasse 5 ⏱ 11am–6pm daily 🌐 art.daimler.com

③ Arkaden

🔲 J6/7 🏠 Alte Potsdamer Strasse 7 ⏱ 10am–9pm Mon-Sat 🌐 potsdamer-platz.net/arkaden

This enormously popular entertainment and shopping complex is spread over three floors, and includes around 140 shops, restaurants and boutiques. The basement houses a food court offering regional specialities from all over Germany.

Did You Know?

The Christmas market at Potsdamer Platz includes alpine thrills like snowboarding and tobogganing.

④ Theatre Complex

🔲 J6 🏠 Marlene-Dietrich-Platz

Situated in a square dedicated to the famous Berlin-born actress Marlene Dietrich, the city's largest musical stage is housed in the **Theater am Potsdamer Platz**, designed by Renzo Piano. It has staged a mix of local musical productions and German versions of Broadway hits.

The exclusive Adagio nightclub is located in the basement of this building and Berlin's most popular casino, **Spielbank Berlin**, can be found here, too.

The theatre complex is also the main forum for the city's annual film festival, the Berlinale (p52). Over the course of the ten-day event,

↑ Potsdamer Platz contains an eclectic mix of modern architectural designs

around 400 films are shown, most of which are world and European premieres. Book ahead if you wish to attend.

Theater am Potsdamer Platz

⌖ 🏠 Marlene-Dietrich-Platz 1 ⏰ 8am–8pm daily 🌐 stage-entertainment.de

Spielbank Berlin

🏠 Marlene-Dietrich-Platz 1 ⏰ 11am–5am daily 🌐 spielbank-berlin.de

---

⑤

Leipziger Platz

📍 J6

This small square just east of Potsdamer Platz is becoming an exciting hub of its own.

The **Mall of Berlin** now occupies the site of the former Wertheim department store, once the largest in Europe. It contains shops and restaurants of every variety as well as a hotel, a running club and the XXL slide that winds from the second floor all the way to the ground-floor atrium.

At the southern end of Leipziger Platz is the **Dalí Museum**, exhibiting hundreds of works by the famous Surrealist artist. A few doors down is the **German Spy Museum**, a multimedia museum exploring the history of secret services around the world, with an emphasis on espionage in Cold War-era Berlin. The museum exhibits collections of authentic and replica espionage equipment, and offers various interactive experiences such a laser maze and Facebook data puzzle.

Mall of Berlin

🍴😊🏠🅿 🏠 Leipziger Pl. 12 ⏰ 10am–9pm Mon–Sat, 1–7pm Sun 🌐 mallofberlin.de

Dalí Museum

⌖😊😊🅿 🏠 Leipziger Pl. 7 ⏰ Opening times vary, see website for details 🌐 daliberlin.de

German Spy Museum

⌖ 🏠 Leipziger Pl. 9 ⏰ 10am–8pm daily 🌐 deutsches-spionagemuseum.de

---

EAT

Teehaus im Englischen Garten

After a few hours exploring the ultra-modern Potsdammer Platz, wander through the Tiergarten and take in the greenery and lakes for a change of scenery. Slightly hidden in a small corner of the park, this cosy café-restaurant is nestled in a cottage with a thatched roof and surrounded by a small formal garden. There is a program of free concerts and themed evenings during summer time.

📍 G5 🏠 Altonaer Str. 2 🕙 Nov–Mar 🌐 das-teehaus.jimdo.com

€€€

EXPERIENCE MORE

4

Philharmonie und Kammermusiksaal

📍 I6 🏠 Herbert-von-Karajan-Strasse 1 📞 25 48 88 00 🚇 & 🚇 Potsdamer Platz 🚇 Mendelssohn-Bartholdy-Park 🚌 200, M48, M85

Home to one of the most renowned orchestras in Europe, the Philharmonic and Chamber Music Hall is among the finest postwar architectural achievements in Europe. The Philharmonic, completed in 1963 to a design by Hans Scharoun, pioneered a new concept in concert hall interiors. The orchestra's podium occupies the central section of the pentagonal hall, around which are galleries for the public, designed to blend into the perspective of the five corners. The exterior reflects the interior and is reminiscent of a circus tent.

The Berlin Philharmonic was founded in 1882 and has been directed by such luminaries as Hans von Bülow, Wilhelm Furtwängler, Sir Simon Rattle and the controversial Herbert von Karajan and Claudio Abbado. The current director is Kirill Petrenko, who took up the position in 2019. The orchestra attained renown not only for the quality of its concerts, but also through its prolific symphony recordings.

The smaller Chamber Music Hall was added in the 1980s. Designed to complement Scharoun's existing architecture, it features a central multisided space covered by a fanciful tent-like roof.

_____

5

Musikinstrumenten-Museum

📍 I6 🏠 Tiergartenstrasse 1 🚇 & 🚇 Potsdamer Platz 🚌 200, M48, M85 ⏱ Opening times vary, see website for details 🚫 Mon 🌐 sim.spk-berlin.de

Hidden behind the Philharmonie, in a small building designed by Edgar Wisniewski and Hans Scharoun between 1979 and 1984, the fascinating Museum of Musical Instruments houses over 750 exhibits in a collection dating from 1888. Intriguing displays enable you to trace each instrument's development, from the 16th century to the present day. You can marvel at the harpsichord of Jean Marius, once owned by Frederick the Great, and the violins made by Amati and Stradivarius.

Most spectacular of all is the silent-film-era cinema organ, a working Wurlitzer dating from 1929. With a range of sounds that extends even to locomotive impressions, the demonstrations of its powers every Saturday at noon attract enthusiastic crowds. However, at all times throughout the week the sounds of other exhibited instruments can be heard via recordings.

The museum also has an excellent archive and library open to the public, and its calendar of events is full of live concerts.

←

The striking home of the Berlin Philharmonic

STAY

Das Stue

Located inside a former embassy, Das Stue ("living room" in Danish), has a plush and playful Nordic-style interior that houses a Michelin-starred restaurant, Susanne Kaufmann Spa and a cool cocktail bar.

📍G6 🏠Drakestrasse 1 🌐das-stue.com

€€€

Ritz Carlton

This distinctive Art Deco skyscraper offers one of the classiest stays in the city. It has a couple of great bars, an atmospheric brasserie and sumptuous rooms.

📍J6 🏠Potsdamer Platz 3 🌐ritzcarlton.com

€€€

Kupferstichkabinett

📍I6 🏠Matthäikirchplatz 8 ⓢ&Ⓤ Potsdamer Platz Ⓤ Mendelssohn-Bartholdy-Park 🚌200, M29, M41, M48, M85 🕐10am-6pm daily 🌐smb.museum

The print collections of galleries in the former East and West Berlin were united in 1994 in the Print Library, located in the Kulturforum (p176). These displays originated with a collection started by the Great Elector (p215) in 1652, which has been open to the public since 1831. Despite wartime losses it has an imposing breadth and can boast around 2,000 engravers' plates, over 520,000 prints and around 110,000 drawings and watercolours. Sadly, only a small fraction of these delicate treasures can be even briefly exposed to daylight; therefore the museum does not have a permanent exhibition, only galleries with temporary displays of selected works. For visitors with a special interest, items in storage can be viewed in the studio gallery by prior arrangement.

The collection includes work from every renowned artist from the Middle Ages to contemporary times. Well represented is the work of Botticelli (including illustrations for Dante's *Divine Comedy*), Dürer, Rembrandt and the Dutch Masters, Watteau, Goya, Daumier and painters of the *Die Brücke* art movement.

Kunstbibliothek

📍I6 🏠Matthäikirchplatz 6 ⓢ&Ⓤ Potsdamer Platz Ⓤ Mendelssohn-Bartholdy-Park 🚌200, M29, M41, M48, M85 🕐10am-6pm Tue-Fri, 11am-6pm Sat & Sun 🌐smb.museum

The Art Library is not only a collection of a vast range of books and periodicals about the arts, making it a valuable resource for researchers; it is also a museum with a huge collection of posters, advertisements and an array of other forms of design. Worth seeing is a display on the history of fashion, as well as a vast collection of items of architectural interest. The latter includes around 30,000 original plans and drawings by architects such as Johann Balthasar Neumann, Erich Mendelsohn and Paul Wallot.

The exhibitions can be seen in the reading and studio rooms, and also in the library's own galleries.

↑ Street organ in the Musikinstrumenten-Museum collection

8

St-Matthäus-Kirche

📍I6 🏠Matthäikirchplatz ⓢ&Ⓤ Potsdamer Platz Ⓤ Mendelssohn-Bartholdy-Park 🚌148, 200, M41, M48, M85 🕐11am-6pm Tue-Sun 🌐stiftung-stmatthaeus.de

St Matthew's Church once stood in the centre of a small square surrounded by buildings. After bomb damage in World War II, the structure was restored, making it the focal point of the Kulturforum. The church was originally built between 1844 and 1846 to a design by Friedrich August Stüler and Hermann Wentzel, in a style based on Italian Romanesque temples.

Each of the three naves is covered by a separate two-tier roof, while the eastern end of the church is closed by a semicircular apse. The exterior is covered in a two-tone brick façade arranged in yellow and red lines. Ironically, this pretty church with its slender tower now creates quite an exotic element among the many ultramodern and sometimes extravagant buildings of the Kulturforum.

⑨

Neue Nationalgalerie

📍I7 🏛Potsdamer Strasse 50 Ⓢ&Ⓤ Potsdamer Platz Ⓤ Mendelssohn-Bartholdy-Park 🚌200, M29, M41, M48, M85 🕐Until 2020 for renovation 🌐smb.museum

The magnificent collection of modern art housed in the New National Gallery has a troubled history. The core of the collection consisted of 262 paintings that belonged to banker J H W Wagener. In the late 1860s, when Wagener died, he bequeathed them to Crown Prince William, who housed them in the Nationalgalerie on Museumsinsel.

However, in 1937, a Nazi programme of cultural cleansing meant that over 400 of the works in the collection, which had grown to include paintings by Monet, Manet and Renoir, were confiscated.

After World War II the Berlin municipal authority decided to rebuild the collection and authorized the construction of a suitable building in West Berlin to house it. The commission was given to the elder statesman of modern architecture, the 75-year-old Mies van der Rohe. The result is a striking, minimalist building with a flat steel roof over a glass hall, which appears to float in mid-air supported only by six slender interior struts.

The collection comprises largely 20th-century art, but begins with artists of the late 19th century, such as Edvard Munch, Ferdinand Hodler and Oskar Kokoschka. German movements, such as *Die Brücke* (*p30*), are well represented, with pieces by Karl Schmidt-Rottluff and Ernst Ludwig Kirchner (notably his evocative oil painting *Potsdamer Platz*).

As well as the Bauhaus movement, represented by Paul Klee and Wassily Kandinsky, the gallery shows works by exponents of a stark realism, such as Otto Dix and George Grosz. Celebrated artists of other European countries are also included – Pablo Picasso, Fernand Léger, de Chirico, Dalí, René Magritte and Max Ernst. Post-World War II art is represented by Barnett Newman, Frank Stella and many others. The sculpture garden houses important works, both figurative and abstract.

Following reunification, new works by artists from the former East Germany were added. Some of the art is sometimes shown at the Hamburger Bahnhof (*p124*), as both museums draw on the same collection.

DRINK

Potsdamer Strasse has come on leaps and bounds over the last decade, with plenty of great new drinking spots among the cool boutiques and galleries.

Kumpelnest 3000

📍I7 🏛Lützowstrasse 23 🕐7pm–6am Mon-Thu, 7pm–8am Fri & Sat 🌐kumpelnest3000.com

Victoria Bar

📍I7 🏛Potsdamer Str 102 🕐6:30pm–3am Sun-Thu, 6:30pm–4am Fri & Sat 🌐victoriabar.de

Tiger Bar

📍I7 🏛Oh Panama, Potsdamer Strasse 91 🕐6pm–midnight Tue-Sat 🌐oh-panama.com

⑩

Urban Nation

📍H8 🏛Bülowstrasse 7 Ⓤ Nollendorfplatz 🚌106, 187, M19 🕐10am–6pm Tue-Sun 🌐urban-nation.com

The Urban Nation Museum For Contemporary Art opened in 2017 in Schöneberg, though its roots as an organization stretch back to 2013. Whereas the collective behind it, under the curation of Yasha Young, had previously used the city's surfaces as canvasses for outdoor street art and installations, now there is an indoor space to show them off, too. As well as exhibiting

←

Contemporary art shown by the nonprofit art collective Urban Nation

→ Tranquil, informal study space in the Staatsbibliothek

the work of international and local artists, the nonprofit venue hosts workshops and events – and it's still possible to find much of their work on the streets around the gallery; look out for the large mural on the corner of Bülowstrasse and Frobenstrasse.

Potsdamer Strasse

📍 I7 🔵 & 🟦 **Potsdamer Platz** 🟦 **Kurfürstenstrasse, Bülowstrasse, Kleistpark** 🚌 **104, 106, 187, 204, M19, M29, M41, M45, M48**

A few years ago, Schöneberg's main drag, Potsdamer Strasse, was known for its seedy sex shops and run-down casinos. These days only slight traces of this insalubrious past remain, as gentrification has ushered in a new generation of shops, galleries, cafés and bars. Sitting alongside established spots like the Victoria Bar (No. 102) and the charming Joseph Roth-Diele at No. 75 are shiny new-comers: art galleries such as Circle Culture (No. 75) and Esther Schipper (No. 81e), stylish restaurants such as Oh Panama (No. 91) and luxury designer shops like Andreas Murkudis (No. 81).

Staatsbibliothek

📍 I7 🏛 **Potsdamer Strasse 33** 🔵 & 🟦 **Potsdamer Platz** 🚌 **200, M29, M48, M85** 🕐 **9am–9pm Mon–Fri (to 7pm Sat)** 🌐 **staats bibliothek-berlin.de**

An unusually shaped building with an east-facing gilded dome, the State Library is home to one of the largest collections of books and manuscripts in Europe and is fondly referred to by Berliners as the "Stabi". After World War II, East and West Berlin each inherited part of the prewar state library collection and the Staatsbibliothek was built to house the part belonging to West Berlin. The building itself was designed by Hans Scharoun and Edgar Wisniewski and constructed between 1967 and 1978.

It is a building where the disciplines of function and efficiency take precedence over that of form. The store rooms hold about five million volumes; the hall of the vast reading room is open-plan, with an irregular arrangement of partitions and floor levels; general noise and the sound of footsteps is muffled by fitted carpets, making the interior a very quiet and cosy

place in which to work. The library itself houses more than four million books and an excellent collection of manuscripts. It is formally linked to the Staatsbibliothek on Unter den Linden (p68).

Shell-Haus

📍 I7 🏛 **Reichpietschufer 60** 🟦 **Mendelssohn-Bartholdy-Park** 🚌 **200, M29, M48, M85**

This building is undoubtedly a gem for lovers of the archi-tecture developed during the period between World Wars I and II. This Modernist office block was designed by Emil Fahrenkamp and was completed in 1932. The most eye-catching wing extends along Landwehrkanal with a zigzag elevation; from a height of five storeys it climbs upwards in a series of steps, finishing up ten storeys high.

Damaged during World War II, Shell-Haus went through several stages of restoration and multiple incarnations, including as the German navy headquarters and as a military hospital. Beautiful proportions and original design place the structure among the finest of Berlin's buildings of its era.

14

Diplomatenviertel

☑ H6 Ⓤ Nollendorfplatz, Potsdamer Platz 🚌 100, 106, 187, 200

Although a number of consulates existed in the Tiergarten area as early as 1918, the establishment of a Diplomatic Quarter along the southern edge of the Tiergarten, between Stauffenbergstrasse and Lichtensteinallee, did not take place until the period of Hitler's Third Reich, when large embassies representing the Axis Powers, Italy and Japan, were built here.

Despite the fact that these monumental buildings were designed by a number of different architects, the Fascist interpretation of Neo-Classicism and the influence of Albert Speer as head architect meant that the group was homogenous, if bleak. Few buildings survived World War II bombing.

Today, the diplomatic area is bounded by Tiergartenstrasse. The Austrian embassy, designed by Hans Hollein, stands at the junction of Stauffenbergstrasse, next door to the embassies of India and the Republic of South Africa. At Tiergartenstrasse Nos. 21–3, the pre-World War II Italian embassy still stands, while next door is a copy of the first Japanese embassy. Between Klingelhöferstrasse and Rauchstrasse stands an imposing complex of five embassies. Completed in 1999, these represent Norway, Sweden, Denmark, Finland and Iceland. The complex has an art gallery and café open to the public.

15

Tiergarten

☑ I5 Ⓢ Tiergarten, Bellevue 🚌 100, 106, 187, 200

This is the largest park in Berlin. Situated at the geographical centre of the city it occupies a surface area of more than 200 ha (495 acres). Once a forest used as the Elector's hunting reserve, it was transformed into a landscaped park by Peter Joseph Lenné in the 1830s. A Triumphal Avenue was built in the eastern section of the park at the end of the 19th century, lined with statues of the country's rulers and statesmen.

World War II inflicted huge damage on the Tiergarten, including the destruction of the Triumphal Avenue, many of whose surviving monuments can now be seen in the Zitadelle Spandau (p239). Replanting, however, has now restored the Tiergarten, which is a favourite meeting place for Berliners. Its avenues are now lined with statues of figures such as Johann Wolfgang von Goethe and Richard Wagner.

By the lake known as Neuer See and the Landwehrkanal

Tiergarten in autumn *(inset)* and summer ↓

are memorials to the murdered leaders of the Spartacus movement, Karl Liebknecht and Rosa Luxemburg. Also worth finding is a collection of gas lamps, displayed near the Tiergarten S-Bahn station.

16

Villa von der Heydt

G H7 **A** Von-der-Heydt-Strasse 18 **C** 266 41 28 88 **U** Nollendorfplatz **Q** 100, 200, M29

This fine villa, built in a late Neo-Classical style, is one of the few surviving reminders that the southern side of the Tiergarten was one of the most expensive and beautiful residential areas of Berlin.

Designed by Hermann Ende and G A Linke, the villa dates from 1862. The neatly manicured gardens and railings around the villa are adorned with busts of Christian Daniel Rauch and Alexander von Humboldt. The statues, by Reinhold Begas, originally lined the Triumphal Avenue in the Tiergarten before being moved here. After restoration

in 1980, the villa became the headquarters of one of the most influential cultural bodies, the Foundation of Prussian Cultural Heritage.

17

Grosser Stern

G G5 **S** Bellevue **U** Hansaplatz **Q** 100, 106, 187

The Great Star roundabout at the centre of the Tiergarten is so-named for the five large roads that radiate from it. At its centre is the enormous Siegessäule (Victory Column; *p175*). Surrounding it are monuments brought over from the nearby Reichstag building *(p173)* in the late

1930s. During the same period, the Strasse des 17 Juni was widened to twice its original size, the square surrounding the roundabout was enlarged and much of the existing statuary removed.

In the northern section of the square stands a vast bronze monument to the first German Chancellor, Otto von Bismarck (1815–98). Around it stand allegorical figures, the work of late 19th-century sculptor Reinhold Begas. Other statues represent various national heroes including Field Marshal Helmuth von Moltke (1800–91), chief of the Prussian general staff between the years 1858 and 1888, who won the Franco-German war.

LANDWEHRKANAL

Built in the 19th century, Berlin's Landwehr Canal meanders through several inner-city districts, passing plenty of interesting sights along the way. As well as the café-lined stretches through Kreuzberg *(p178)*, it also passes Potsdamer Platz *(p162)*, the celebrated Neue Nationalgalerie *(p168)*, the distinctive Bauhaus-Archiv *(p174)* and through the Tiergarten. In summer, stop off at the Tiergarten's charming Café am Neuen See, where you can row on the small lake.

18 Haus der Kulturen der Welt

📍 I5 🏛 John-Foster-Dulles-Allee 10 🚇 & Ⓤ Hauptbahnhof, Bundestag 🚌 100 🕐 10am–7pm daily 🌐 hkw.de

The House of World Culture, designed by the American architect Hugh Stubbins, was intended as the American entry in the international architecture competition "Interbau 1957", from which the Hansaviertel apartment blocks also originated. It soon became a symbol of freedom and modernity in West Berlin during the Cold War, particularly when compared to the GDR-era architecture of Karl-Marx-Allee (p146) in East Berlin.

Unfortunately its roof failed to withstand the test of time and the building partially collapsed in 1980. After reconstruction it was reopened in 1989, with a change of purpose: to bring world cultures to a wider German audience via events, exhibitions and performances. It is known for its jazz festivals in particular.

Standing nearby is the black tower of the Carillon, built in 1987 to commemorate

↑ The squat structure and parabolic roof of the Haus der Kulturen der Welt, affectionately called the "pregnant oyster"

the 750th anniversary of Berlin. Suspended in the tower is the largest carillon in Europe, comprising 67 bells. Daily, at noon and 6pm, the bells give a brief computer-controlled concert.

19 Sowjetisches Ehrenmal

📍 J5 🏛 Strasse des 17 Juni 🚇 & Ⓤ Brandenburger Tor 🚌 100, 248

The huge Monument to Soviet Soldiers near the Brandenburg Gate was unveiled on 7 November 1945, on the anniversary of the start of the October Revolution in Russia. Flanked by the first two tanks into the city, the monument commemorates over 300,000 Soviet soldiers who perished in the battle for Berlin at the end of World War II. The vast column was made from marble taken from the headquarters of the Chancellor of the Third Reich when it was being dismantled.

The monument is also a cemetery for around 2,500 Soviet casualties. Following the partition of Berlin, the site ended up in the British

← A heroic figure standing watch atop the Sowjetisches Ehrenmal monument

sector, but formed a kind of non-territorial enclave to which Soviet soldiers posted to East Berlin had access.

20 Schloss Bellevue

📍 G5 🏛 Spreeweg 1 🚇 Bellevue 🚌 100, 187

The captivating Bellevue Palace with its dazzlingly white Neo-Classical façade is now the official residence of the German Federal President, and is a very pretty sight from the northern edge of the Tiergarten park. Built in 1786 to a design by Michael Philipp Boumann for the Prussian Prince August Ferdinand, the palace served as a royal residence until 1861. In 1935 it was refurbished to house a Museum of German Ethnology. Refurbished again in 1938, it became a hotel for guests of the Nazi government.

Following bomb damage during World War II, the palace was carefully restored to its former glory, with the oval ballroom rebuilt to a design by Carl Gotthard Langhans. The palace is set within an attractive park laid out to the original late 18th-century design, though unfortunately the picturesque garden pavilions that once stood here did not survive World War II.

↑ Visitors taking an audiotour of the materials in the Reichstag's dome, designed as a spectacular viewing gallery

㉑ Ⓜ Ⓨ

Reichstag

📍 J5 🏠 Platz der Republik Ⓤ Bundestag 🚌 100, 248 🕐 8am–midnight daily 🕐 Occasionally for cleaning, see website for details 🌐 bundestag.de

Built to house the German Parliament, the Reichstag was intended to symbolize the national unity and aspirations of the new German Empire, declared in 1871. The Neo-Renaissance design by Paul Wallot captured the prevailing spirit of German optimism. Completed in 1894, it was funded by money paid by the French as wartime reparations. The Reichstag became a potent symbol that would be exploited in the years to come. It was here that in 1918 Philipp Scheidemann declared the formation of the Weimar Republic. On the night of 28 February 1933, a fire destroyed the main hall. The Communists were blamed, accelerating a political witch-hunt driven by the Nazis, who subsequently came to power.

When World War II began, the building was not rebuilt. Yet its significance resonated beyond Germany, as shown by the photograph of the Soviet flag flying from the Reichstag in May 1945, which became a symbol of the German defeat.

Between 1957 and 1972, the dome and most of the ornamentation was removed. What remained made a spectacular backdrop for huge festivals and rock concerts, much to the annoyance of the East German authorities.

On 2 December 1990, the Reichstag was the first meeting place of a newly elected Bundestag following German reunification. On 23 June 1995, the artist Christo and his wife Jeanne-Claude wrapped the Reichstag in fabric – an artistic statement that lasted for two weeks.

The latest phase of rebuilding, between 1995 and 1999 to a design by Lord Norman Foster, transformed the Reichstag into a modern meeting hall beneath an elliptical dome. Visits to the cupola's viewing gallery are free and the views are breathtaking. Advance registration is required, either online or at least two hours in advance at the service centre on Scheidemannstrasse.

↑ The Regierungsviertel's Marie-Elisabeth-Lüders-Haus office building (2003) is named for one of Germany's first female politicians

22

Regierungsviertel

📍I4 Ⓢ Brandenburger Tor Ⓤ Bundestag 🚌100, 248

This bold concept for a government district fit for a 21st-century capital was the winning design in a competition held in 1992. Construction of the complex was completed in 2003. Axel Schultes and Charlotte Frank's grand design proposed a rectangular site cutting across the meander of the Spree just north of the Reichstag (p173).

While many of the buildings have been designed by other architects to fit within the overall concept, Schultes and Frank designed the Bundeskanzleramt, opposite the Reichstag – the official residence of the German Chancellor. The whole project is complemented by the neighbouring Hauptbahnhof railway station, an impressive glass-and-steel construction with several levels above and below ground. The city's newest U-Bahn line, the U55, connects Hauptbahnhof to the Bundestag and Brandenburg Gate (p78), and will eventually be extended to Alexanderplatz (p106).

23

Bauhaus-Archiv

📍H7 🏛 Klingelhöferstrasse 14 📞 25 40 02 78 Ⓤ Nollendorfplatz 🚌100, 106, 187, M29 🔒Closed for restoration until 2022

The Bauhaus school of art, started by Walter Gropius in 1919, was one of the most influential art institutions of the 20th century. The belief of the Bauhaus group was that art and technology should combine in harmonious unity.

Originally based in Weimar, and from 1925 in Dessau, this school provided inspiration for numerous artists and architects. Staff and students included Mies van der Rohe, Paul Klee, Wassily Kandinsky, Theo van Doesburg and László Moholy-Nagy. The school moved to Berlin in 1932, but was closed down by the Nazis in 1933.

After the war, the Bauhaus-Archiv was relocated to Darmstadt. In 1964 Walter Gropius designed a building to house the collection, but it was never realized. The archive was moved to Berlin in 1971, where the design was adapted to the new site. The gleaming white building with its distinctive glass-panelled gables was completed in 1979, and while the interior is closed for renovation, the exterior is magnificent. Some of the archive (together with its Bauhaus shop) can be seen in its temporary home in the Hardenberg Haus, on the corner of Knesebeckstrasse and Hardenbergstrasse, not far from Berlin Zoo (p203).

24

Siegessäule

📍 G5 🏛 Grosser Stern 📞 391 29 61 Ⓢ Bellevue Ⓤ Hansaplatz 🚌 100, 106, 187 🕐 Apr-Oct: 9:30am-6:30pm daily; Nov-Mar: 10am-5pm daily

The Victory Column is based on a design by Johann Heinrich Strack and was built to commemorate Prussia's triumph in the Prusso-Danish war of 1864.

After further Prussian victories, "Goldelse", a gilded figure by Friedrich Drake representing Victory, was added to the top. The monument stood in front of the Reichstag building until the Nazi government moved it here in 1938. The base is decorated with bas-reliefs commemorating battles. Higher up the column, a mosaic frieze depicts the 1871 founding of the German Empire. An observation terrace at the top offers magnificent vistas over Berlin.

25

Bendlerblock (Gedenkstätte Deutscher Widerstand)

📍 H6 🏛 Stauffenbergstrasse 13-14 📞 26 99 50 00 Ⓤ Potsdamer Platz, Kurfürstenstrasse 🚌 M29, M48 🕐 9am-6pm Mon-Fri (to 8pm Thu), 10am-6pm Sat & Sun

The collection of buildings known as the Bendlerblock was originally built during the Third Reich as an

extension to the German State Naval Offices. During World War II these buildings were the headquarters of the Wehrmacht (German Army). It was here that a group of officers planned their famous and ultimately unsuccessful assassination attempt on Hitler on 20 July 1944. Four of the conspirators were shot in the Bendlerblock courtyard, and a monument commemorating this event, designed by Richard Scheibe in 1953, stands where the executions were carried out. On the upper floor of the building is an exhibition documenting the history of the German anti-Nazi movements.

26

Hansaviertel

📍 G4 Ⓢ Bellevue Ⓤ Hansaplatz 🚌 100, 106, 187

This area to the west of Schloss Bellevue (p172) is home to some of the most interesting modern architecture in Berlin, built for an international exhibition in

1957. Taking on a World War II bomb site, prominent architects from around the world designed 45 projects, of which 36 were realized, to create a varied residential development set in an environment of lush greenery. The list of distinguished architects involved in the project included Walter Gropius (Händelallee Nos. 3–9), Alvar Aalto (Klopstockstrasse Nos. 30–32) and Oscar Niemeyer (Altonaer Strasse Nos. 4–14). The development also includes a school, a commercial services building and two churches.

In 1960, a new headquarters for the **Akademie der Künste** (Academy of Arts) was built at Hanseatenweg No. 10. Designed by Werner Düttmann, the academy has a concert hall, an exhibition area, archives and a library. In front of the main entrance is a magnificent piece, *Reclining Figure*, by eminent British sculptor Henry Moore.

Akademie der Künste
📍 G5 🏛 Hanseatenweg 10 🕐 11am-8pm Tue-Sun 🌐 adk.de

→
The Siegessäule, or Victory Column, bathed in golden sunlight

A SHORT WALK
AROUND THE KULTURFORUM

Distance 1 km (0.5 miles) **Nearest station** Potsdamer Platz **Time** 10 minutes

The idea of creating a new cultural centre in West Berlin was put forward in 1956. The first building to go up was the Berlin Philharmonic concert hall, built to an innovative design by Hans Scharoun in 1961. Most of the plans for the various other components of the Kultur-forum were realized between 1961 and 1987, and came from such famous architects as Ludwig Mies van der Rohe. The area is now a major cultural centre with fascinating museums and stunning architecture to enjoy as you explore.

The Kunstgewerbemuseum (Museum of Arts and Crafts) contains a unique collection of items including fashion and furniture, dating from the Middle Ages to the present day (p156).

The Kupferstichkabinett (Gallery of Prints and Drawings; p167)

The Kunstbibliothek (Art Library) has a rich collection of books, graphic art and drawings, many of which are displayed in its exhibition halls (p167).

Important works by Old Masters such as Jan van Eyck and Jan Vermeer are exhibited in the Gemäldegalerie (p158).

REICHPIETSCHUFER

LANDWEHRKANAL

← Gallery of fashion at the Kunstgewerbemuseum

Its outside covered in a layer of golden aluminium, the Berlin Philharmonie concert hall is known all over the world for its superb acoustics (p166).

Locator Map
For more detail see p154

The Musikinstrumenten-Museum (Museum of Musical Instruments) contains a unique collection of instruments dating from the 16th to the 20th centuries (p166).

St-Matthäus-Kirche is a picturesque 19th-century church that stands out among the modern buildings of the Kulturforum (p167).

Hans Scharoun designed the public lending and research Staatsbibliothek (State Library) in 1978 (p169).

SCHAROUNSTRÄSSE

MATTHÄI KIRCH PLATZ

POTSDAMER STRASSE

UNDSTRASSE

FINISH

| 0 metres | 100 |
| 0 yards | 100 |

N ↑

START

Sculptures by Henry Moore and Alexander Calder stand outside the streamlined building of the Neue Nationalgalerie, designed by Ludwig Mies van der Rohe (p168).

→ The bright exterior of St-Matthäus-Kirche

KREUZBERG

The area covered in this chapter is only a part of the district of the same name. The evolution of Kreuzberg began in the late 19th century, when it was a working-class area. After World War II, unrepaired buildings were abandoned by those who could afford to move, leaving a population of artists, foreigners, the unemployed and members of a variety of subcultures.

Kreuzberg has become an area of contrasts, with luxury apartments next to dilapidated buildings. Some parts of Kreuzberg are mainly Turkish, while others are inhabited by affluent young professionals. The district's attractions are its wealth of restaurants and Turkish bazaars, as well as an interesting selection of nightclubs, cinemas, theatres and galleries.

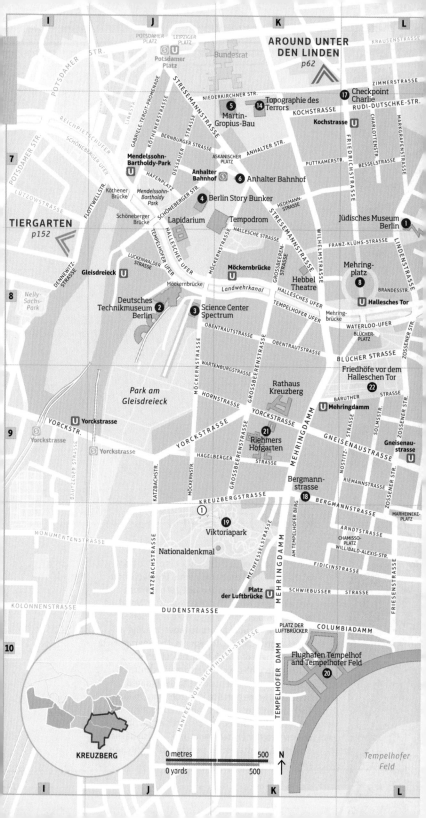

I J K L

7

8

9

10

KRAUSENSTRASSE
ZIMMERSTRASSE
17 Checkpoint
Charlie
RUDI-DUTSCHKE-STR.

POTSDAMER
PLATZ
LEIPZIGER
PLATZ

Bundesrat

Potsdamer
Platz

NIEDERKIRCHNER STR.

KOCHSTRASSE

5 Martin-
Gropius-Bau

14 Topographie des
Terrors

6 Kochstrasse

CHARLOTTENSTR.

FRIEDRICHSTRASSE

MARKGRAFENSTRASSE

BESSELSTRASSE

Mendelssohn-
Bartholdy-Park

HAFENPLATZ

ASKANISCHER
PLATZ

ANHALTER STR.

PUTTKAMERSTR

FRANZ-KLÜHS-STRASSE

4 Berlin Story Bunker

Anhalter
Bahnhof

6 Anhalter Bahnhof

HEDEMANN-
STRASSE

1 Jüdisches Museum
Berlin

LINDENSTRASSE

Köthener
Brücke

Mendelssohn-
Bartholdy
Park

Schöneberger
Brücke

Lapidarium

Tempodrom

TIERGARTEN
p152

Nelly-
Sachs-
Park

Gleisdreieck

Deutsches
Technikmuseum
Berlin **2**

3 Science Center
Spectrum

Möckernbrücke

Landwehrkanal

Hebbel
Theatre

Mehring-
platz
8

BRANDESSTR.

8 Hallesches Tor

Mehring-
brücke

WATERLOO-UFER

BLÜCHER-
PLATZ

ZOSSENER STR.

BLÜCHER STRASSE

OBENTRAUTSTRASSE

OBENTRAUTSTRASSE

Friedhöfe vor dem
Halleschen Tor
22

BARUTHER STRASSE

Park am
Gleisdreieck

WARTENBURGSTRASSE

Rathaus
Kreuzberg

Mehringdamm

GNEISENAUSTRASSE

Gneisenau-
strasse

HORNSTRASSE

YORCKSTRASSE

21

Riehmers
Hofgarten

HAGELBERGER STRASSE

Bergmann-
strasse

NOSTITZSTRASSE

RIEMANNSTRASSE

ZOSSENER STR.

Yorckstrasse

Yorckstrasse

YORCKSTR.

KREUZBERGSTRASSE

18

BERGMANNSTRASSE

MARHEINEKE-
PLATZ

19

Viktoriapark

Nationaldenkmal

AM TEMPELHOFER BERG

ARNDTSTRASSE

CHAMISSO-
PLATZ

WILLIBALD-ALEXIS-STR.

FIDICINSTRASSE

FRIESENSTRASSE

MEHRINGDAMM

**Platz
der Luftbrücke**

SCHWIEBUSSER STRASSE

DUDENSTRASSE

KOLONNENSTRASSE

PLATZ DER
LUFTBRÜCKE

COLUMBIADAMM

MONUMENTENSTRASSE

Flughafen Tempelhof
and Tempelhofer Feld
20

KATZBACHSTRASSE

MANFRED VON-RICHTHOFEN-STRASSE

TEMPELHOFER DAMM

Tempelhofer
Feld

KREUZBERG

0 metres   500
0 yards   500

N

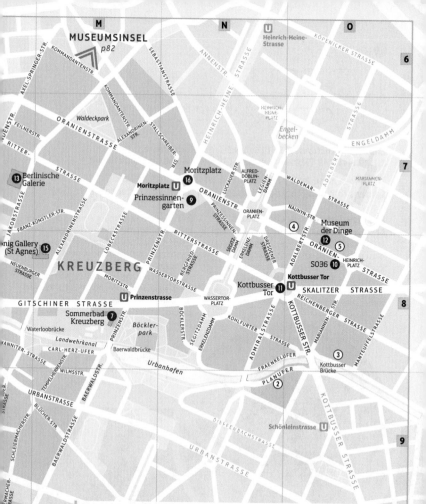

MUSEUMSINSEL p82

KREUZBERG

Must Sees

① Jüdisches Museum Berlin
② Deutsches Technikmuseum Berlin

Experience More

③ Science Center Spectrum
④ Berlin Story Bunker
⑤ Martin-Gropius-Bau
⑥ Anhalter Bahnhof
⑦ Sommerbad Kreuzberg
⑧ Mehringplatz
⑨ Prinzessinnengarten
⑩ SO36
⑪ Kottbusser Tor
⑫ Museum der Dinge
⑬ Berlinische Galerie
⑭ Topographie des Terrors
⑮ König Gallery (St Agnes)

⑯ Moritzplatz
⑰ Checkpoint Charlie
⑱ Bergmannstrasse
⑲ Viktoriapark
⑳ Flughafen Tempelhof and Tempelhofer Feld
㉑ Riehmers Hofgarten
㉒ Friedhöfe vor dem Halleschen Tor

Eat

① Tomasa
② Defne
③ Cocolo

Drink

④ Luzia

Shop

⑤ Voo Store

1 ⚡ 🏍 🖥 🛍

JÜDISCHES MUSEUM BERLIN

📍L7 🏛Lindenstrasse 9-14 🚇Hallesches Tor, Kochstrasse
🚌M29, M41, 248 🕐10am-8pm daily 🚫Some Jewish hols 🌐jmberlin.de

The Jewish Museum is a mix of exhibition spaces, archives and gardens that bring the memories and stories of Jewish culture alive.

History Through Architecture

Designed by Daniel Libeskind, a Polish-Jewish architect based in the United States, the museum complex is an exciting and imaginative example of late 20th-century architecture. The complex contains a library and gardens, but the highlight of the museum is the Libeskind Building, whose shape, style and interior arrangement are part of a philosophical programme to illustrate the history and culture of Germany's Jewish community, and the repercussions of the Holocaust. The long, narrow galleries with slanting floors and sharp zigzagging turns are designed to evoke the feeling of loss and dislocation. These are interspersed by "voids" that represent the vacuum left behind by the destruction of Jewish life.

Iron plate faces *(inset)* cry up at visitors where they lie discarded on the floor in Menashe Kadishman's *Shalekhet* installation ↓

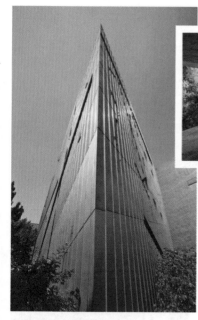

↑ The Garden of Exile symbolizes the forced exile of Germany's Jews

↑ The Libeskind Building is likened to a deconstructed Star of David

MUSEUM GUIDE

Entrance to the main museum (the Libeskind Building) is via an underground tunnel. The exhibition is divided into 14 sections, taking visitors through German Jewish history and culture from early history up to the present day.

2 🗺️ 🛵 🍴 📺 🛍️

DEUTSCHES TECHNIKMUSEUM BERLIN

📍J8 🏠Trebbiner Strasse 9 Ⓤ Gleisdreieck 🚌M29, M41 🕐9am–5:30pm Tue–Fri, 10am–6pm Sat & Sun 🌐sdtb.de/stiftung/startseite

The Museum of Technology takes visitors on a multimedia journey through recent human history by exploring its technological achievements.

A Grand-Scale Museum

The Museum of Technology was established by grouping together more than 100 smaller, specialized collections under one roof. The current collection is arranged on the site of a former trade hall, the size of which allows many of the museum's exhibits – such as locomotives, aircraft, boats and water towers – to be displayed full-size and in their original condition. Highlights of the collection include vintage cars and motorcycles, and dozens of locomotives and railway carriages from different eras. There are also exhibitions dedicated to flying, printing, weaving, engineering and computer technology. Adjacent to the museum is a beautiful park containing two windmills and the museum's rail transport exhibit in the former Anhalter Bahnhof station.

↑ The plane on the roof is a Douglas C-47B Skytrain "Raisin Bomber" dating from 1948–9

EAT

Tomasa
This red-brick villa has a well-stocked playroom, a great kids' menu and a courtyard and garden. It's a good spot for breakfast or brunch before the museum, which is a pleasant 1.5 km (1 mile) walk away through Park am Gleisdreieck.

📍J10 🏠Kreuzbergstrasse 62 🕐9am–midnight Sun–Wed (to 1am Thu) 🌐tomasa.de

€€€

Did You Know?

The exhibitions on paper-making and shipping are great for children.

Three floors are dedicated to shipping and navigation ↑

↑ The Aerospace exhibition
celebrates 200 years of
German aviation

EXPERIENCE MORE

3
Science Center Spectrum

⊙ J8 **⌂** Möckernstrasse 26
Ⓢ Anhalter Bahnhof
Ⓤ Möckernbrücke, Gleisdreieck **⯃** M29, M41, 248
⊙ Opening times vary, see website for details
ⓦ sdtb.de/spectrum

This annexe to the Deutsches Technikmuseum (p184) focuses on interactive exhibits. With its own distinct building next to the main museum, it occupies some 1,400 sq m (15,000 sq ft) of space across four floors, and features around 150 interactive exhibits arranged by themes such as Sound, Light & Sight and Power. There's a big room full of cars and motorbikes, a rainbow suspended in the air without the use of water, and masses of hands-on experiments, including swings and bridges to operate, the option to create colour tones by mixing light surfaces originating from real sunlight, and a Foucault's Pendulum that shows how the earth rotates. Last but not least there's a fun hall of mirrors for some stretchy selfies.

↑ Colour-mixing, just one of the absorbing interactive activities on offer at the Science Center Spectrum

4
Berlin Story Bunker

⊙ J7 **⌂** Schöneberger Strasse 23A **Ⓢ** Anhalter Bahnhof **Ⓤ** Mendelssohn-Bartholdy-Park **⯃** M29, M41 **⊙** 10am–7pm daily
ⓦ berlinstory.de

The bunker that houses this idiosyncratic museum was used during the war by those working in and living around the nearby Anhalter Bahnhof train station, which is now a memorial ruin. Today it contains the Berlin Story Museum, which illuminates some of the most significant aspects of Berlin's 800-year history through multimedia stations that combine photographs, films and art installations.

A separate exhibition was added in 2017 entitled "Hitler – how could it happen." It follows the timeline of Adolf Hitler's rise and fall via photographs, films, documents and recreations of parts of the infamous Führerbunker (p76).

5
Martin-Gropius-Bau

⊙ K7 **⌂** Niederkirchner Strasse 7 (corner of Stresemannstrasse) **☎** 25 48 60 **Ⓢ** & **Ⓤ** Potsdamer Platz **⯃** 200, M29, M41 **⊙** 10am–7pm Wed–Mon

The innovative Martin-Gropius-Bau building was originally built to fulfil the requirements of an arts and crafts museum. It was designed by Martin Gropius with the participation of Heino Schmieden and constructed in 1881. The building's style is reminiscent of an Italian Renaissance palace, with a magnificent glazed interior courtyard, an impressive atrium and unusual, richly decorated elevations. Located between the windows are the crests of German cities, and within the friezes are reliefs illustrating different arts and crafts. In the plaques between the windows of the top storey are beautiful mosaics containing allegorical figures representing the cultures of different eras and countries. From 1922 Martin-Gropius-Bau accommodated the Museum of Ethnology, but after World War II the building was abandoned and left in ruins. Although plans for an inner-city motorway threatened it until the 1970s, a reconstruction programme eventually commenced in 1981, led by architects Winnetou Kampmann and Ute Weström.

This was followed in 1999 by a further refurbishment, and since then the building has housed a changing series of exhibitions on art, photography and architecture.

6

Anhalter Bahnhof

🔲 K7 🔲 Askanischer Platz 6-7 🔲 Anhalter Bahnhof 🔲 Potsdamer Platz, Mendelssohn-Bartholdy-Park 🚌 M29, M41

Only a tiny fragment now remains of the Anhalter Bahnhof station, which was named after the Saxon royal family. It was once Berlin's largest ,and Europe's second-largest, railway station.

The hugely ambitious structure was designed by Franz Schwechten and constructed in 1880. The station was intended to be the biggest and most elegant in Europe in order to impress official visitors to the capital of the German Empire. Some of the most famous people to alight at Anhalter Bahnhof were the Italian King Umberto, who was welcomed by Kaiser Wilhelm II himself, and the Russian Tsar Nicholas.

The station was taken out of public use in 1943 after its roof was destroyed by Allied bombing. Only the front portico remains, crowned by still-damaged sculptures and the hole that housed a large electric clock, as well as fragments of its once glorious façade. On the vast grounds behind rises the soaring, tent-like roof of the entertainment venue, Tempodrom.

Did You Know?

Kreuzberg is also known as X-Berg (based on "kreuz", which means "cross" in German).

HANSA-TONSTUDIO

Hansa Studio is one of Berlin's most famous music recording studios. Built in 1912, it has recorded albums by such internationally renowned names as David Bowie, Depeche Mode, U2 and R.E.M., as well as German luminaries such as Nina Hagen and Udo Jürgens. Only one studio is active these days, but it's possible to tour the building and also see the rooms where many of these prominent artists once recorded.

→ Fragment of the Anhalter Bahnhof, once the gateway to southern Germany

SHOP

Voo Store

Situated inside a former locksmiths, this swanky industrial-design shop sells a highly curated mix of clothing, home decor and fashion accessories. Great coffee shop, too.

⊙ 08 **⌂** Oranienstrasse 24 **🕐** 10am–8pm Mon–Sat **🖥** vooberlin.com

7 ⬙

Sommerbad Kreuzberg

⊙ M8 **⌂** Prinzenstrasse 113–119 **☎** 30 22 19 00 11 **Ⓤ** Prinzenstrasse **🚌** 140, 248 **🕐** 7am–8pm daily

Known more commonly as Prinzenbad due to its proximity to the Prinzen-strasse U-Bahn station, this cult Kreuzberg swimming pool was made famous by its appearance in Sven Regener's 2001 book *Herr Lehmann* – and it subsequently featured in the hit film, too. While not the most refined of the city's pools, its two 50-m (164-ft) pools are hugely popular not only for their outdoor location, but also because they're big on character. Expect to find a rich and varied mix of hipsters, Middle Eastern families, elderly Berliners and water-sliding youngsters gathered here on any warm day.

8

Mehringplatz

⊙ L8 **Ⓤ** Hallesches Tor **🚌** 248, M41

Mehringplatz was planned in the 1730s when the boundaries of the city were extended. Its original name was Rondell, meaning "circus", an appropriate name, as Wilhelmstrasse, Friedrich-strasse and Lindenstrasse all converged here.

Rondell was originally the work of Philipp Gerlach; then, in the 1840s, Peter Joseph Lenné designed the decoration of the square. At the centre is the Column of Peace, commemorating the Wars of Liberation in 1815. The column is crowned by the figure of Victory by Christian Daniel Rauch. Two sculptures were added in the 1870s: *Peace* by Albert Wolff and *Clio* (the Muse of History) by Ferdinand Hartzer. In the 19th and early 20th centuries the area was populated with politicians, diplomats and aristocrats, and in 1947 the square was named after the writer Franz Mehring. The current buildings date from the 1970s.

9

Prinzessinnengarten

⊙ N7 **⌂** Prinzenstrasse 35–38 **Ⓤ** Moritzplatz **🚌** 140, 248, M29 **🕐** 10am–10pm Mon–Sat (to 8pm Sun) **🖥** prinzessinnen garten.net

It would be easy to under-estimate the influence of this small, nonprofit public garden. Started in 2009 by a couple of green-fingered entrepreneurs, plus a constant stream of local volunteers, it transformed a site off Moritz-platz *(p191)* that was a forlorn wasteland into a thriving garden full of flowers, vegetables and herbs.

Today it also has an organic café on site that sells food made from the garden's own ingredients and holds regular workshops on every-thing from beekeeping to gardening, as well as community events such as summer flea markets.

→ Sharing gardening tips at a plant stall in the Prinzessinnengarten

↑ Alternative music venue SO36, providing techno and indie sounds for a lively mixed crowd

Did You Know?

Kreuzberg has long been a prominent district for Berlin's LGBT+ community.

SO36

📍 O8 🏠 Oranienstrasse 190
Ⓤ Kottbusser Tor
🚍 M29, 140 🕐 9pm–5am
Tue–Sat 🌐 so36.de

One of Berlin's best-known alternative music venues, SO36 – the name is a reference to the district's Berlin Wall-era postal code – grew famous during the 1970s and 1980s, when it was run by artist Martin Kippenberger and hosted punk and post-punk acts like Einstürzende Neubauten, Iggy Pop and Nick Cave. Today it regularly hosts big-name bands, mostly of a rock and indie persuasion, as well as up-and-coming local bands in its basic, large main room. Look out also for regular specials such as roller

discos, Turkish LGBT+ pop event Gayhane and even the occasional flea market.

⓫ Kottbusser Tor

📍 N8 🏠 Kottbusser Strasse
Ⓤ Kottbusser Tor
🚍 140, M29, N8

Nicknamed "Little Istanbul", Kottbusser Tor has long been the Turkish heartland of inner city Berlin. Originally a city gate leading to the city of Cottbus, today it's ostensibly a roundabout surrounded by 1970s- and 1980s era residential housing bedecked with tell-tale satellite dishes (so that residents can tune into Turkish and Middle Eastern TV channels). It's a vibrant area whether day or night, with a constant flow of foot and car traffic and a procession of food markets, street vendors and coffee shops. Although its reputation for low-level crime can't be disregarded, these days it's

mostly frequented by a mix of local families and hipsters who congregate at weekends in search of the many inconspicuous bars and clubs – Monarch, Palermo, Möbel Olfe – as well as the mix of cheap falafel spots and trendy US-style burger joints like The Bird.

Museum der Dinge

📍 O8 🏠 Oranienstrasse 25
Ⓤ Kottbusser Tor
🚍 140, M29 🕐 noon–7pm
Thu–Mon 🌐 museum derdinge.de

Kreuzberg's Museum of Things houses the archive of the Deutscher Werkbund: a federation of craftsmen, designers, architects and manufacturers, formed in 1907, which was a forerunner of the more famous Bauhaus. Both movements aimed to make well-designed, high-quality goods available to all, and the shelves and cabinets in this airy space are stacked with a fascinating array of everyday items, from Manoli ashtrays and Art Deco fondue sets to GDR-era toiletries.

One of the museum's main attractions, in a room of its own, is the "Frankfurt Kitchen"; designed by Viennese architect Margarete Schütte-Lihotzky in 1926, its folding cupboards, countertops and slew of appliances makes it a direct forerunner of today's standard fitted kitchens. There's a a decent gift shop featuring plenty of designer-friendly objects and a range of related books.

→ Early electric kettles at the Museum der Dinge

↑ A juxtaposition of white space and colour *(inset)* at the Berlinische Galerie

⑬ Berlinische Galerie

♠L7 ⌂Alte Jakobstrasse 124-8 ⓊKochstrasse 🚌248, M29 ⏰10am-6pm Wed-Mon 🌐berlinische galerie.de

The city's museum for modern art, design and architecture is one of the finest regional museums in the country. Changing themed exhibitions draw upon its huge collection of German, East European and Russian paintings, photographs, graphics and architectural artifacts.

One of the highlights is the 5,000-strong painting collection, which covers all the major art movements from the late 19th century until today. It includes works by Max Liebermann *(p245)*, Otto Dix, Georg Baselitz, Alexander Rodchenko, Iwan Puni and Via Lewandowsky.

The museum's collection of sketches, prints and posters encompasses the Berlin Dadaists George Grosz, Hannah Höch and Werner Heldt, as well as works by Ernst Ludwig Kirchner and Hanns Schimansky.

Among the architectural items held by the Galerie are drawings and models for buildings that were never built, offering fascinating glimpses into how the city might have looked. A fine example is the shell-like Expressionist Sternkirche (Star Church), designed by Otto Bartning in 1922.

⑭ Topographie des Terrors

♠K7 ⌂Stresemannstrasse 110 (entrance on Nieder-kirchner Strasse 8) Ⓢ&ⓊPotsdamer Platz, Kochstrasse ⓈAnhalter Bahnhof 🚌M29, M41 ⏰10am-8pm daily 🌐topographie.de

During the Third Reich, three of the most terrifying Nazi political departments had their headquarters in a block here, making this area the government district of National Socialist Germany. Prinz-Albrecht palace at Wilhelmstrasse No. 102 became the headquarters of the Third Reich's security service (SD). Prinz-Albrecht-

---

THE BERLIN BLOCKADE (1948-9)

On 24 June 1948, due to rising tensions between East Germany and West Berlin, Soviet authorities blockaded all the roads leading to West Berlin. In order to ensure food and fuel for the residents, US General Lucius Clay ordered that provisions be flown into the city. British and American planes made a total of 212,612 flights, transporting almost 2 million tonnes (2.3 million tons) of goods, among which were parts of a power station. In April 1949, at the height of the airlifts, planes were landing every 63 seconds. The blockade ended in May 1949. Although the airlifts were successful, there were casualties: 70 airmen and 8 ground crew lost their lives.

Strasse No. 8 was occupied by the head of the Gestapo, Heinrich Müller, while the Hotel Prinz Albrecht at No. 9 became the headquarters of Himmler's SS.

After World War II, the ruins of the heavily bombed buildings were pulled down. In 1987, however, an exhibition was installed on this site by committed citizens of Berlin. This well-researched and exhaustive exploration of Nazi crimes and terror in all its forms, including propaganda, deportation, forced labour and genocide, builds a chilling picture of the decisions that must have been taken on this very site. A preserved section of the Berlin Wall runs alongside the building, on Niederkirchner Strasse.

15 📖

König Gallery (St Agnes)

📍 M8 🏛 Alexandrinen-strasse 118-121 Ⓤ Prinzen-strasse, Moritzplatz 🚌 140, 248, N41 🕐 11am-7pm Tue-Sat, noon-7pm Sun 🌐 koeniggalerie.com

The striking, almost window-less Brutalist church of St Agnes was built in the 1960s. It houses the Johann König Gallery, which opened

here in 2015 following a renovation by Arno Brandlhuber. The gallery features two distinctive spaces – one on the main floor and one on an upper floor supported by a concrete slab – plus a sculpture garden that also forms part of the exhibitions. In addition to solo shows and group exhibitions, the gallery hosts regular readings, performances and presentations. There's a pleasant café inside too, and some of the surrounding buildings are used by artists during their residencies.

16

Moritzplatz

📍 N7 Ⓤ Moritzplatz 🚌 140, M29

For several decades – before and after the fall of the Wall – the area around Moritzplatz was a somewhat bleak vision of 1970s residential blocks and the occasional kebab shop. In recent years, it has been transformed almost beyond recognition by a flurry of developments beginning with the celebrated Prinzessinnengarten (p188). In more recent years, it has been joined by the creative centre Aufbau Haus, craft and arts shop Modular, the upscale Parker Bowles deli and the Prince Charles nightclub.

17

Checkpoint Charlie

📍 L6 🏛 Friedrichstrasse 43-45 Ⓤ Kochstrasse 🚌 M29

Between 1961 and 1990, Checkpoint Charlie was the only crossing point for foreigners between East and West Berlin. During that time, it represented a symbol of both freedom and separation for the many East Germans trying to escape from the GDR regime. It was also witness to dramatic events during the Cold War, including a tense two-day standoff between Russian and American tanks in 1961.

Little remains of the check-point: no gates, barriers or barbed wire. Instead there is a replica checkpoint booth and the famous huge sign on the old Western side that reads "You are leaving the American Sector".

At the museum nearby, **Haus am Checkpoint Charlie**, look out for the exhibits connected with the escape attempts of East Germans to the West. The ingenuity and bravery of these escapees are astonishing, using devices such as secret compartments built into cars and specially constructed suitcases.

Haus am Checkpoint Charlie
🔃 🕐 🔃 🔃 9am-10pm daily
🌐 mauermuseum.de

→
Replica of
Checkpoint Charlie

↑ Pavement dining in summer on busy Bergmannstrasse

EAT

Defne

Long-running, canalside restaurant whose Turkish and Mediterranean menu includes delicious classics like *imam bayildi*, lamb skewers and seafood pasta.

Q N9 **A** Planufer 92C **⊙** Opening times vary, see website for details **W** defne-restaurant.de

€€€

Cocolo

The second branch of Berlin's best ramen spot. Cocolo's menu is small but consistently top-notch: think ramen with sweet pork belly or miso and vegetables, plus extras like Japanese dumplings.

Q O8 **A** Paul-Lincke-Ufer 39 **⊙** noon–11pm Mon–Sat **W** kuchi.de/restaurant/cocolo-x-berg

€€€

18

Bergmannstrasse

Q K9 **U** Südstern, Geneisenaustrasse **🚌** 248, N7, N6, N42

Kreuzberg is unofficially divided between its gritty and hip east side and its more gentrified western counterpart. Here, entire blocks of 19th-century houses have been restored and the area's main artery, Bergmannstrasse, has been revitalized. Pedestrianized and furnished with antique streetlamps to enhance the atmosphere, it bristles with independent shops, galleries, cafés and restaurants. Also refreshed is the popular Marheineke Markthalle: a covered market filled with not only fruit and vegetables but also cafés, delis and even exhibitions. Just off the street is the charming Chamissoplatz, which draws crowds to its Saturday

→
Viktoriapark's Neo-Gothic memorial

morning organic farmers' market. To the west, the street leads to one of the main parks in the area, Viktoriapark, ideal for a green breather after the bustle of the streets.

---

19 🖵

Viktoriapark

Q K10 **U** Platz der Luftbrücke **🚌** 104, 140, M19

This rambling park, with several artificial waterfalls, short trails and a small hill, was designed by Hermann Mächtig and built between 1884 and 1894. The Neo-Gothic Memorial to the Wars of Liberation at the summit of the hill is the work of Karl Friedrich Schinkel *(p28)*, which commemorates the Prussian victory against Napoleon's army in the Wars of Liberation. The cast-iron tower is well ornamented. In the niches of the lower section are 12 allegorical figures by Christian Daniel Rauch, Friedrich Tieck and Ludwig Wichmann. Each figure symbolizes a battle and is linked to a historic figure – either a military leader or a member of the royal family. The park contains the popular Golgotha pub and beer garden, perfect for refreshment after a stroll.

⑳ Flughafen Tempelhof and Tempelhofer Feld

📍 K10 🏠 Platz der Luftbrücke 📞 200 03 74 41 Ⓤ Platz der Luftbrücke 🚌 104, 248

The disued Tempelhof Airport was once Germany's biggest. Built in 1923, it was enlarged during the Third Reich. You can take a guided tour of the building (1:30pm on Wed, Fri, Sat and Sun), which is typical of Third Reich architecture, even though the eagles that decorate it predate the Nazis. In 1951, a monument was added in front of the airport. Designed by Eduard Ludwig, it commemorates the airlifts of the Berlin Blockade *(p190)*. The three spikes on the top symbolize the air corridors used by Allied planes. The airport was permanently closed to air traffic in 2008. It has now been transformed into a park that is popular with cyclists, roller-bladers and skaters who come here to enjoy the unobstructed airport runways.

㉑ Riehmers Hofgarten

📍 K9 🏠 Yorckstrasse 83-86, Grossbeerenstrasse 56-57 & Hagelberger Strasse 9-12 Ⓤ Mehringdamm 🚌 140, 248, M19

Riehmers Hofgarten is the name given to the 20 or so exquisite houses arranged around a picturesque garden within the area bordered by the streets Yorckstrasse, Hagelberger Strasse and Grossbeerenstrasse. These houses were built between 1881 and 1899 to the detailed designs of Wilhelm Riehmer and Otto Mrosk, respected architects who not only designed the houses' intricate, Renaissance-style and Neo-Baroque façades but also gave equal splendour to the elevations overlooking the courtyard garden. The streets of Riehmers Hofgarten have been carefully restored and Yorckstrasse also has quite a few cafés. Next to Riehmers Hofgarten is the church of St Bonifaz, designed by Max Hasak. Adjacent to the church is a similar complex of houses built in an impressive Neo-Gothic style.

㉒ Friedhöfe vor dem Halleschen Tor

📍 L9 🏠 Mehringdamm, Blücher-, Baruther & Zossener Strasse 📞 691 61 38 Ⓤ Hallesches Tor 🚌 140, 248, M41 🕐 Dec & Jan: 8am-4pm daily; Feb & Nov: 8am-5pm daily; Mar & Oct: 8am-6pm daily; Apr & Sep: 8am-7pm daily; May-Aug: 8am-8pm daily

Beyond the city walls, next to the Halleschen Gate, are four cemeteries established in 1735. Some of the beautiful gravestones commemorate some of the great Berlin artists including the composer Felix Mendelssohn-Bartholdy, architects Georg Wenzeslaus von Knobelsdorff, David Gilly and Carl Ferdinand Langhans, and the writer, artist and composer E T A Hoffmann.

←

Picnickers relaxing on the disused runway spaces of Flughafen Tempelhof

A SHORT WALK
MEHRINGPLATZ AND FRIEDRICHSTRASSE

Distance 1.5 km (1 mile) **Nearest station** Potsdamer Platz **Time** 15 minutes

The areas north of Mehringplatz are the oldest sections of Kreuzberg. Now full of modern developments such as the Friedrichstadt Passagen – a huge complex of shops, apartments, offices, galleries and restaurants – only a few buildings recall the earlier splendour of this district, which was laid out in 1734. However, a walk through this area is a must for those who want to know more about World War II- and GDR-era Berlin, as it's home to some key sights such as the Jüdisches Museum Berlin and Checkpoint Charlie.

A small hut marks the place of Checkpoint Charlie, the notorious border crossing between East and West Berlin (p191).

Martin-Gropius-Bau is an interesting, multicoloured Neo-Renaissance building that houses the city's main temporary art exhibition space (p186).

START

KOCHSTRASSE

WILHELMSTRASSE

FRIEDRICHSTRASSE

PUTTKAMERSTRASSE

HEDEMANNSTRASSE

A shocking exhibition known as Topographie des Terrors (Topography of Terrors) details Nazi crimes (p190).

← The Topographie des Terrors exhibition

↑ The jagged edges of the Jüdisches Museum Berlin

Locator Map
For more detail see p180

KREUZBERG

RUDI-DUTSCHKE STRASSE

CHARLOTTENSTRASSE

MARKGRAFENSTRASSE

LINDENSTRASSE

BESSELSTRASSE

STRASSE

ANZ-KLUHS-STRASSE

This shopping and restaurant complex is located inside the Axel-Springer-Hochhaus, a 1960s high-rise built adjacent to the Berlin Wall as a highly visible political statement.

Did You Know?

The Topographie des Terrors is housed on the site of the former Gestapo and SS headquarters.

0 metres   150   N
0 yards   150   ↑

Windows made to resemble cracks create a striking effect in the metallic facing of the Jüdisches Museum Berlin (Berlin Jewish Museum), designed by architect Daniel Libeskind (p182).

Mehringplatz was formerly known as Rondell, and then for many years as Belle-Alliance-Platz. Completely destroyed during World War II, it was rebuilt by Hans Scharoun, who followed the original design (p188).

FINISH

AROUND KURFÜRSTENDAMM

The area around Kurfürstendamm boulevard (the Ku'damm) was developed in the 19th century. Luxurious buildings were constructed along the avenue, while the areas of Breitscheidplatz and Wittenbergplatz became replete with hotels and department stores.

After World War II, with the old centre (Mitte) situated in East Berlin, this area became the centre of West Berlin. Traces of wartime destruction were removed very quickly and this area was transformed into the heart of West Berlin, and dozens of new company headquarters and trade centres were built. The situation changed after the reunification of Berlin and, although many tourists concentrate on the Mitte district, the heart of the city continues to beat around Kurfürstendamm.

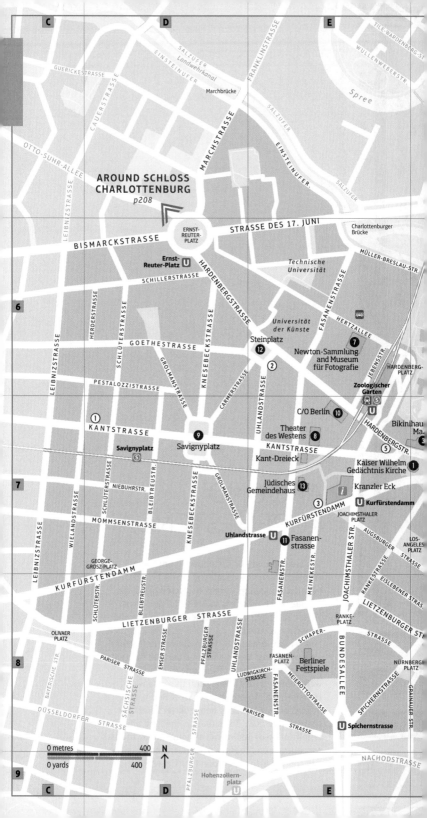

AROUND KURFÜRSTENDAMM

Must See

① Kaiser Wilhelm Gedächtnis Kirche

Experience More

② KaDeWe
③ Bikinihaus Mall
④ Europa-Center
⑤ Tauentzienstrasse
⑥ Zoo Berlin
⑦ Newton-Sammlung and Museum für Fotografie
⑧ Theater des Westens
⑨ Savignyplatz

⑩ C/O Berlin
⑪ Fasanenstrasse
⑫ Steinplatz
⑬ Jüdisches Gemeindehaus

Eat & Drink

① Lon Men's Noodle House
② Bar am Steinplatz

Stay

③ Hotel Zoo
④ 25hours Hotel Bikini
⑤ Waldorf Astoria

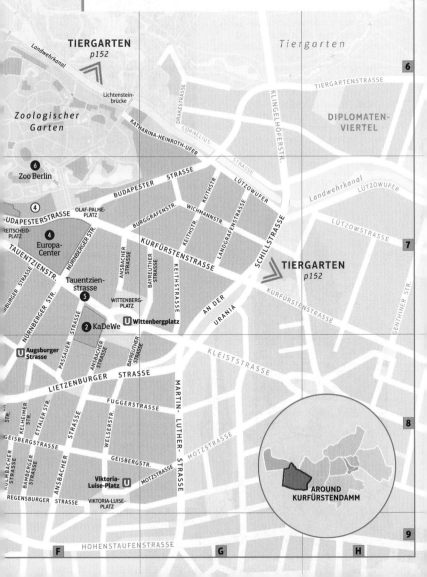

❶ 🖉

KAISER WILHELM GEDÄCHTNIS KIRCHE

📍F7 🚇Breitscheidplatz Ⓢ&Ⓤ Zoologischer Garten Ⓤ Kurfürstendamm
🚌100, 109, 110, 200, 204, 245, M19, M29, M46, X9, X10, X34 🕘9am–7pm daily
🌐 gedaechtniskirche-berlin.de

The damaged tower of Kaiser Wilhelm Memorial Church is a symbol of peace and the city's determination to rebuild after World War II.

This church-monument is one of Berlin's most famous landmarks, surrounded by a lively crowd of street traders, buskers and beggars. The vast Neo-Romanesque church was designed by Franz Schwechten and consecrated in 1895. It was almost completely destroyed by Allied bombs in 1943, and after World War II the ruins were removed, leaving only the massive front tower at the base of which the *Gedenkhalle* (Memorial Hall) is situated. This hall documents the history of the church and contains some of its original ceiling mosaics, marble reliefs and liturgical objects. In 1961, Egon Eiermann designed an octagonal church in blue glass and a new freestanding bell tower.

↑ The vast figure of *Christ on the Cross* is the work of Karl Hemmeter

The hexagonal bell tower on the site of the former main nave

The damaged roof of the old tower is one of Berlin's best-known landmarks.

COVENTRY AND BERLIN

In the main entrance of the old church you'll find a surprisingly modest crucifix. It was fashioned from nails found in the ashes of Coventry Cathedral, England, which was destroyed during German bombing raids in 1940.

Walls of concrete and blue glass form a dense grid

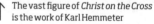

←
The old spire, completed in 1895, and the new church and bell tower, completed in 1961

Splendid mosaics decorate
the arches, walls and ceilings
of the old church ↑

Food with a view at legendary department store KaDeWe

EXPERIENCE MORE

② KaDeWe

♀ F7 ⊕ Tauentzienstrasse 21-24 Ⓤ Wittenbergplatz ⊞ M19, M29, M46 ◷ 10am-8pm Mon-Thu, 10am-9pm Fri, 9:30am-8pm Sat ⓦ kadewe.de

Kaufhaus des Westens, or KaDeWe, is the largest department store in Europe. It was built in 1907 to a design by Emil Schaudt, but it has been extended several times. From the very beginning it was Berlin's most exclusive department store, with a slogan that ran "In our shop a customer is a king, and the king is a customer". After World War II, KaDeWe became the symbol of the economic success of West Berlin.

You can buy everything here; however, the main attraction must be the Food Hall, a gourmet's paradise, with exotic fruits and vegetables, live fish and seafood, 100 varieties of tea, more than 2,400 wines and a host of other gastronomic delights. KaDeWe also has a restaurant, the Wintergarten.

③ Bikinihaus Mall

♀ F7 ⊕ Budapester Strasse 38-50 Ⓢ&Ⓤ Zoologischer Garten Ⓤ Kurfürstendamm ⊞ 100, 110, 200, 204, 245, 249, M45 ◷ 10am-8pm Mon-Sat ⓦ bikiniberlin.de

The three-floor Bikinihaus Mall, named for the 1950s building that houses it, has an inspired feature: its ground floor houses 70 wooden "pop-ups", crate-like mini-shops that independent stores can rent for up to a year. This keeps things fresh and exciting while the surrounding brand outlets – Carhaart, Scotch & Soda, Gant – offer a solid range of mid-range fashion and home design.

④ Europa-Center

♀ F7 ⊕ Breitscheidplatz Ⓢ&Ⓤ Zoologischer Garten ⊞ 100, 109, 200, X9

The Europa-Center stands on the site of the legendary Romanisches Café, a famous meeting place for Dada artists in the 1920s. The current building dates from 1965, and since that time it has been one of the largest complexes of its type in the whole of Germany. Designed by Helmut Hentrich and Hubert Petschnigg, it comprises a group of low-rise buildings housing a trade centre, numerous restaurants and pubs, the deluxe Hotel Palace Berlin and the political cabaret *Die Stachelschweine*.

Around the Center are some intriguing fountains, including the "Flow of Time Clock", designed by Bernard Gitton. Seconds, minutes and hours are measured in vials and spheres of green liquid.

△ GREAT VIEWS
Monkey Bar

As well as amazing cocktails, the Monkey Bar at the 25hours Hotel Bikini has a wrap-around terrace with excellent views over the adjacent zoo and Kaiser Wilhelm Gedächtnis Kirche.

5

Tauentzienstrasse

F7 **Wittenbergplatz**
M19, M29, M46

This is one of the most important streets for trade and commerce in this part of Berlin. Some shops here are not as expensive or as elegant as on Kurfürstendamm – but they attract more visitors for this reason. One of the highlights of the street is the unusual façade of the department store Peek & Cloppenburg. Designed by Gottfried Böhm, the walls of the building are covered with transparent, gently slanting and undulating "aprons".

Also unmissable, literally, is the amazing sculpture, *Berlin*. Representing the divided Berlin of the Wall era, it was installed in 1987 to mark the 750th anniversary of the city.

6

Zoo Berlin

F7 **Hardenbergplatz 8/ Budapester Strasse 34**
Zoologischer Garten
100, 109, 110, 200, 204, 245, 249, M45, M46, M49, X9, X10, X34 **Opening times vary, see website for details** **zoo-berlin.de**

Zoo Berlin is one of Berlin's greatest attractions and many animal "stars" are to be found here. Part of the Tiergarten (*p170*), it dates from 1844,

which makes it the oldest zoo in Germany. You can enter from Hardenbergplatz through the Lion's Gate, and from Budapester Strasse through the decorative Oriental-style Elephant Gate.

The zoo offers a number of attractions, including the monkey house, with its family of gorillas, and a darkened pavilion for nocturnal animals. The hippopotamus pool has a glazed wall so they can be seen underwater. Since 2017, the zoo has also been home to a pair of giant pandas. The aquarium, one of the largest in Europe, contains sharks, piranhas and unusual animals from coral reefs. There is also a huge terrarium with an overgrown jungle that is home to a group of crocodiles.

7

Newton-Sammlung and Museum für Fotografie

E6 **Jebensstrasse 2**
& Zoologischer Garten
10am–6pm Tue, Wed & Fri–Sun (to 8pm Thu)
smb.museum

Society and art photographer Helmut Newton (1931–2004) bequeathed his life's work to the city of Berlin. Newton, who was born and received his first training as a photographer in Berlin, became one of the 20th century's most well-known photographers with his stark black-and-white

images of nudes and portraits of the rich and famous.

This museum serves as the city's museum of photography, and is constantly expanding its collections. It displays photographs dating back to the 19th century, and its exhibits on Newton contain selections of his work – including fashion and landscapes – as well as a collection of his cameras.

←

One of Berlin Zoo's two giant pandas, Meng Meng and Jiao Qing, on loan from China

8

Theater des Westens

📍 E7 🏠 Kantstrasse 9-12
☎ 0180 544 44
Ⓢ & Ⓤ Zoologischer Garten
🚌 100, 109, 110, 200, M49,
X9, X10, X34

The Theater of the West,
one of the most picturesque
of all Berlin's theatres, was
built in 1896 to a design by
Bernhard Sehring. The composition of its façade links Neo-
Classical elements with
Palladian and Art Nouveau
details. The interior of the
theatre has been designed
in a splendid Neo-Baroque
style, while the back and the
section that houses the stage
have been rebuilt within
a Neo-Gothic structure,
incorporating the decorative
elements of a chess set.

From its very beginning
the theatre focused on
lighter forms of musical
entertainment. Operettas
and vaudeville have been
staged here, and in more
recent times musicals such as
Les Misérables. Some of the
world's greatest stars have
appeared on the stage here,
including Josephine Baker,
who performed her famous
banana dance in 1926. Near

the theatre is the renowned
Delphi cinema and popular
jazz club Quasimodo.

9

Savignyplatz

📍 D7 Ⓢ Savignyplatz
🚌 M49, X34

Savignyplatz is enclosed on
the south side by the arcade
of a railway viaduct, under
which Sally (Liza Minnelli) and
Brian (Michael York) scream in
the film *Cabaret* by Bob Fosse.
During the day the square
does not look interesting –
there are no remarkable
buildings, only carefully tended
greenery and flowerbeds.
However, the area around the
square truly comes alive at
night, when the dozens of
cafés and restaurants fill up.
During summer the entire
edge of Savignyplatz and
neighbouring streets turn into
one big garden filled with
tables and umbrellas. People
come from outlying districts
to visit popular restaurants
and cafés such as Dicke Wirtin.
The arcades in the viaduct
contain many cafés and
bars, and one section has
been taken up by the
Bücherbogen bookshop.

> **During summer,
> the entire edge of
> Savigny Platz
> and neighbouring
> streets turn into
> one big garden filled
> with tables and
> umbrellas.**

10 🖼🎭📷📖🎨

C/O Berlin

📍 E7 🏠 Hardenbergstrasse
22-24 Ⓤ Zoologischer
Garten 🚌 100, 200, 245,
M49, X10, X34 🕐 11am-
8pm daily 🌐 co-berlin.org

This photography exhibition
centre showcases work by
renowned photographers as
well as young talent, and
holds artist talks, lectures and
guided tours. It is housed in
Amerika Haus, the former
American culture and
information centre, built
during the international
building exhibition in 1956–7
to a light and airy design by
Bruno Grimmek.

11

Fasanenstrasse

📍 E7 Ⓤ Uhlandstrasse
🚌 109, 110, M49, X10, X34

The discreet charm of
Fasanenstrasse, particularly
between Lietzenburger
Strasse and Kurfürstendamm,
has attracted the most
exclusive designer shops in
the world. *Fin-de-siècle* villas
set in tranquil gardens and
elegant shop windows of
jewellers, art galleries and
fashion shops will all entice
you to take an afternoon stroll
along this street.

It is worth seeing the villas
at No. 23–25, which are called
the Wintergarten-Ensemble.
The first one, No. 23, dates
from 1889. Tucked away in a
garden, the villa is home to
the Literaturhaus, which
organizes interesting

↑ The magnificent façade of the Theater des Westens,
matched by an equally opulent interior

exhibitions and readings. It also houses an excellent café that extends into a conservatory. No. 25, built in 1892 by Hans Grisebach, accommodates an auction house and art gallery.

---

⑫
Steinplatz

♿E7 🅰Steinplatz
🅂& Ⓤ Zoologischer Garten
🚌245, M45, N2

Because of the two nearby universities (Berlin University of the Arts and the Technical University of Berlin), this square was a popular meeting place for artists, intellectuals and students in the years of West Berlin. A green oasis surrounded by beautiful architecture, the square is still a lovely meeting spot, and makes a great place to take a break between exploring the galleries between Herzallee and Kantstrasse.

The square also contains a monument dedicated to the victims of Stalinism and National Socialism. It is made of stones from Fasanenstrasse Synagogue, which was destroyed during World War II.

⑬
Jüdisches Gemeindehaus

♿E7 🅰Fasanenstrasse 79/80 📞88 02 80
🅂& Ⓤ Zoologischer Garten
Ⓤ Uhlandstrasse or Kurfürstendamm 🚌245, M49, X10, X34

The Jewish Community House is the headquarters of the local Jewish community, constructed on the site of a synagogue that was burned down by the Nazis and their supporters during Kristallnacht on 9 November 1938. The new building, designed by Dieter Knoblauch and Heinz Heise, was constructed in 1959. The only reminders of the splendour of the former synagogue are the portal at the entrance to the building and some decorative fragments on the façade.

Inside there are offices and a prayer room covered by three glazed domes. At the rear there is a courtyard with a place of remembrance. There is also an emotive statue at the front of the building, depicting a broken scroll of the Torah (the holy book of Jewish law).

↑ Crowds outside the C/O Berlin photography exhibit centre

A SHORT WALK
BREITSCHEIDPLATZ AND KU'DAMM

Distance 1.5 km (1 mile) **Nearest U-Bahn station** Kurfürstendamm **Time** 15 minutes

The area surrounding the eastern end of the Ku'damm – especially Tauentzienstrasse and Breitscheidplatz – is the centre of the former West Berlin. Years ago, this ultra-modern district attracted visitors from all over the world. In terms of shopping and leisure, it's becoming overshadowed by Potsdamer Platz and the arcades of Friedrichstrasse, but the Ku'damm still retains its unique character and is the perfect place for a city stroll. Nowhere else in Berlin is there a place so full of life as Breitscheidplatz, a department store with such style as KaDeWe, or streets as refined as Fasanenstrasse.

Designed by Josef Paul Kleihues, the Kant-Dreieck (Kant Triangle) building contains only right angles. The "sail" on the roof makes it instantly recognizable.

KANTSTRASSE

Literaturhaus contains a charming café and a good bookshop.

Fragments of the old synagogue are incorporated into the façade of the Jüdisches Gemeindehaus (Jewish Community House; p205).

FASANENSTRASSE

KURFÜRSTENDAMM

MEINEKESTRASSE

START

AUGSBURGER STRASSE

JOACHIMSTALER STRASSE

Fasanenstrasse is a tranquil street that features some of the most expensive shops in Berlin (p204).

A stroll along the Ku'damm is a walk into the heart of Berlin, and an essential part of any visit to the city.

| 0 metres | 100 |
| 0 yards | 100 |

The structure of the Berlin Stock Exchange at Ludwig-Erhard-Haus is based on parabolic arches.

The façade of the Theater des Westens is fittingly decorated with dancing women (p204).

Bahnhof Zoo

↑ Chinese-inspired gazebo at Zoo Berlin

BUDAPESTER STRASSE

AUENTZIENSTRASSE

The Oriental-style Elephant Gate is one of two entrances to the Berlin Zoo (p203).

● FINISH

The juxtaposition of old and new buildings at Kaiser Wilhelm Gedächtnis Kirche has created one of the most iconic sights in Berlin (p200).

One of the attractions of the Europa-Center is a glazed courtyard containing a fountain with moving parts (p202).

AROUND SCHLOSS CHARLOTTENBURG

The area surrounding Schloss Charlottenburg is one of the most enchanting regions of the city, full of greenery and attractive buildings dating from the end of the 19th century. Originally a small settlement called Lützow, it was only when Elector Friedrich III (later King Friedrich I) built his wife's summer retreat here at the end of the 17th century that this town attained significance. Initially called Schloss Lietzenburg, the palace was renamed Schloss Charlottenburg after the death of Queen Sophie Charlotte.

By the 18th century Charlottenburg had become a town, and was for many years an independent administration, inhabited by wealthy people living in elegant villas. It became officially part of Berlin in 1920 and, despite World War II and the ensuing division of the city, the central section of this area has kept its historical character.

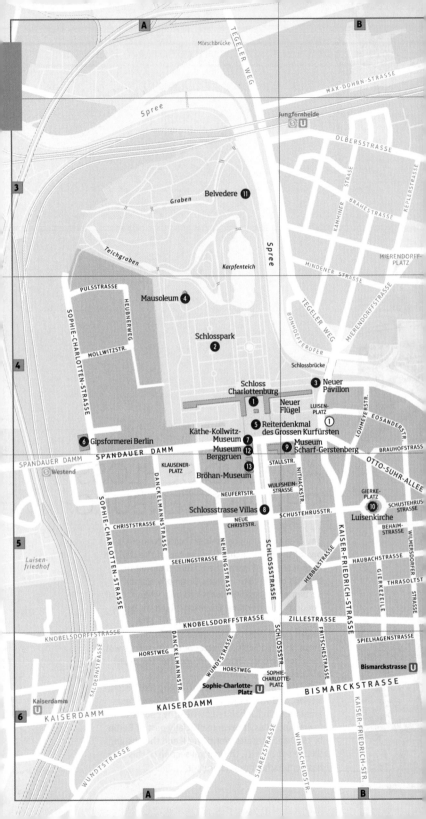

A

B

Mörschbrücke

TEGELER WEG

MAX-DOHRN-STRASSE

Spree

Jungfernheide Ⓢ Ⓤ

OLBERSSTRASSE

3

Graben

Belvedere ⑪

KAMMINER STRASSE

BRAHESTRASSE

KEPLERSTRASSE

STRASSE

MIERENDORFF-PLATZ

Teichgraben

Spree

MINDENER STRASSE

MIERENDORFFSTRASSE

Karpfenteich

Schlossbrücke

TEGELER WEG

BONHOEFFERUFER

PULSSTRASSE

Mausoleum ④

HEUBNERWEG

Schlosspark ②

MOLLWITZSTR.

SOPHIE-CHARLOTTEN-STRASSE

4

Schloss Charlottenburg ①

Schlossbrücke

Neuer Flügel

③ Neuer Pavillon

LUISEN-PLATZ

LOHMEYERSTR.

EOSANDERSTR.

⑤ Reiterdenkmal des Grossen Kurfürsten

⑥ Gipsformerei Berlin

Käthe-Kollwitz-Museum ⑦

①

BRAUHOFSTRASS

SPANDAUER DAMM

SPANDAUER DAMM

Ⓢ Westend

Museum Berggruen ⑫

⑨ Museum Scharf-Gerstenberg

STALLSTR.

NITHACKSTR.

OTTO-SUHR-ALLEE

KLAUSENER-PLATZ

DANCKELMANNSTRASSE

Bröhan-Museum ⑬

WULFSHEIN-STRASSE

NEUFERTSTR.

Schlossstrasse Villas ⑧

SCHUSTEHRUSSTR.

GIERKE-PLATZ

⑩ Luisenkirche

SCHUSTEHRUS-STRASSE

SOPHIE-CHARLOTTEN-STRASSE

CHRISTSTRASSE

NEUE CHRISTSTR.

HEBBELSTRASSE

BEHAIM-STRASSE

WILMERSDORFER

5

Luisen-friedhof

SEELINGSTRASSE

NEHRINGSTRASSE

SCHLOSSSTRASSE

HAUBACHSTRASSE

KAISER-FRIEDRICH-STRASSE

GIERKEZEILE

THRASOLTST

STRASSE

KNOBELSDORFFSTRASSE

ZILLESTRASSE

SPIELHAGENSTRASSE

KNOBELSDORFFSTRASSE

DANCKELMANNSTR.

HORSTWEG

WUNDTSTRASSE

HORSTWEG

SCHLOSSSTR.

FRITSCHESTRASSE

Bismarckstrasse Ⓤ

SALDERNSTRASSE

SOPHIE-CHARLOTTE-PLATZ

Sophie-Charlotte-Platz Ⓤ

BISMARCKSTRASSE

KAISER-FRIEDRICH-STR.

Kaiserdamm Ⓤ

6

KAISERDAMM

KAISERDAMM

WUNDTSTRASSE

SUAREZSTRASSE

WINDSCHEIDSTR.

A

B

AROUND SCHLOSS CHARLOTTENBURG

Must See
1 Schloss Charlottenburg

Experience More
2 Schlosspark
3 Neuer Pavillon
4 Mausoleum
5 Reiterdenkmal des Grossen Kurfürsten
6 Gipsformerei Berlin
7 Käthe-Kollwitz-Museum
8 Schlossstrasse Villas
9 Museum Scharf-Gerstenberg
10 Luisenkirche
11 Belvedere
12 Museum Berggruen
13 Bröhan-Museum

Eat
1 Brauhaus Lemke am Schloss

AROUND KURFÜRSTENDAMM p196

AROUND SCHLOSS CHARLOTTENBURG

0 metres 400
0 yards 400

N

❶ 🛝 🄼

SCHLOSS CHARLOTTENBURG

📍A4 🚇Spandauer Damm 20–24 🅂Jungfernheide, Westend 🅄Richard-Wagner-Platz, Sophie-Charlotte-Platz 🚌109, 309, M45 🕐Apr–Oct: 10am–6pm Tue–Sun; Nov–Mar: 10am–5pm Tue–Sun 🌐spsg.de

Charlottenburg Palace is made up of two magnificent buildings: the Altes Schloss (Old Palace) and Neuer Flügel (New Wing).

Built in 1695, the palace in Charlottenburg was intended as a summer home for Sophie Charlotte, Elector Friedrich III's wife. Between 1701 and 1713 Johann Friedrich Eosander enlarged the palace, crowning it with a cupola and adding the orangery wing. This section of the palace is now known as the Altes Schloss. The Neuer Flügel extension was undertaken by Frederick the Great (Friedrich II), and designed by Georg Wenzeslaus von Knobelsdorff in the mid-18th century. Restored to their former elegance following World War II, its collection of richly decorated interiors is unequalled in Berlin.

↑ Schlosspark, a favourite weekend spot for locals

This sculpture replaced the original destroyed in World War II.

↑ The Goldene Galerie, a Rococo garden ballroom, dating from 1746

→ *Fortuna* by Ricard Scheibe crowns the palace.

GALLERY GUIDE

The ground floor of Altes Schloss houses the opulent chambers of Friedrich III, a Portrait Gallery and the Porcelain Cabinet. The upper floors include the apartment of Friedrich Wilhelm IV and a silver and tableware collection.

💬 INSIDER TIP
Neuer Flügel

The New Wing has a separate entrance from the main section of the palace, and requires a separate ticket. It holds the elegant apartments and exquisite furniture of Friedrich Wilhelm II, and hosts art and history exhibitions.

↑ The central section of the palace is the work of Johann Arnold Nering

Cherubs striking playful poses in royal Schlosspark

EXPERIENCE MORE

②

Schlosspark

📍A4 🚇Luisenplatz
Ⓢ Westend 🚇 Richard-
Wagner-Platz, Sophie-
Charlotte-Platz
🚌 109, 309, M45

The extensive palace park that surrounds Schloss Charlottenburg (p212), crisscrossed with tidy gravel paths, is a favourite place for Berliners to stroll at the weekend. The park is largely the result of reconstruction work carried out after World War II, when 18th-century prints were used to help recreate the varied layout of the original grounds.

Immediately behind Schloss Charlottenburg is a French-style Baroque garden, made to a strict geometrical design with a vibrant patchwork of flowerbeds, carefully trimmed shrubs and ornate fountains. Further away from the palace, beyond the curved carp lake, is a less formal English-style landscaped park, originally laid out in the 1820s under the direction of the renowned royal gardener, Peter Joseph Lenné. The lakes and waterways of the park are the habitat of various waterfowl,

including herons. A bike path runs along the Spree from the palace park to the Tiergarten (p170) and beyond.

---

③

Neuer Pavillon (Schinkel-Pavillon)

📍B4 🚇Luisenplatz (Schlosspark Charlottenburg) ☎ 30 32 09 11 Ⓢ Westend 🚇 Richard-Wagner-Platz, Sophie-Charlotte-Platz 🚌 109, 309, M45 🕐 Apr–Oct: 10am–5:30pm Tue–Sun; Nov–Mar: noon–4pm Tue–Sun

This charming Neo-Classical pavilion, with its clean lines and first-floor balcony, was built for Friedrich Wilhelm III and his second wife, Princess Auguste von Liegnitz. During a visit to Naples, the king was so impressed by the Villa Reale del Chiamonte that he commissioned Karl Friedrich Schinkel (p28) to build him something similar. The pavilion was finished for the king's birthday on 3 August 1825. Schinkel designed a two-storey structure with a central staircase and ranged the rooms around it in perfect

symmetry. Pillared galleries on the first floor added variety to the eastern and western elevations. A cast-iron balcony runs around the entire structure. Like many other Schloss Charlottenburg buildings, the pavilion burned down completely in World War II and was rebuilt in 1960.

EAT

Brauhaus Lemke am Schloss
Set right beside the Schloss Charlottenburg, this classic brewhouse makes a convenient spot for post-tour sustenance. The interior is as reassuringly traditional as the menu, which features home-brewed beer and filling, meat-heavy German food.

📍B4 🚇Luisenplatz
🕐noon–midnight daily
🌐lemke.berlin

€€€

The display inside the pavilion reveals the original splendour of the aristocratic interiors, enhanced with pictures and sculptures of the period. The prize picture is a renowned panorama of Berlin dated 1834, painted by Eduard Gärtner from the roof of the Friedrichswerdersche Kirche. You can also admire paintings by Schinkel, not only a great architect but also a fine painter of fabulous architectural fantasies.

4

Mausoleum

📍A4 🚇Luisenplatz (Schlosspark Charlotten-burg) ☎32 09 14 46 🚍Westend 🚇Richard-Wagner-Platz, Sophie-Charlotte-Platz 🚌109, 309, M45 🕐Apr-Oct: 10am-5:30pm Tue-Sun 🚫Nov-Mar

Queen Luise, the beloved first wife of Friedrich Wilhelm III, was laid to rest in this modest, dignified building, set among the trees in Schlosspark. The mausoleum was designed by Karl Friedrich Schinkel, in the style of a Doric portico-fronted temple.

In the original design, the queen's sarcophagus was housed in the crypt while the tombstone (a cenotaph sculpted by Christian Daniel Rauch) stood in the centre of the mausoleum. After the death of Friedrich Wilhelm in 1840, the mausoleum was refurbished, an apse added and the queen's tomb moved to one side, leaving room for her husband's tomb, also designed by Rauch. The second wife of the king, Princess Auguste von Liegnitz, was also buried in the crypt of the mausoleum.

Between 1890 and 1894, the tombs of Kaiser Wilhelm I and his wife, Auguste von Sachsen-Weimar, were added to the crypt. Both monuments are the work of Erdmann Encke.

5

Reiterdenkmal des Grossen Kurfürsten

📍A4 🚇Luisenplatz 🚍Westend 🚇Richard-Wagner-Platz, Sophie-Charlotte-Platz 🚌109, 309, M45

The Monument to the Great Elector (Friedrich Wilhelm) is the finest in Berlin and was paid for by his son, Elector Friedrich III (later King Friedrich I). Designed by Andreas Schlüter to be cast in one piece, the statue was completed in 1703, and erected near the former Berlin palace, by Lange Brücke (now called Rathausbrücke). The statue was moved to safety in World War II, but ironically, on the return journey, the barge transporting the monument sank in the port of Tegel.

In 1949 the statue was retrieved intact from the water and erected here on a copy of the base. The original base finally ended up in the Bode-Museum topped with a replica of the statue.

The statue portrays the Great Elector as a warrior on horseback, triumphant over the figures of prisoners of war around the base. The base itself is decorated with patriotic reliefs of allegorical scenes. One scene depicts the kingdom surrounded by figures representing Peace, History and the Spree river; another shows it protected by embodiments of Bravery, Faith and Strength (represented by the figure of Hercules).

6

Gipsformerei Berlin

📍A4 🚇Sophie-Charlotten-Strasse 17-18 ☎32 67 69 11 🚍Westend 🚇Sophie-Charlotte-Platz 🚌309, M45 🕐9am-4pm Mon-Fri (to 6pm Wed); may vary during exhibitions

Founded by Friedrich Wilhelm III in 1819, the Berlin Replica Workshop produces original-sized replicas from items in Berlin museums and other collections, and also repairs damaged sculptures. Visitors are welcome to this modest brick building west of Schloss Charlottenburg and can purchase items on the spot or choose from cata-logues to have them made to order and shipped home. Sculptures are generally copied in white plaster or painted true to the original. Most moulds originate from the Middle Ages, the Renaiss-ance and the 19th century.

THE GREAT ELECTOR (1620-88)

The Elector Friedrich Wilhelm was one of the most famous rulers of the Hohenzollern dynasty. He inherited the position of ruler of Brandenburg-Prussia in 1640, and one of his first duties was to rebuild the region after the devastation of the Thirty Years' War (1618-48). In 1660 he wrested the Duchy of Prussia territory from Poland. During the course of his reign, Berlin became a powerful city, and rich families from all over Europe - fleeing persecution in their own land - chose to settle here.

7

Käthe-Kollwitz-Museum

Q A4 **A** Spandauer Damm 19 **S** Westend **U** Richard-Wagner-Platz, Sophie-Charlotte-Platz **⊞** 109, 309, M45 **◯** 11am-6pm daily **W** kaethe-kollwitz.de

This museum provides a unique opportunity to become acquainted with the work of Käthe Kollwitz (1867–1945). Born in Königsberg, the artist settled in Berlin, where she married a doctor who worked in Prenzlauer Berg, a working-class district (p118). Her drawings and sculptures portrayed the social problems of the poor, as well as human tragedy and suffering. She frequently took up the theme of motherhood and war after losing a son and grandson in World Wars I and II.

The museum exhibits her work, including sculptures, posters and drawings, as well as letters and photographs.

8

Schlossstrasse Villas

Q A5 **A** Schlossstrasse 65-67 **U** Sophie-Charlotte-Platz **⊞** 309

Most of the historic villas and buildings that once graced Schlossstrasse no longer exist.

However, careful restoration of a few villas enables the visitor to get a feel for what the atmosphere must have been like at the end of the 19th century. It is worth taking a stroll down Schlossstrasse to look at the renovated villas, especially No. 67, which was built in 1873 in a Neo-Classical style to a design by Georg Töbelmann. If you continue the walk down nearby Schustehrusstrasse, you'll see an interesting school building at No. 39–43. Just up the road at No. 55 is the fine Villa Oppenheim, home of the Charlottenburg-Wilmersdorf Museum, open to the public except on Mondays.

9

Museum Scharf-Gerstenberg

Q B4 **A** Schlossstrasse 70 **U** Richard-Wagner-Platz, Sophie-Charlotte-Platz **S** Westend **⊞** 309, M45 **◯** 10am-6pm Tue-Fri, 11am-6pm Sat & Sun **W** smb.museum

The two 1850s pavilions on either side of Schlossstrasse were intended as officers' barracks for the King's Guard du Corps. Adjoining the eastern one is the Marstall, or stable block, and in this can be found the Museum Scharf-Gerstenberg. The museum presents paintings, sculptures, works on paper and even films by Surrealist and associated artists such as Dalí, Magritte, Max Ernst, Paul Klee and Jean Dubuffet, and also older works by Goya, Piranesi and Redon. More than 250 objects are presented over three floors, explaining the history of surreal art, with pieces from almost all the leading Surrealists.

←
Spiral staircase below the cupola of the Museum Scharf-Gerstenberg

Did You Know?

The pavilions on either side of Schlossstrasse were inspired by a design by King Friedrich Wilhelm IV.

10

Luisenkirche

Q B5 **A** Gierkeplatz 4 **C** 341 90 61 **U** Richard-Wagner-Platz, Sophie-Charlotte-Platz **⊞** 109, M45 **◯** 9am-1pm Mon, Tue, Thu & Fri, 2-6pm Wed

This small church dates back to 1716, but its original Baroque styling was removed in rebuilding undertaken by Karl Friedrich Schinkel (p28) in the 1820s, when the church was renamed in memory of Queen Luise (1776–1810).

The shape of the church is based on a traditional Greek cross, with a tower at the front. The interior fixtures and fittings are not the originals, and the elegant stained-glass windows were made in 1956.

11

Belvedere

Q A3 **A** Spandauer Damm 20-24 (Schlosspark Charlottenburg) **C** 32 09 10 **S** Westend **U** Richard-Wagner-Platz, Sophie-Charlotte-Platz **⊞** 109, 309, M45 **◯** Apr-Oct: 10am-5:30pm Tue-Sun **◯** Nov-Mar

The Belvedere is a summer house in the Schlosspark which served as a tea pavilion for Friedrich Wilhelm II and, in times of war, as a watchtower. It dates from 1788 and was designed by Carl Gotthard Langhans. The architect mixed Baroque and Neo-Classical elements, giving the building an oval central

→ A formal green avenue leading up to the Belvedere

structure with four straight-sided annexes. The building is crowned by a low dome topped with a sculpture of three cherubs supporting a basket of flowers.

Though the Belvedere was ruined during World War II, the summer house was reconstructed between 1956 and 1960 and adapted to serve as an exhibition space. The exhibition is a large collection of exquisite porcelain from the Berlin Königliche Porzellan-Manufaktur (Royal Porcelain Workshop), which has pieces from the Rococo period up to late Biedermeier, including some outstanding individual items.

⓬ ⊘ ▣ 🏛

Museum Berggruen

**Ⓠ A4 ⌂ Schlossstrasse 1
Ⓢ Westend ⓤ Richard-Wagner-Platz, Sophie-Charlotte-Platz 🚌 109, 309, M45 🕐 10am–6pm Tue-Fri, 11am–6pm Sat & Sun 🆆 smb.museum**

Heinz Berggruen assembled this tasteful collection of art dating from the late 19th and first half of the 20th century. Born and educated in Berlin, he emigrated to the US in 1936, spent most of his later life in Paris, but later

> **The Belvedere is a summer house in the Schlosspark which served as a tea pavilion for Friedrich Wilhelm II and, in times of war, as a watchtower.**

entrusted his collection to the city of his birth. The museum opened in what was once the west pavilion of the barracks using space freed up by moving the Antiken-sammlung to Museumsinsel. The exhibition halls were modified according to the designs of Hilmer and Sattler, who also designed the layout of the Gemäldegalerie (p158). The Museum Berggruen is particularly well known for its large collection of quality paintings, drawings and gouaches by Pablo Picasso. The collection begins with a drawing from his student days in 1897 and ends with works he painted in 1972, one year before his death.

In addition to these, the museum displays more than 60 works by Swiss artist Paul Klee and more than 20 works by Henri Matisse. The museum also houses paintings by other major artists, such as Georges Braque and Paul Cézanne. The collection is supplemented by some excellent sculptures, particularly those of Henri Laurens and Alberto Giacometti.

⓭ ⊘

Bröhan-Museum

**Ⓠ A5 ⌂ Schlossstrasse 1a
Ⓢ Westend ⓤ Richard-Wagner-Platz, Sophie-Charlotte-Platz 🚌 109, 309, M45 🕐 10am–6pm Tue-Sun 🆆 broehan-museum.de**

This small but interesting museum, set in a late Neo-Classical building, houses a collection of decorative arts amassed by Karl H Bröhan, who from 1966 collected works of art from the Art Nouveau (Jugendstil or Secessionist) and Art Deco periods. The paintings of the artists particularly connected with the Berlin Secessionist movement, such as Karl Hagemeister and Hans Baluschek, are especially well represented. Alongside the paintings there are fine examples of arts and crafts in other media: furniture, ceramics, silverwork and textiles. There is glasswork by Émile Gallé and porcelain from some of the finest European manufacturers.

A SHORT WALK
AROUND THE SCHLOSS

Distance 2 km (1.5 miles) **Nearest U-Bahn station** Richard-Wagner-Platz **Time** 20 minutes

The park surrounding the former royal summer residence in Charlottenburg is one of the most picturesque places in Berlin, making for a beautiful walk in every season. Visitors are drawn here by the luxury Baroque complex and outlying structures, which were meticulously rebuilt after World War II. The marvellous interiors were once home to Prussian nobles, and now the wings of the palace and its pavilions house interesting exhibitions.

↑ French-style garden in Schlosspark

The central section of Schloss Charlottenburg is called Nering-Eosanderbau, in honour of the architects who designed the building (p212).

Did You Know?

The *Ortsteil* (locality) of Charlottenburg includes much of the Kurfürstendamm area.

Kleine Orangerie

The monument to the Great Elector at the entrance of Schloss Charlottenburg was funded by his son King Friedrich I and designed by Andreas Schlüter (p215).

START

Neuer Flügel, the palace's newest wing, was once home to the royal art collection. Today the building houses changing art and history exhibits.

In the Neo-Classical Mausoleum built for Queen Luise, members of the royal family are laid to rest (p215).

Locator Map
For more detail see p210

AROUND SCHLOSS CHARLOTTENBURG

0 metres   150
0 yards   150

FINISH

In 1960 Karl Bobeck created the group of statues that surmount the Belvedere, in imitation of the original figures which were designed by Johann Eckstein (p216).

The Schlosspark is a French-style park, laid out in a geometric pattern, extending behind the palace (p214).

In front of the western elevation of the Neuer Pavillon are two granite columns (1840), topped by statues of Victory, the work of Christian Daniel Rauch (p214).

→ The Belvedere's Baroque flourishes and Neo-Classical lines

BEYOND THE CENTRE

In 1920 seven towns were incorporated into Berlin, along with 59 communes and 27 country estates – each of which had been evolving independently for many years. Over the following decades the faces of many of these boroughs changed, but some places have kept their small-town or rural character. Thanks to this diversity, a stay in Berlin can simultaneously equate to visiting several cities. A short journey by S-Bahn enables you to travel from the cosmopolitan city centre of the 21st century to the vast forests of the Grunewald or the beach at Wannsee lake. You can explore everything from Dahlem's tranquil streets lined with villas, to Spandau's Renaissance citadel, cobbled lanes and the vast Gothic church of St-Nikolai-Kirche – all just half an hour away from the centre of Berlin and well worth a visit.

BEYOND THE CENTRE

Must See

① Neukölln

Experience More

② Schloss Britz
③ Alt-Rixdorf
④ Britzer Garten
⑤ Treptower Park
⑥ Schloss Friedrichsfelde & Tierpark Zoo
⑦ Deutsch-Russisches Museum
⑧ Stasi-Museum
⑨ Stasi-Prison
⑩ Köpenick
⑪ Gethsemanekirche
⑫ Zeiss-Grossplanetarium
⑬ Mauerpark
⑭ Schloss Schönhausen
⑮ Jüdischer Friedhof Weissensee
⑯ Schloss Tegel
⑰ Haus des Rundfunks
⑱ AEG-Turbinenhalle
⑲ Gedenkstätte Plötzensee
⑳ Villa Borsig
㉑ Wedding
㉒ Le Corbusier Haus
㉓ Messegelände
㉔ Funkturm
㉕ Georg-Kolbe-Museum
㉖ Spandau
㉗ Olympiastadion
㉘ Strandbad Wannsee
㉙ Königskolonnaden
㉚ Rathaus Schöneberg
㉛ Grunewaldturm
㉜ Grabstätte von Heinrich von Kleist
㉝ Haus der Wannsee-Konferenz
㉞ Museumsdorf Düppel
㉟ Villenkolonie Alsen
㊱ Dahlem
㊲ Potsdam

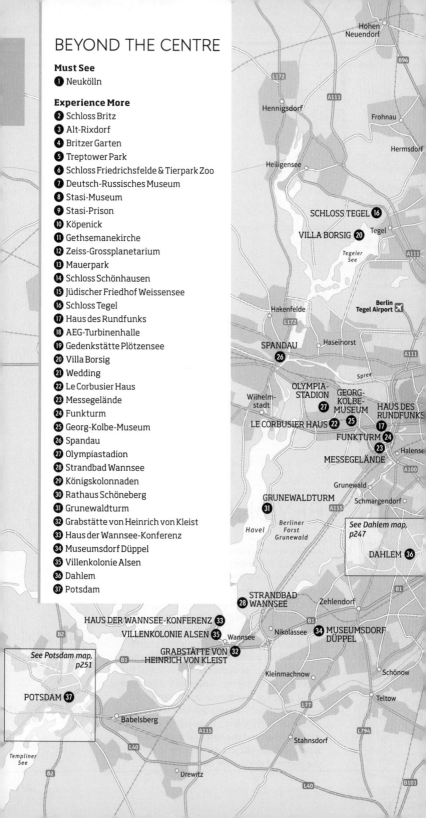

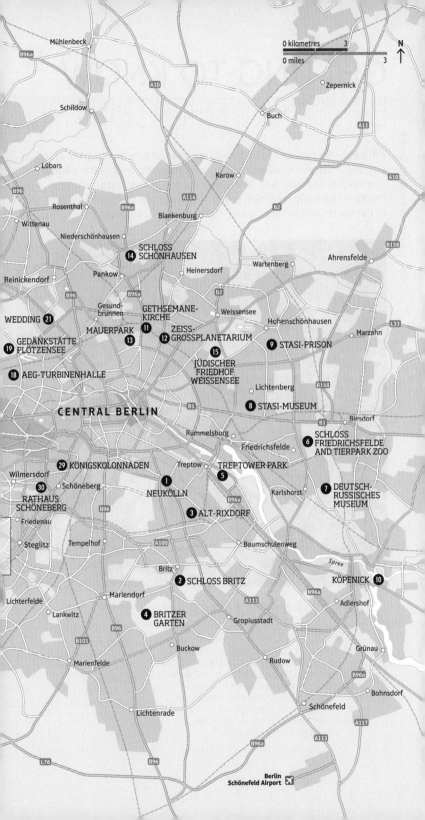

0 kilometres 3
0 miles 3

N

Mühlenbeck

B96a

A10

Schildow

Buch

Zepernick

A11

Lübars

B96

Rosenthal

B96a

A114

Blankenburg

Karow

A10

B2

B158

Wittenau

Niederschönhausen

14 SCHLOSS
SCHÖNHAUSEN

Heinersdorf

Wartenberg

Ahrensfelde

Reinickendorf

Pankow

B96

B96a

Gesund-
brunnen

**GETHSEMANE-
KIRCHE**

Weissensee

Hohenschönhausen

Marzahn

L33

WEDDING **21**

MAUERPARK

11

13

12 ZEISS-
GROSSPLANETARIUM

9 STASI-PRISON

B2

19 GEDÄNKSTÄTTE
PLÖTZENSEE

15

JÜDISCHER
FRIEDHOF
WEISSENSEE

18 AEG-TURBINENHALLE

Lichtenberg

B158

CENTRAL BERLIN

B1

8 STASI-MUSEUM

B1

Biesdorf

Rummelsburg

Friedrichsfelde

6 SCHLOSS
FRIEDRICHSFELDE
AND TIERPARK ZOO

29 KÖNIGSKOLONNADEN

Treptow

TREPTOWER PARK

5

Karlshorst

7 DEUTSCH-
RUSSISCHES
MUSEUM

Wilmersdorf

30

Schöneberg

1

NEUKÖLLN

**RATHAUS
SCHÖNEBERG**

B96

Friedenau

3 ALT-RIXDORF

B96a

Steglitz

Tempelhof

A100

Baumschulenweg

Spree

Britz

2 SCHLOSS BRITZ

KÖPENICK 10

Lichterfelde

Lankwitz

4 BRITZER
GARTEN

Mariendorf

A113

Gropiusstadt

Adlershof

B96

B101

Buckow

B96a

Marienfelde

Rudow

Grünau

B96a

Lichtenrade

Bohnsdorf

Schönefeld

A117

B96a

A113

L76

B96

**Berlin
Schönefeld Airport** ✈

GETTING TO KNOW
BEYOND THE CENTRE

Although most visitors to Berlin will spend their time roaming the inner city, the *Ortsteile* (localities) in the surrounding boroughs offer plenty more sights and surprises. The GDR-era museums and architecture of the East, the mellow districts in the northwest and the sparkling lakes of the southwest are all just an S-Bahn or bicycle ride away.

EAST OF THE CENTRE

PAGE 226

East of Friedrichshain lie the less gentrified districts of Lichtenberg, Hohenschönhausen, Marzahn and Treptow-Köpenick. Largely demonised in the nineties, the areas' prefabricated residential blocks today draw a mix of former East Berliners, immigrants and students priced out of the city centre. You'll find a clutch of GDR-era sights well worth exploring, including the Gedenkstätte Hohenschönhausen and the Stasi-Museum Berlin, plus more natural attractions such as the charming but low-key Tierpark.

Best for
GDR history and architecture, strolls, local culture

Home to
Neukölln, Tierpark, Stasi-Museum, Köpenick, Mauerpark

Experience
The cobbled-streets of medieval Alt Rixdorf

PAGE 236

NORTHWEST OF THE CENTRE

The many forests, parks, lakes and rivers of the northwest act as a natural magnet for city-dwellers looking for a weekend getaway. The area is also dotted with local attractions and impressive structures that exemplify key moments in Berlin's fascinating history: from the medieval Spandau and its Renaissance citadel to the enormous Third Reich-era Olympiastadion and the modernist (and monolithic) Le Corbusier Haus.

Best for
Architecture, strolls, culture

Home to
Zitadelle Spandau, Olympiastadion

Experience
A sporting event or pop concert, as well as architecture and history, at the Nazi-era Olympiastadion

PAGE 240

SOUTHWEST OF THE CENTRE

This area contains some of the city's finest natural beauty and is the place to head in the summer months. The sandy lido at the villa-lined lake Wannsee is a major warm-weather destination, and there is a plethora of beautiful outdoor attractions in the towns of Dahlem and Potsdam. For German culture and history, you can find a top-notch collection of German Expressionism at the Brücke Museum and a medieval atmosphere at Museumsdorf Düppel.

Best for
Nature, walks, beaches

Home to
Strandbad Wannsee, Rathaus Schöneberg

Experience
A stroll along the crisscrossing pathways of Grunewald forest to the striking hilltop Grunewaldturm

❶ NEUKÖLLN

🚇 Hermannplatz 🚌 171, 194, M29, M41, N7, N9, N94

This thriving neighbourhood has become home to a large population of people from around the world, as young students, creatives and professionals flock here for the cheap rents and cool atmosphere.

Characterized by a vibrant mixture of international expats, Neukölln is one of the city's fastest-growing – and fastest-gentrifying – districts. Some tourists would ignore the neighbourhood after seeing traffic-heavy drags like Sonnenallee and the bleak main square, Hermannplatz – but those willing to explore further will soon see why it's so popular with the locals. Areas such as those around Schillerstrasse and Weserstrasse – not to mention Kreuzkölln – are lined with bistros, galleries and boutiques. While there aren't many major sights in the area there are still a few places worth visiting, such as the pretty Körnerpark, the Kindl Centre for Contemporary Art, Schloss Britz *(p228)*, Britzer Garten and Neukölln's historic centre, Alt-Rixdorf.

The central Berlin skyline from Klunkerkranich rooftop bar ↓

KREUZKÖLLN

Reuterstrasse and Hobrechtstrasse are the streets directly south of the Landwehrkanal between Kotbusser Damm and Pannierstrasse. They have been nicknamed Kreuzkölln since they overlap both the Kreuzberg and Neukölln districts. These streets are characterized by a particularly dense concentration of boutiques, bars, galleries, cafés and restaurants. The Maybachufer embankment of the canal also hosts a vibrant Turkish market on Tuesdays and Fridays, and a flea market on Sundays.

↑ Kreuzkölln's cool vibe makes it the most up-and-coming area in Berlin

←

Britzer Garten, one of the city's best green spots

Did You Know?

Neukölln is the name of both the district and the borough in which it is located.

EAST OF THE CENTRE

↑ Pretty Schloss Britz, occasionally a venue for exhibitions and concerts

Schloss Britz

🏛 Alt-Britz 73 Ⓤ Parchimer Allee 🚌 181, M44, M46
🕐 11am–6pm Tue–Sun
🌐 schlossbritz.de

Originally a small manor house built in 1706 for Sigismund von Erlach, Schloss Britz was extended to its current size in the 1880s to a design by Carl Busse. It is a one-storey palace with a modest Neo-Classical aspect adorned with Baroque statues and a tower.

As well as housing a museum, the building is often used as a venue for concerts and exhibitions. The palace displays furnishings from the *Gründerzeit* – the years after the founding of the German Empire in 1871. The 19th-century interiors are excellent, but it is also worth strolling through the lovely park, where there is a bust of one of the palace's former owners, Rüdiger von Ilgen, which once stood in the Tiergarten.

Next to the palace there stands a housing estate called Hufeisensiedlung (Horseshoe Colony), built in the late 1920s to a design by Bruno Taut and Bruno Schneidereit. The architects' aim was to create spacious and affordable housing for Berliners.

Alt-Rixdorf

Ⓢ & Ⓤ Berlin-Neukölln
Ⓢ Sonnennallee
Ⓤ Karl-Marx-Strasse
🚌 171, M41, N7

Nestled gently between the bustling and unattractive thoroughfares of Karl-Marx-Strasse and Sonnenallee, charming Alt Rixdorf (Old Rixdorf) is a wonderful hidden spot to explore. This is the historical heart of the Neukölln neighbourhood, with pretty Richardplatz at the centre, founded in the mid-18th century by Protestant refugees from Bohemia. The cobbled streets lined with historical buildings still retain their old-world charm. Along Kirchgasse are the mid-19th-century remnants of the Bohemian village, whose history is told at the nearby **Museum im Böhmischen Dorfes** (Museum in a Bohemian Village) via exhibits on the traditions, beliefs, art, crafts and lives of its inhabitants, then and now. Other attractions include picturesque Bethlehemskirche, which sometimes hosts small concerts; the old village forge, dating back to 1624 and still working today; and a similarly historical coach house.

Museum im Böhmischen Dorfes

🏛 Kirchgasse 5 🕐 2–5pm Thu, noon–2pm 1st & 3rd Sun of the month 🌐 museum imboehmischendorf.de

---

PLÄNTERWALD (SPREE PARK)

The small stretch of protected forest (Plänterwald) that leads down from Treptower Park is a pleasant place to stroll. It's best known, though, as the location of the "Kulturpark", which was built in 1969 as the first theme park in the GDR. Following reunification, its rusting ruins and fallen dinosaurs became a pilgrimage destination for urbex thrill-seekers but is now owned by the city, who run official tours of the site while they decide what to do with it.

Steps leading to the Red Army monument, rising above Treptower Park ↓

2,500,000

The number of Red Army soldiers involved in the Battle of Berlin.

Britzer Garten

🏠 Sangerhauser Weg 1
Ⓤ Alt-Mariendorf 🚌 179, 181, M44 ⏰ Opening times vary, see website 🌐 gruen-berlin.de/britzer-garten

This 4-ha (10-acre) park is something of a city secret. Located in the south of Neukölln (p226), it's vast enough to contain a multitude of sights, from scenic lakes and springs, themed gardens and playgrounds to a domestic animal enclosure with sheep, goats and donkeys, and several café-restaurants. Its size and rolling terrain make it feel more natural than its landscaped heritage suggests, with patches of grassland, streams and shrubs mixed in with rose and herb gardens, and a tremendous, crowd-pulling display of tulips (over 500,000) in spring. Other attractions include a "witch garden", a small train that carries visitors around and the largest sundial in Europe. Of the three restaurants, the one inside the Britzer Mühle (mill) is the most interesting, though the Britzer See-terrassen has the nicest views from its outdoor tables.

5

Treptower Park

🏠 Alt-Treptow
Ⓢ Treptower Park
🚌 166, 265

The vast park in Treptow was laid out in the 1860s on the initiative and design of Johann Gustav Meyer. In January 1919 it was where revolutionaries Karl Liebknecht, Wilhelm Pieck and Rosa Luxemburg assembled a 150,000-strong group of striking workers during the Spartacist uprising.

The park, however, is best known for the colossal Soviet War Memorial. Built between 1946 and 1949, it stands on the grave of 5,000 Soviet soldiers killed in the battle for Berlin in 1945. The gateway is marked by a vast granite sculpture of a grieving Russian Motherland surrounded by statues of Red Army soldiers. This leads to the mausoleum, topped by an 11-m- (35-ft-) high figure of a soldier rescuing a child and resting his mighty sword on a smashed swastika.

In the furthest section of the park is the astronomical observatory, **Archenhold Sternwarte**, built for a decorative arts exhibition held here in 1896. Given a permanent site here in 1909, the observatory was used by Albert Einstein for a lecture on the Theory of Relativity in 1915. It is also home to the longest refracting telescope in the world (21 m, or 70 ft) and a small planetarium. You can take a tour at 3pm on weekends and at 8pm on Thursdays.

Archenhold Sternwarte
🏠 Alt-Treptow 1
⏰ 2–4:30pm Wed-Sun
🌐 planetarium.berlin

↑ The Baroque Schloss Friedrichsfelde, and zebras from Tierpark Zoo (inset)

6 ♿

Schloss Friedrichsfelde

🏛 Am Tierpark 125
🚇 Tierpark 🚌 194, 296, 396 🚊 27, 37, M17
🕐 Summer: 10am-6pm daily; rest of year: 10am-4:30pm daily 🌐 schloss-friedrichsfelde.de

The Baroque Friedrichsfelde Palace was built for Dutchman Benjamin von Raule around 1695, to a design by Johann Arnold Nering. A redesign in 1786 gave the residence its present-day appearance, typical of the style during the transition from Baroque to Neo-Classical. It now houses a museum of interiors, chiefly furnished with 18th- and 19th-century pieces.

The palace's park was remodelled to become the East Berlin **Tierpark Zoo** in 1957. The animal inhabitants include all of the usual favourites and there are masses of family-friendly, hands-on experiences.

Tierpark Zoo

♿🅿️😊🍴🅿️🕐 Nov-Feb: 9am-4:30pm daily; March, Sep & Oct: 9am-6pm daily; Apr-Sep 9am-6:30pm daily
🌐 tierpark-berlin.de

7

Deutsch-Russisches Museum (Berlin-Karlshorst)

🏛 Zwieseler Strasse 4/ Rheinsteinstrasse 🚇 Karlshorst 🚌 296 🚊 27, 37, M17
🕐 10am-6pm Tue-Sun
🌐 museum-karlshorst.de

This building was erected in the 1930s for the engineering corps of the Wehrmacht (the armed services of the Third Reich). It was here on the night of 8 May 1945 that Hitler's successor Grossadmiral Karl Dönitz, Field Marshal Wilhelm Keitel, Admiral Hans-Georg von Friedeburg and General Hans-Jürgen Stumpff signed the unconditional surrender of Germany's armed forces. You can visit the officers' mess hall in which the signing took place and the office of

---

EAT

Inselcafé

The main restaurant on the Insel der Jugend (Island of Youth) has a menu that stretches to goulash, coconut curry and pasta dishes, as well as coffee, cake and waffles throughout the day. In summer there are deckchairs set out right by the river.

🏛 Insel der Jugend
🕐 Apr-Oct: noon-6pm daily; Nov-Mar: noon-6pm Sun
🌐 inselberlin.de

€€€

Marshal Zhukov, and see an exhibition documenting the history of World War II.

8

Stasi-Museum

🏠 **Ruschestrasse 103 (Haus 1)** Ⓤ **Magdalenen-strasse** 🕐 **10am–6pm Mon-Fri, 11am–6pm Sat & Sun** 🌐 **stasimusem.de**

Under the GDR, this huge complex of buildings housed the Ministry of the Interior and the infamous Stasi (GDR secret service) headquarters. The Stasi's "achievements" in infiltrating its own community were without equal in the Eastern bloc.

One of the buildings houses a museum that describes the organizational structure, history and ideology of the Stasi. It includes photographs and documents depicting the Stasi's activities. The breakup of the Stasi is covered, as well as an overview of subsequent events leading up to the reunification of Germany.

A model of the headquarters is on display, as well as equipment used for bugging and spying on citizens. You can see the office of the infamous Stasi chief Erich Mielke, commander of the Ministry for State Security and a Big Brother-like figure. Mielke's legacy of suffering still lives on in the memory of millions

Spy camera designed to be concealed under clothing, on show at the Stasi-Museum

of German citizens. The interior is just as it was when the Stasi used the complex. Tours are held in English on Saturday, Sunday and Monday at 3pm.

9

Stasi-Prison (Gedenkstätte Berlin-Hohenschönhausen)

🏠 **Genslerstrasse 13a** Ⓢ & Ⓤ **Lichtenberg, then** 🚌 **256 to Liebenwalder-strasse/Genslerstrasse** 🚊 **16 to Genslerstrasse, M5 to Freienwalder, M6** 🕐 **9am–6pm daily** 🌐 **stiftung-hsh.de**

This museum is housed in the former custody building of the Stasi – the dreaded security service of the GDR. The custody building was part of a huge complex built in 1938. In May 1945 the occupying Russian authorities created a special transit camp here, in which they interned war criminals subsequently transported to Siberia. Shortly thereafter they started to bring anyone under political suspicion to the camp. During this time more than 20,000 people passed through here.

From 1946 this group of buildings was refashioned into the custody area for the KGB, and in 1951 it was given over for the use of the Stasi.

Visitors can see prisoners' cells and interrogation rooms. Housed in the cellars was the "submarine" – cells for the most "dangerous" suspects.

Tours are offered daily in both German and English. Many of the German-language guides are former inmates.

🔍 HIDDEN GEM
Insel der Jugend

A charming steel bridge takes you from Treptower Park to Berlin's "Island of Youth", named in the GDR-era for its role as a former youth club. Though small, the island hosts a café and restaurant as well as occasional events (concerts, open-air cinema) and serves as a pleasant picnic spot.

The grim exterior of the Stasi-Prison, a feared destination

10

Köpenick

Ⓢ Spindlersfeld, then 🚌167 or Ⓢ Köpenick, then 🚌164 🚊60, 61, 62, 67, 68

Köpenick is much older than Berlin. In the 9th century AD this island contained a fortified settlement called Kopanica, inhabited by Slavs. From the late 12th century, Köpenick belonged to the Margrave of Brandenburg. In about 1240 a castle was built, around which a town began to evolve, though over the years it lost out in importance to Berlin. Craftsmen settled here, and after 1685 a large colony of Huguenots followed suit.

In the 19th century Köpenick recreated itself as an industrial town. Despite wartime devastation, it has retained its historic character. By the old market square and in nearby streets, such as Alt Köpenick and Grünstrasse, modest houses have survived which recall the 18th century, next to buildings from the end of the 19th century.

At Alt Köpenick No. 21 is a vast brick town hall designed in the style of the Brandenburg Neo-Renaissance by Hans Schütte and Hugo Kinzer. It was here on 16 October 1906 that a famous swindle took place. Wilhelm Voigt dressed himself in a Prussian officer's uniform and proceeded to "arrest" the mayor and then fraudulently empty everything from the city treasury. This incident inspired a comedy, *The Captain from Köpenick* by Carl Zuckmayer, which is still popular today.

Köpenick's greatest attraction is a magnificent palace, **Schloss Köpenick**, on the island in the southern part of town. It was built in the late 17th century for the heir to the throne, Friedrich (later King Friedrich I), to a design by the Dutch architect Rutger van Langefeld. The three-storey Baroque building that resulted was extended to a design by Johann Arnold Nering, but until 1693 only part of the extension was completed: the chapel, entrance gate and a small gallery wing. In 2004 the Kunstgewerbemuseum (*p156*) opened a series of Renaissance and Baroque rooms in the Köpenick palace.

Schloss Köpenick

Ⓒ Ⓒ Ⓒ Ⓐ Schlossinsel 1
🕐 11am–5pm Tue–Sun
🌐 smb.museum

🔍 HIDDEN GEM
Müggelsee

Köpenick is home to Müggelsee, Berlin's largest lake. It's a great city escape for both locals and tourists, with hills, forests and plenty of bathing areas.

↓ Köpenick's robustly grand town hall, completed in 1904

Stunning imagery at the Zeiss-Gross-planetarium ↑

🕕 Gethsemanekirche

🏠 Stargader Strasse 77
Ⓢ & Ⓤ Schönhauser Allee
Ⓦ ekpn.de

The Neo-Gothic red-brick building of Gethsemane Church is perhaps the most famous church in northeast Berlin, playing as it did a crucial role in East Germany's peaceful revolution. This Protestant church, solidly built in oxblood-red brick in 1890, dominates the neighbourhood. It was one of several built on the order of Emperor Wilhelm II, who wanted to increase religious worship among the mostly Social Democratic working classes living in Prenzlauer Berg and other areas. The building was designed by August Orth, one of the period's most important architects of churches and railway stations.

The Protestant community of Gethsemanekirche is proud to have pioneered civil rights movements, and hosted anti-Nazi rallies from 1933 to 1945. The congregation also questioned the Socialist regime after World War II, while the church itself served as an assembly hall for peaceful opponents in October 1989. On 2 October that year, the praying crowd was brutally attacked by the East German secret service police, marking the start of the Communist regime's demise.

Today, the square is surrounded by beautiful restored buildings, housing many sidewalk restaurants, cafés and quaint little shops. Only a few steps away is Kollwitzplatz (p132), a welcoming, leafy square with an atmosphere reminiscent of Paris. Nearby Kollwitzstrasse is home to an organic farmers' market on Saturdays.

🕛 Zeiss-Gross-planetarium

🏠 Prenzlauer Allee 80 (Ernst-Thälmann-Park)
Ⓢ Prenzlauer Allee, then
🚌 156 🚊 M2 ⏰ 9am–5pm Tue, 9am–8pm Wed & Thu, 9am–9:30pm Fri, 1–9:30pm Sat, 11:30am–6:30pm Sun
Ⓦ planetarium.berlin

The silvery dome visible from afar is a huge planetarium built in the grounds of a park dedicated to the memory of the interwar Communist leader Ernst Thälmann, who died at Buchenwald concentration camp. The foyer houses an exhibition of optical equipment and various accessories produced by the renowned factory of Carl-Zeiss-Jena.

> The Protestant community of Gethsemanekirche is proud to have pioneered civil rights movements, and hosted anti-Nazi rallies from 1933 to 1945.

13

Mauerpark

🅐 Mauerpark, Gleimstrasse
🅤 Bernauer Strasse,
Eberswalder Strasse
🚋 M10

Formerly part of the Berlin Wall (hence the name "Wall Park"), this largely treeless expanse of lawn in Prenzlauer Berg is a magnet for young locals and tourists alike. Although it can be a little claustrophobic on warm days, it is a great spot for people-watching.

Children love the park and an artificial rock can be climbed under professional supervision. From around 3pm on Sundays, aspiring pop stars can attempt karaoke at the amphitheatre and perform to a packed audience. The giant eclectic flea market held next to the park from 10am to 6pm on Sundays attracts huge crowds of mostly 20-somethings on the lookout for a special bargain, be it junk or vintage. Vegan burgers and cold beers complete the experience, which can be a welcome restorative treat after a visit to the haunting Wall Memorial nearby (p122).

The Mauerweg, a shared walking and bicycle path, follows the path of the old Wall right across Mauerpark.

14

Schloss Schönhausen

🅐 Tschaikowskistrasse 1
🅢 & 🅤 Pankow 🚌 150, 250
🚋 M1 🕐 Jan-Mar: 10am-4pm Sat, Sun & hols;
Apr-Oct: 10am-5:30pm
Tue-Sun; Nov & Dec: 10am-5pm Sat, Sun & hols
🅦 spsg.de

This palace, located in an extensive and picturesque park, belonged to the von Dohna family during the 17th century. Ownership of the estate passed to the Elector Friedrich III in 1691, for whom Johann Arnold Nering designed the palace. In 1704 it was extended to a design by Johann Friedrich Eosander von Göthe, who added side wings. The palace was home to Queen Elisabeth Christine, estranged wife of

↑ Catching some free entertainment at Mauerpark

Frederick the Great, between 1740 and 1797. In 1763 further extensive refurbishment was undertaken by architect Johann Boumann. The property remained in the hands of the Prussian royal family for the next hundred years. Among those who resided here were Princess Auguste von Liegnitz, following the death of her husband, King Friedrich Wilhelm III.

After World War II the rebuilt palace was occupied by the president of the German Democratic Republic, Wilhelm Pieck. In 1990, after discussions here, the treaty to reunify Germany was signed on 3 October that year. Make time for a stroll through the vast park, which has kept the pleasant character bestowed on it by Peter Joseph Lenné in the 1820s.

15

Jüdischer Friedhof Weissensee

🏠 Herbert-Baum-Strasse 45 Ⓢ Greifswalder Strasse, then 🚋 12, M4, M13 🚌 156, 200 🕐 Opening times vary, see website 🌐 jg-berlin. org/judentum/friedhoefe/ weissensee.html

This extensive Jewish cemetery, established in 1880 according to a design by Hugo Licht, is the final resting place of more than 115,000 Berliners, many of whom were victims of Nazi persecution. It is chilling to note that many surnames listed on gravestones simply no longer exist in Germany, due to whole families being eradicated or driven out of the country.

By the main entrance is a place of remembrance for the victims of the Holocaust, with plaques bearing the names of the concentration camps. Buried here are renowned figures from Berlin's Jewish cultural and commercial past. Among others, here rest the publisher Samuel Fischer and the restaurateur Berthold Kempinski.

Some tombstones are outstanding works of art, such as that of the Panowsky family, designed by Ludwig Hoffmann, or the Cubist tombstone of Albert Mendel, designed by Walter Gropius. Some family graves are adorned with temple-like structures. The Nazis left this burial ground largely unharmed, but in 1999 the cemetery was desecrated in an act of anti-Semitic vandalism. More than 100 headstones were kicked over and some were smeared with swastikas.

Still in use today, most of the new graves in this plot belong to Jewish immigrants from the former Soviet Union, who outnumber the German-born Jews in Berlin.

↓ Entrance hall to the Jüdischer Friedhof Weissensee

NORTHWEST OF THE CENTRE

16 ⚡ Ⓜ
Schloss Tegel

📍 Adelheidallee 19–21
📞 886 71 50 Ⓤ Alt Tegel
🚌 133, 222 🕐 May–Sep:
10am, 11am, 3pm & 4pm
Mon ⓧ Oct–Apr

Schloss Tegel is one of the most interesting palace complexes in Berlin. In the 16th century there was already a manor house on this site, which in the second half of the 17th century was rebuilt into a hunting lodge for the Elector Friedrich Wilhelm (*p215*). In 1766 the ownership of the property passed to the Humboldt family, and, from 1820 to 1824, Karl Friedrich Schinkel (*p28*) thoroughly rebuilt the palace, giving it its current style.

There are tiled bas-reliefs decorating the elevations on the top floor of the towers. These were designed by Christian Daniel Rauch and depict the ancient wind gods. Some of Schinkel's marvellous interiors have survived, along with several items from what was once a large collection of antique sculptures. The palace is still privately owned by descendants of the Humboldt family, but guided tours are offered at 10am, 11am, 3pm and 4pm on Mondays from May to September. It is also worth visiting the park. On its western limits lies the Humboldt family tomb, designed by Schinkel and decorated with a copy of a splendid sculpture by Bertel Thorwaldsen; the original piece stands inside the palace.

17
Haus des Rundfunks

📍 Masurenallee 8–14
Ⓢ Messe Nord/ICC
Ⓤ Theodor-Heuss-Platz
🚌 104, 218, X34, X49

This building's depressing, flat, brick-covered façade hides an interior of startling beauty. The huge edifice was constructed as a radio station between 1929 and 1931 to a design by Hans Poelzig. The building has a triangular shape, with three studio wings radiating from the central five-storey hall. The impressive Art Deco interiors, which are spectacularly lit from above, are enhanced by geometrically patterned rows of balconies and large, pendulous, octagonal lamps. They represent one of the finest architectural achievements of this era in Berlin.

From the studio concert hall, concerts are often broadcast on the RBB radio station (Rundfunk Berlin-Brandenburg).

18
AEG-Turbinenhalle

📍 Huttenstrasse 12–19
Ⓤ Turmstrasse, then
🚌 M27

This building is one of the most important textbook examples of modern architecture dating from the beginning of the 20th century. It was commissioned by the electronics company AEG in 1909 and designed by Peter Behrens in conjunction with Karl Bernhardt. While former Berlin's industrial buildings were mostly red-brick and fortress-like, the Turbinenhalle was among the earliest structures not to incorporate any element, decorative or otherwise, that reflected previous architectural styles.

A huge hangar of a building, it has enormous windows and stretches 123 m (400 ft) down Berlichingenstrasse. The principal design imperative was to maintain a streamlined profile, while making no effort to disguise the construction materials. Today, the building is part of the Siemens company and is still used as a factory.

19
Gedenkstätte Plötzensee

📍 Hüttigpfad Ⓢ Beusel-
strasse, then 🚌 123 🕐 Mar–
Oct: 9am–5pm daily; Nov–
Feb: 9am–4pm daily
🌐 gedenkstaette-
ploetzensee.de

A narrow street leads from Saatwinkler Damm to the Plötzensee Memorial, marking the site where nearly 2,500 people convicted of crimes against the Third Reich were hanged. It is a simple memorial in a brick hut, which still has the iron hooks from which the victims were suspended.

↑ Urban landscape in the district of Wedding

↑ Schloss Tegel, designed by Karl Friedrich Schinkel

Did You Know?

Plötzensee is also home to one of the city's finest outdoor beaches – Strandbad Plötzensee.

While the main figures in the unsuccessful assassination attempt on Hitler, on 20 July 1944, were executed in Bendlerblock (p175), the rest of the conspirators were killed here. Count Helmuth James von Moltke, one of the leaders of the German resistance movement, was also executed here. The count organized the Kreisauer Kreis – a political movement which united German opposition to Hitler.

⑳ Villa Borsig

⌂ Reiherwerder Ⓤ Alt Tegel 🚌 133, 222, 224, then a 15-minute walk

This villa sits on a peninsula which cuts into the Tegeler See, reminiscent of Schloss Sanssouci in Potsdam (p254). It was built much later, however, between 1911 and 1913. It was designed by Alfred Salinger and Eugen Schmohl for the Borsigs, one of the wealthiest industrialist families in Berlin. This villa is particularly picturesque when seen from the lake, so it is worth looking out for it from a boat cruise.

㉑ Wedding

Ⓢ & Ⓤ Wedding, Gesundbrunnen Ⓤ Seestrasse, Osloer Strasse 🚌 133, 222, 224, then a 15-minute walk

Wedding is an interesting, up-and-coming area. Artists are taking over abandoned industrial buildings, a lively theatre and gallery scene is developing and the area is becoming more attractive to renters and buyers. Volkspark Rehberge, a beautiful park, is a hidden gem.

㉒ Le Corbusier Haus

⌂ Flatowallee 16 Ⓢ Olympiastadion 🚌 149, 218 ⓦ corbusierhaus-berlin.org

This apartment building by Le Corbusier, on a hill near the site of the Olympiastadion (p239), was the architect's entry to the 1957 Internationale Bauausstellung. His innovative design for what he called a *Unité d'Habitation* was an attempt to create fully self-sufficient housing estates in answer to a Europe-wide housing shortage. He built three of these complexes, the most famous being in Marseilles. For his Berlin design, Le Corbusier wanted to build over 500 two-storey apartments with integral services, such as a post office, shops, a sports hall and nursery school. Financial pressures prevented all of Le Corbusier's aspirations from being fulfilled; nevertheless, the monolithic building was a milestone for West Berlin's postwar architecture. For some, it will always be the "*Wohnmaschine*" (dwelling machine) and they criticize the jail-like hallways, called "streets" by the architect. Others praise the Bauhaus-inspired clear lines, airy, light-filled apartments and the architectural departure from ornamental features.

The apartments are mostly privately owned, but you can see the interior on tours that take place on Saturdays; check the website for details.

← The Georg-Kolbe-Museum, with its collection of 20th-century sculpture

23 Messegelände

🏠 Hammarskjöldplatz
🚇 Messe Nord/ICC
Ⓤ Kaiserdamm 🚌 104, 139, 349, X49

The pavilions of these vast exhibition and trade halls cover more than 160,000 sq m (1,700,000 sq ft). Many of the international events organized here are among the largest events of their kind in Europe.

The original exhibition halls on this site were built before World War I, but nothing of those buildings remains. The oldest part is the Funkturm and the group of pavilions which surround it. The huge building at the front – Ehren-halle – was built in 1936 to a design by Richard Ermisch, and is one of the few surviving buildings in Berlin designed in a Fascist architectural style.

The straight motorway that lies at the rear of the halls, in the direction of Nikolassee, is the famous Avus, the first German Autobahn, built in 1921. It was adapted for motor racing and became Germany's first car-racing track. It was here that the world speed record was broken before World War II. Now it forms part of the Autobahn system.

24 Funkturm

🏠 Hammarskjöldplatz
🚇 Messe Nord/ICC Ⓤ Kaiser-damm 🚌 104, 218, 349, X34
🕐 Opening times vary, see website for details
🌐 funkturm-messeberlin.de

This radio tower, which resembles Paris's Eiffel Tower, has become one of Berlin's most recognizable landmarks. Built in 1924 to a design by Heinrich Straumer, it rises 150 m (500 ft) into the air. It now operates as both an air-traffic control tower and radio mast. Visitors can enjoy views on the observation terrace at 125 m (400 ft), or dine at the Funkturm's lofty restaurant at 55 m (180 ft). The terrace may close for safety in bad weather.

25 Georg-Kolbe-Museum

🏠 Sensburger Allee 25
🚇 Heerstrasse 🚌 218, X34, X49 🕐 10am–6pm daily
🌐 georg-kolbe-museum.de

One of the most renowned German sculptors, Georg Kolbe (1877–1947) bequeathed the house in which he lived and worked for almost his entire life to the city of Berlin.

Trained as a painter and draughtsman, Kolbe became famous for his expressive works that came to symbolize the early freedoms of the Weimar era (p57).

Kolbe also left the city 180 of his sculptures and his art collection, which includes works by the Expressionist painter Ernst Ludwig Kirchner and the sculptor Wilhelm Lehmbruck. The museum has expanded its collection to include many more sculptures by Kolbe's peers. Visiting here is not only a rare chance to get to know Kolbe's works but also an opportunity to see his house and workshop, which displays tools and various devices for lifting a heavy sculpture.

Workshops with sculptors are held here regularly, and exhibitions on challenging and topical subjects, for example contemporary body image, draw large audiences.

A castle was first built on the site of the Zitadelle Spandau (Spandau citadel) in the 12th century, but today only the 36-m (120-ft) Juliusturm (Julius tower) remains.

26

Spandau

🚇 Altstadt Spandau, Zitadelle 🚌 X33

Spandau is one of the oldest towns in the Greater Berlin area. Evidence of the earliest settlement dates back to the 8th century, although the town of Spandau was only granted a charter in 1232.

The area was spared the worst of the World War II bombing, so the town has managed to retain a distinctive, historical character. The heart of the town is a network of medieval streets with a picturesque market square and a number of original timber-framed houses. In the north of Spandau sections of the 15th-century town wall still stand, and in the centre of town is the magnificent Gothic St-Nikolai-Kirche, dating from the 14th century.

A castle was first built on the site of the **Zitadelle Spandau** (Spandau citadel) in the 12th century, but today only the 36-m (120-ft) Juliusturm (Julius tower) remains. The fortress was built between 1560 and 1590, to a design by Francesco Chiaramella da Gandino. Though the citadel had a jail, Rudolf Hess, Spandau's most infamous resident, was incarcerated a short distance away in a military prison after the 1946 Nuremberg trials.

Today, the Zitadelle is a fascinating place to explore, and hosts a popular music festival in summer.

Zitadelle Spandau

🚲🕐🚗😊🅿️ 🕐 Am Juliusturm 64 🕐 10am–5pm daily 🌐 zitadelle-berlin.de

---

27

Olympiastadion

📍 Olympischer Platz 🚇 & 🚇 Olympiastadion 🚌 218, M49 🕐 Opening times vary, see website for details 🌐 olympiastadion. berlin

The plans for this stadium were conceived in 1933, when Adolf Hitler ordered the construction of a grandiose sporting complex for the 1936 Olympic Games in Berlin. It was designed by Werner March in the Nazi architectural style and was inspired by the architecture of ancient Rome.

To the west of the stadium lie the Maifeld and the Waldbühne. The Maifeld is an enormous assembly ground fronted by the Glockenturm, a 77-m (250-ft) bell tower with a viewing platform. The bell inside the tower is a replica of the original, which was damaged during World War II and is now on display outisde the stadium. The Waldbühne is an open-air amphitheatre with a design inspired by the ancient theatre of Epidaurus in Greece.

Following a €236-million refurbishment, the stadium reopened in 2004 as a high-tech arena. The Deutsches Sportmuseum next to the stadium also hosts concerts and shows.

The Olympiastadion, built for the historic 1936 Berlin Olympics ↓

ZITADELLE SPANDAU

This magnificent, perfectly proportioned 16th-century citadel stands where the Spree and Havel rivers meet. Both the main citadel and its 19th-century additions are still in excellent condition. It holds museums of local history and an observation terrace on the Juliusturm.

Key

① Bastion Kronprinz
② Bastion Brandenburg
③ Palace
④ Main gate
⑤ Bastion König
⑥ Bastion Königin
⑦ Juliusturm
⑧ Ravelin Schweinekopf

SOUTHWEST OF THE CENTRE

28

Strandbad Wannsee

🏠 Wannseebadweg 2s
🕐 30 22 19 00 11
Ⓢ Nikolassee 🚌 218

The vast, picturesque lake of Wannsee, situated on the edge of the Grunewald forest, is a principal destination for Berliners who are looking for recreation. Here you can take part in water sports, enjoy a lake cruise, bathe or simply enjoy relaxing on the shore.

Near S-Bahn Wannsee there are yachting marinas and harbours, while further north is one of the largest inland beaches in Europe – Strandbad Wannsee. It has been in use since the beginning of the 20th century, and was developed between 1929 and 1930 with the construction of a complex of changing rooms, shops, and cafés on top of man-made terraces.

On sunny summer days, sun-worshippers completely cover the sandy shore, while the lake is filled with yachts and windsurfers. It is also quite pleasant to take a walk around Schwanenwerder island. It has many elegant villas, one of which, Inselstrasse No. 24/26, was built for Axel Springer, the German newspaper publisher.

29

Königskolonnaden (Kleistkolonnaden)

🏠 Potsdamer Strasse
Ⓤ Kleistpark
🚌 106, 204, M46

A short walk north of U-Bahn Kleistpark, the unremarkable architecture of Potsdamer Strasse suddenly transforms dramatically. Leading to the park, the elegant sandstone Königskolonnaden (Royal Colonnade) captivates the passer-by with its Baroque ornamental sculptures. Designed by Carl von Gontard and built between 1777 and 1780, it once graced the route from Königsstrasse to Alexanderplatz (p106). In 1910, to protect it from traffic, it was moved to this new site.

The huge Kammergericht at the far boundary of the park was built between 1909

EAT

In summer, the sparkling Wannsee lake is a favoured destination for locals and visitors alike, so there are plenty of great dining options here for those who want a day trip out from the city centre.

Bootshaus Bolle
🏠 Am Grosser Wannsee 60
🕐 noon-8pm Thu-Sun
🚫 Mon-Wed
🌐 bootshaus-bolle.de

€€€

Wannseeterrassen
🏠 Wannseebadweg 35
🕐 noon-11pm Wed-Sun
🚫 Mon-Tue
🌐 wannseeterrassen. berlin

€€€

Clubrestaurant am Wannsee im MYCvD
🏠 Scabellstrasse 10-11 🕐 1-9pm Wed & Sun, 3-9pm Fri & Sat
🚫 Mon-Tue & Thu
🌐 restaurant-wannsee.de

€€€

→
Strandbad Wannsee, ideal for taking a break from city life

and 1913 to a design by Carl Vohl, Rudolf Mönnich and Paul Thömer. The site of the notorious Nazi Volksgericht or "People's Court", it was also used to try members of the failed July 1944 bomb plot against Hitler. From 1945 to 1958 it was the official seat of the Allied Control Council, and is now the Supreme Court of the state of Berlin.

30

Rathaus Schöneberg

⌂ John-F-Kennedy-Platz 1
Ⓤ Rathaus Schöneberg
🚌 104, M46

The gigantic building with a tower dominating the Schöneberg district's main square is its town hall, built in 1914. From 1948 to 1990 it was used as the main town hall of West Berlin. It was here, on 26 June 1963, that US President John F Kennedy gave his famous speech. More than 300,000 Berliners

 HIDDEN GEM
Grunewaldturm

For those who don't like heights, the Grunewald Tower is still worth a visit, not only for the ground-floor restaurant but also the mosaic decorating the ceiling of the memorial hall. The Neo-Byzantine design was created by August Oetken (1868–1951), a German painter and mosaic artist.

assembled to hear the young president say, *"Ich bin ein Berliner"* – "I am a Berliner" – as an expression of solidarity from the democratic world to a city defending its right to freedom. (An urban myth has since claimed that the phrase actually means "I am a small doughnut", but this is incorrect – although there is, indeed, a small doughnut in Germany known as a *berliner*.)

↑ Statue of Kaiser Wilhelm in the Grunewaldturm

31

Grunewaldturm

⌂ Havelchaussee 61 🚌 218
🕙 10am–10pm daily

The Neo-Gothic tower built on a hill at the edge of the Havel river is one of the most prominent features of the area. This type of tower became popular in Germany during the 19th century as a way of commemorating important events or people. The Grunewaldturm was built in 1899 on the centenary of the birth of Wilhelm I. After 1871 he was the first Emperor of the Second Reich and the tower was initially named "Kaiser-Wilhelm-Turm". The 56-m (185-ft) tower was designed by Franz Schwechten and is made of red brick with plaster details. The tower is made all the more striking by the green background provided by the surrounding leafy trees. The view from the top of this structure is well worth climbing the 204 steps for.

Sunset over the Havel river

32

Grabstätte von Heinrich von Kleist

🏠 Bismarckstrasse (near No. 3) Ⓢ Wannsee 🚌 114, 316, 318

A narrow street running from Königstrasse at the viaduct of the S-Bahn Wannsee leads to the gravesite of the playwright Heinrich von Kleist. It is the spot where he committed first murder and then suicide; on 21 November 1811 he shot his companion Henriette Vogel and then turned the pistol on himself. They are both buried here. Modest stones mark their grave, on which flowers are left by well-wishers.

33

Haus der Wannsee-Konferenz

🏠 Am Grossen Wannsee 56/58 Ⓢ Wannsee, then 🚌 114 🕙 10am–6pm daily 🌐 ghwk.de

This is one of the most beautiful of the luxury holiday villas on the shores of Lake Wannsee, and yet because of its past, it is also the most abhorrent. Built in 1915 to a design by Paul Baumgarten, it is in the style of a small Neo-Baroque palace with an elegant portico. In 1940 the villa was sold to the Nazi SS. On 20 January 1942, a

↑ The gravestone of Heinrich von Kleist and Henriette Vogel

meeting took place here between Reinhard Heydrich and 14 other officers from the secret service and the SS, among them Adolf Eichmann. It was then that the decision was taken about "the final solution on the question of Jews". Their plans for the outright extermination of 11 million Jews embraced the whole of Europe, including Great Britain and neutral countries.

Since 1992 this has been a museum and place of remembrance. An exhibition depicts the history of the Holocaust with some shocking documents and photographs from the ghettos and extermination camps. For security reasons, the gate to the villa is always locked, and to enter the park you have to announce yourself through the intercom.

34

Museumsdorf Düppel

🏠 Clauertstrasse 11 Ⓢ Mexikoplatz or Ⓤ Krumme Lanke, then 🚌 118, 622 🕙 Late Mar–early Oct: 10am–6pm Sat, Sun & public hols 🌐 dueppel.de

This reconstruction of a medieval village has been made on the site of a 13th-century settlement. It is a living village surrounded by still-cultivated gardens and fields, where traditional breeds of pigs and sheep are raised in pigsties and sheds.

On Sundays the village puts on displays of traditional crafts. Here you can see how primitive saucepans and tools were fashioned; how wool was spun, dyed and woven and how baskets were made.

↑ Max-Lieberman Villa, part of Wannsee's Villenkolonie Alsen

35 🖼 🖼

Villenkolonie Alsen

📍 Am Grossen Wannsee
🚇 Wannsee, then 🚌 114

This clutch of villas on Lake Wannsee forms a delightful holiday resort – the oldest of its kind in Berlin. The villas are thought to be the most beautiful in the district, not just because of their picturesque lakeside location, but also because of the quality of their architecture.

Strolling along Am Grossen Wannsee, it is worth looking at the villa at No. 39/41, known as Haus Springer. It was designed by the architect Alfred Messel in 1901 and is covered with shingles, a reflection of contemporary American designs.

Another must-see is the **Max-Lieberman Villa** at No. 42, designed by Paul Baumgarten in 1909 for the painter Max Liebermann (1847–1935). Liebermann spent many summers here painting in the garden on the lake shore. The villa is now a museum and houses around 40 of Liebermann's paintings.

Max-Lieberman Villa
🖼 🖼 🖼 🖼 Times vary, see website for details
🌐 liebermann-villa.de

MAX LIEBERMANN (1847–1935)

One of the greatest German painters, Max Liebermann was also one of the most interesting and controversial figures of Berlin's elite circles at the start of the 20th century. A sensitive observer as well as an outstanding portraitist, Liebermann was famously stubborn – he could stand up even to the Kaiser himself. From 1920 he was president of the Akademie der Künste (Academy of Arts; *p73*), but in view of his Jewish origin he was removed from office in 1933. He died just two years later, alone, and his wife committed suicide to escape being sent to a concentration camp.

↑ Sculpture by Bernhard Heiliger in the gardens of Kunsthaus Dahlem

36

DAHLEM

Ⓢ Botanischer Garten, Rathaus Steglitz Ⓤ Onkel Toms Hütte, Oskar-Helene-Heim, Freie Universität (Thielplatz), Dahlem Dorf, Podbielskiallee, Breitenbachplatz 🚌 115, 110, M2, M48, M85, X10, X11, X83

First referenced in documents from the 13th century, Dahlem is one of the most interesting suburbs in Steglitz-Zehlendorf, a borough southwest of central Berlin. An affluent and tranquil city suburb, the district was confirmed as a major cultural and educational centre after World War II with the establishment of a university and a museum complex.

①

Brücke-Museum

⌂ Bussardsteig 9 🚌 115 ⏲ 11am–5pm Wed–Mon Ⓦ bruecke-museum.de

One of the more interesting museums dedicated to 20th-century art is hidden away on a leafy, tranquil street lined with picturesque villas, in an elegant Functionalist building designed by architect Werner Düttmann. The museum houses a collection of German Expressionist paintings linked to the artistic group known as *Die Brücke* (p32), which originated in Dresden in 1905 and was based in Berlin from 1910. The members of this group included Karl Schmidt-Rottluff, Emil Nolde, Max Pechstein, Ernst Ludwig Kirchner and Erich Heckel.

The collection is based on almost 80 works by Schmidt-Rottluff, bequeathed to the town in 1964. The collection quickly grew, thanks to donations and acquisitions. In addition to displaying other works of art contemporary to *Die Brücke* (which was disbanded in 1913), there are also some paintings from the later creative periods of these artists, and works by other closely associated figures.

Nearby, at Käuzchensteig No. 8, lie the foundation's headquarters, established in the former studio of the sculptor Bernhard Heiliger. The garden, which borders the Brücke-Museum, has a display of his metal sculptures.

②

Kunsthaus Dahlem

⌂ Käuzchensteig 8 🚌 115, X10 ⏲ 11am–5pm Wed–Mon Ⓦ kunsthaus-dahlem.de

This exhibition venue was built between 1939 and 1942 as a studio for the sculptor Arno Breker, one of the most prolific sculptors of the Third Reich, on grounds provided by the government.

In 1949, renowned sculptor Bernhard Heiliger, who was a student of Breker, moved into the east wing of the building and lived and worked in the complex until his death in 1995. In the garden adjacent to the Kunsthaus, more than 20 of his striking

> The Onkel-Tom-Siedlung project in Zehlendorf was the realization of the English concept of garden cities.

sculptures are exhibited. During Heiliger's time at the site, different parts of the complex were leased to other prominent artists from around the world.

Since 2015, the building has served as an exhibition space for postwar German Modernist art from both East and West Germany, and also promotes contemporary art.

③

Onkel-Tom-Siedlung

🅰 Riemeister Strasse/ Argentinische Allee
Ⓤ Onkel Toms Hütte

This housing estate, known as "Uncle Tom's Estate", represents one of the most interesting urban architectural achievements of the Weimar Republic (p57). It was built from 1926 to 1932, to a design by Bruno Taut, Hugo Häring and Otto Rudolf Salvisberg. Their primary intention was to solve the city's housing shortage by building large developments that were both pleasant to live in and fairly inexpensive. The Onkel-Tom-Siedlung project in Zehlendorf was the realization of the English concept of garden cities.

The result is an enormous housing estate comprising single- and multiple-family houses. Set in lush greenery on the borders of Grunewald, it accommodates nearly 15,000 people.

EAT

Miss Wu

For something different, head to Miss Wu, which combines friendly service with a surprisingly broad repertoire of Chinese classics, as well as several more unusual dishes. Vegetarian-friendly too.

🅰 Königin-Luise-Strasse 71, 14195 Ⓒ noon–11pm daily 🅦 misswu.de

€€€

→
The colourful Onkel-Tom-Siedlung housing estate

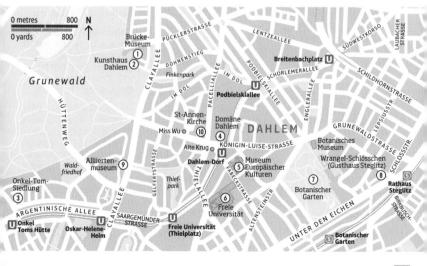

DRINK

Alter Krug

For something traditional and German, this classic wood-panelled pub-restaurant offers a smart interior, German menu and a beer garden large enough to seat 500 people.

🄰 Königin-Luise-Strasse 52 🕙 10am–midnight daily 🌐 alter-krug-berlin.de

---

④ 🚲 🍴 🍹 🛍
Domäne Dahlem

🄰 Königin-Luise-Strasse 49 Ⓤ Dahlem Dorf 🚌 110, X11, X83 🕙 Opening times vary, see website for details 🌐 domaene-dahlem.de

Domäne Dahlem, a city-farm that combines a manor house and farming estate, is a rare oasis of country life in the Berlin suburbs. The Baroque house was built for Cuno Johann von Wilmersdorff around 1680 and still retains its original character. Part of the Stadtmuseum Berlin (Berlin City Museum), it boasts period interiors, while the 19th-century farm buildings hold a collection of agricultural tools and a large and varied collection of beehives.

Domäne Dahlem is a working farm as well as a museum, with gardens, workshops and farm animals. There is a small charge to enter the museum; the grounds are free. Festivals and markets held here demonstrate rural crafts and skills, and there is plenty for children to see and do. There is a farm shop selling local, sustainable foods, including the farm's produce, and an organic food market on Saturday mornings.

---

⑤ 🚲 🍹
Museum Europäischer Kulturen

🄰 Arnimallee 25 Ⓤ Dahlem Dorf 🚌 110, X11, X83 🕙 10am–5pm Tue–Fri, 11am–6pm Sat & Sun 🌐 smb.museum

The Museum of European Culture is an ethnographic museum that specializes in European folk art and culture, and documents the daily life of its inhabitants. It hosts long-running exhibitions, often in conjunction with museums from other European countries. Among the exhibits on display are earthenware items, costumes, jewellery, toys and tools.

---

⑥
Freie Universität

🄰 Henry-Ford-Bau, Garystrasse 35–39 Ⓤ Freie Universität 🚌 110 🌐 fu-berlin.de

The Free University was established on 4 December 1948 on the initiative of a group of academics and activists, led by Ernst Reuter. This was a reaction to the restrictions introduced at the Humboldt Universität in the Soviet sector, and further evidence of the competition between the two halves of the city. The university was initially located in rented buildings. It was only thanks to the American Ford Foundation that the Henry-Ford-Bau, housing the rector's office, the auditorium and the library, was built. Designed by Franz-Heinrich Sobotka and Gustav Müller and completed in 1954, the building is distinguished by its fine proportions.

Another architectural highlight is the Humanities and Social Science building, designed by Norman Foster and finished in 2005. It has a glass-domed centrepiece

housing the Philological Library, which is nicknamed the "Berlin Brain" due to its cranial shape.

---

⑦ 🚲 Ⓜ 🍹 🍹 🛍
Botanischer Garten

🄰 Unter den Eichen 5–10 & Königin-Luise-Strasse 6–8 Ⓢ Botanischer Garten Ⓤ Dahlem-Dorf 🚌 M48, X83 🕙 9am–8pm daily 🌐 bgbm.org

The Botanical Garden is one of the most beautiful places in Berlin. It was created towards the end of the 19th century and has a romantic character, dotted with gentle hills and picturesque lakes. Of particular interest is the 19th-century palm house, designed by Alfred Koerner. The huge greenhouses were constructed between 1984 and 1987 to a design by Engelbert Kremser.

↑ The magnificent Palm House and Chinese pavilion *(inset)* in the Botanical Gardens

The most popular plants are the exotic species such as the orchids and cacti. There is also the Botanisches Museum (Botanical Museum), home to an excellent collection of plant specimens.

⑧
Wrangel-Schlösschen (Gusthaus Steglitz)

🏛 Schlossstrasse 48 📞 902 99 39 24 Ⓤ Rathaus Steglitz 🚌 M2, M48, M85

This compact Neo-Classical palace derives its name from Field Marshal Wrangel, the building's mid-19th-century owner. However, the house was built much earlier, in 1804. The simplicity and clarity of its details make it a prime example of early Neo-Classical architecture. It currently houses the cultural centre for the district of Steglitz.

⑨ Ⓜ
Alliiertenmuseum

🏛 Clayallee 135 Ⓤ Oskar-Helene-Heim 🕙 10am–6pm Thu–Tue 🌐 alliierten museum.de

In the heart of the former US military sector of Berlin is the Allied Museum, which combines exhibition space with open-air grounds.

A fascinating exhibition of everyday objects, military memorabilia, photographs and films explains life during the Cold War and the story of Berlin and its inhabitants between 1945 and 1994. Tours are by appointment.

⑩
St-Annen-Kirche

🏛 Königin-Luise-Strasse 55 📞 831 38 13 Ⓤ Dahlem Dorf 🚌 110, X11, X83 🕙 11am–1pm Sat & Sun

At the centre of a small leafy cemetery stands the Gothic 14th-century St-Annen-Kirche. The church was built initially with a plain roof. The chancel was completed in the 15th century, the vaulting in the 17th century and the tower was added in the 18th century.

Inside, 14th-century wall paintings depict scenes from the life of St Anna, alongside items of ecclesiastical furnishings. These include a 15th-century painting of the Crucifixion and 11 late Gothic figures of saints.

The cemetery, which dates back to the 13th century, is also worth exploring. It has a 1996 monument dedicated to the victims of Nazi tyranny. During the war, the pastor here was Martin Niemöller, a founder of the Confessing Church, a Protestant move-ment that resisted the Nazification of churches. He was sent to a concentration camp in 1938, but he survived his imprisonment.

COUNTRY CHURCHES

The establishment of Greater Berlin in 1920 swallowed up nearly 60 villages, some of which were older than the city itself. Now they have evolved into large residential estates, and more than 50 of the parish churches have survived. The most treasured, dating from the 13th century, are in the south of Berlin, for instance in Britz by Backbergstrasse, Buckow (Alt-Buckow), Mariendorf (Alt Mariendorf) and Marienfelde (Alt Marienfelde).

37

POTSDAM

Ⓢ & 🚉 Potsdam Hauptbahnhof 🚋 Park Sanssouci, Charlottenhof 🚌 605, 606, 610, 631, N14, X5, X15 🚊 91, 94, 98 🛈 Luisenplatz 3; 9:30am-6pm Mon-Sat, 10am-4pm Sun & hols; www.potsdamtourismus.de

Southwest of Berlin lies Potsdam, the capital of Brandenburg and one of the most interesting cities in Germany. Tourists flock here to see the royal Park Sanssouci where an eclectic and lovely mix of buildings seem to bloom along with the plants and flowers in beautifully landscaped gardens.

① Park Sanssouci

🏛 Schopenhauerstrasse/ Zur Historischen Mühle 🚌 612, 614, 695

This vast park (whose name means "without worries" in French), covers some 3 sq km (1 sq mile). It was established in 1725 on the site of an orchard, however, it was only transformed into an enormous landscaped park when construction work began on Schloss Sanssouci (p254). Today, the park is made up of smaller gardens dating from different eras, each of which has been maintained in the original style. At the foot of Schloss Sanssouci is the oldest section, containing the Dutch garden, a number of fountains and the French-style Lustgarten (pleasure garden), with a symmetrical layout and lovely rose beds.

The eastern part of the park is called the Rehgarten, a beautifully landscaped park in the English style designed by Peter Joseph Lenné. This park extends right up to the Neues Palais (p252). To the south, surrounding the small palace, extends the Charlottenhof Park, also designed by Lenné. In the northern section of the park, next to the Orangerie (p259), is the Nordischer Garten and the Paradiesgarten.

The range of different garden styles makes a simple stroll through this park particularly pleasant. There are also a large number of sculptures, columns, obelisks and grottoes for the visitor to explore. The vistas and perspectives that suddenly open up across the park and the picturesque groupings of trees are also beautiful.

② Communs

🏛 Am Neuen Palais 🚌 605, 695

This area of Park Sanssouci consists of a pair of two-

← Vineyards leading up to one of the palaces in Park Sanssouci

↑ The Communs, tucked away behind the Neues Palais

storey pavilions linked by a semicircular colonnade. They are unusually elegant buildings considering they were used for servants' quarters and the palace kitchens. However, they also served to screen from view the cultivated fields that extended past the park from the palace.

The Communs were built in 1769 by Carl von Gontard, to a design by Jean-Laurent Le Geay. The buildings are enclosed by an elegant courtyard. The kitchen was in the south pavilion, linked to the palace by an underground passageway, and the north pavilion accommodated the servants of the king's guests. Today, the rectors' offices and part of the medicine department of the University of Potsdam are located in the Communs.

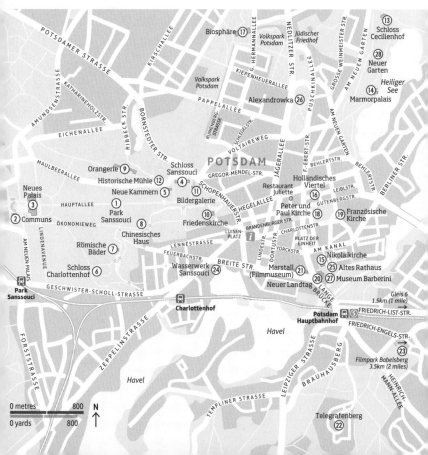

POTSDAM

Biosphäre ⑰
Volkspark Potsdam
Jüdischer Friedhof
Schloss Cecilienhof ⑬
Neuer Garten ㉘
Volkspark Potsdam
Alexandrowka ㉖
Heiliger See
Marmorpalais ⑭
Orangerie ⑨
Schloss Sanssouci ④
Historische Mühle ⑫
Neue Kammern ⑤
Bildergalerie ⑪
Holländisches Viertel
Restaurant Juliette
Neues Palais ③
Park Sanssouci ①
Friedenskirche ⑩
Peter und Paul Kirche ⑱
Französische Kirche ⑲
Communs ②
Chinesisches Haus ⑧
Römische Bäder ⑦
Schloss Charlottenhof ⑥
Wasserwerk Sanssouci ㉔
Marstall (Filmmuseum) ㉑
Nikolaikirche ⑮
Altes Rathaus ㉕
Museum Barberini ㉗
Neuer Landtag ⑳
Park Sanssouci
Charlottenhof
Potsdam Hauptbahnhof
Gleis 6 1.5km (1 mile)
FRIEDRICH-LIST-STR.
Havel
Filmpark Babelsberg 3.5km (2 miles) ㉓
Havel
Telegrafenberg ㉒

0 metres 800
0 yards 800
N ↑

③ ⚒ Ⓜ 🍴 🖥 🛍

NEUES PALAIS

🏛 Am Neuen Palais 🚌 605, 606, 695 🕐 Apr-Oct: 10am-6pm Wed-Mon; Nov-Mar: 10am-5pm Wed-Mon 🌐 spsg.de

The stunning New Palace was designed to be an impressive display of Prussia's glory and power after its victory in the Seven Years' War.

This imposing Baroque palace, on the main avenue in Park Sanssouci, was built at the request of Frederick the Great. The initial plans were prepared in 1750 by Georg Wenzeslaus von Knobelsdorff. However, construction only began in 1763, after the Seven Years' War (1756–63), to a design by Johann Gottfried Büring, Jean Laurent Le Geay and Carl von Gontard. The result was a vast two-storey building, decorated with hundreds of sculptures and more than 200 richly adorned rooms, which together make up one of Germany's most beautiful palaces.

↑ The entrance to the Neues Palais is through the gate on the western façade

Did You Know?

The palace was rarely used as a royal residence, but instead hosted guests for celebrations.

→ Neues Palais, built after the Seven Years' War

INSIDER TIP
Baroque Nights

For a few evenings in the summer, the Baroque era is brought back to life during the annual Potsdam Palace Nights. Brilliant lights transform Park Sanssouci into a magical world of music, theatre and history.

The Rococo interior of the Upper Gallery is decorated with Italian paintings and a beautiful inlaid floor.

EXPERIENCE Potsdam

The central dome is topped by a gilded royal crown, carried by a sculpture of three nymphs.

The elegant Upper Vestibule was designed by Carl von Gontard. The walls are covered with Silesian marble and the ceiling depicts Venus and the Graces.

The vast Marmorsaal ballroom features walls inlaid with marble and a beautiful painting on the ceiling. The gallery was used by the orchestra.

① In the Grottensaal, images of sea creatures on the wall are made of mosaics of shells and coral.

② The Silver Room, with details made of real silver leaf.

③ Hundreds of detailed statues decorate the façade of the Neues Palais, as well as the grounds and the palace interior.

④ 🛝 🎢 🏛

SCHLOSS SANSSOUCI

📍 Park Sanssouci 🚌 612, 614, 650, 695 🚊 91, 94, X8 🕐 Apr–Oct: 10am–5:30pm Tue–Sun; Nov & Dec: 10am–5pm Tue–Sun; Jan–Mar: 10am–4:30pm Tue–Sun 🌐 spsg.de

A terraced vineyard creates a peaceful approach to Sanssouci Palace, the oldest building in the Park Sanssouci complex. Designed as an intimate royal hideaway, this miniature Rococo palace has captivated visitors for centuries.

The name Sanssouci is French for "without a care" and gives a good indication of the flamboyant character of this enchanting Rococo palace, built in 1745. The original sketches, made by Friedrich II (Frederick the Great) himself, were finalized by Georg Wenzeslaus von Knobelsdorff. The glorious interiors were designed by Knobelsdorff and Johann August Nahl. The king clearly loved this palace, as his final wishes were that he should be buried here, near the tomb of his Italian greyhounds. He was actually interred in the Garnisonkirche, Potsdam, but his wishes were eventually carried out in 1991.

The Voltaire Room is decorated with naturalistic carvings.

Bacchanalian sculptures by Friedrich Christian Glume adorn the façde.

An oxidized green dome covers the Marmorsaal (marble hall).

Frederick the Great wanted the Marmorsaal to be loosely based on the Pantheon in Rome.

The walls of the Konzertzimmer (concert room) are decorated with paintings based on Greek mythology.

← Despite its grand, traditional style, the Marmorsaal is open and inviting

← The Rococo style façade on the garden side

→ Picturesque arbours and pergolas decorated with sun motifs complete the palace design

Did You Know?

The grand wings of the palace were built 63 years after the death of its most famous resident, Friedrich II.

The colonnade frames the view of Ruinenburg Hill.

GREAT VIEW
The Ruins

From the north side of the palace you can see some imposing ruins on the Ruinenberg Hill. They are completely artificial, built in the mid-18th century purely as a decoration.

The library of Friedrich II contains about 2,100 books. The walls are lined with cedar panelling to create a contemplative atmosphere.

↑ Schloss Sanssouci, an intimate royal summer residence

EXPERIENCE MORE

⑤ Neue Kammern

🏛 Zur Historischen Mühle (Lustgarten) 📞 0331 969 42 00 🚌 695 🕐 Apr-Oct: 10am-5:30pm Tue-Sun

The New Chambers is a Rococo pavilion containing residential apartments. It is the mirror image of the Bildergalerie (p258) and was originally built as an orangery in 1747 to a design by Georg Wenzeslaus von Knobelsdorff. In 1777 Frederick the Great (Friedrich II) ordered the building to be remodelled as guest accommodation. The architect, Georg Christian Unger, left the elegant Baroque exterior of the orangery largely untouched and instead concentrated on converting the interior. As well as the sumptuous guest suites, the new design included four elegant halls. The best of these is the Ovidsaal, with its rich reliefs and marble floors. The interior decor has been maintained in Frederick's Rococo style. The building also houses a collection of Meissen figurines.

POTSDAM TOWN GATES

The city of Potsdam was enclosed by a wall in 1722. This wall did not serve a defensive purpose – it was supposed to contain criminals and prevent soldiers from deserting. When the borders of the town were extended in 1733, new districts were also enclosed by the wall. There was a total of five city gates, of which three remain. One of these is the Jägertor, which has survived in its original condition and dates from 1733.

JÄGERTOR

⑥ Schloss Charlottenhof

🏛 Geschwister-Scholl-Strasse 34a (Park Charlottenhof) 🚌 605, 606 🚋 91, 94 🕐 1 May–31 Oct: 10am–5pm Tue–Sun 🌐 spsg.de

The small Neo-Classical Charlottenhof Palace is located in the southern extension of Park Sanssouci, Park Charlottenhof. It was designed by Karl Friedrich Schinkel (p28) in 1829 for the heir to the throne, later King Friedrich Wilhelm IV. This small one-storey building was built in the style of a Roman villa. The rear of the palace has a portico that opens out onto the garden terrace. Some of the wall paintings designed by Schinkel, which were made in the so-called Pompeiian style, are still in place. The most interesting part of the interior is the blue-and-white-striped Humboldt Room, also called the

↑ Italianate styling at the Römische Bäder, or Roman baths

Tent Room due to its resemblance to a tent. The palace is surrounded by a picturesque landscaped park which was designed by Peter Joseph Lenné.

---

⑦ Römische Bäder

🏛 Lenné-Strasse (Park Charlottenhof) 🚌 605, 606 🚋 91, 94, 98 🕐 May–Oct: 10am–5:30pm Tue–Sun 🌐 spsg.de

A picturesque group of pavilions, situated by the edge of a lake, forms the "Roman Baths", which actually served as accommodation for the king's guests. It was designed by Karl Friedrich Schinkel, with the involvement of Ludwig Persius, between 1829 and 1840. At the front is the gardener's house, which is adjacent to an asymmetrical low tower in the style of an Italian Renaissance villa. In the background, to the left, extends the former bathing pavilion, which is currently used for

> **The small Neo-Classical Charlottenhof Palace is located in the southern extension of Park Sanssouci, Park Charlottenhof.**

↑ Gilded figures *(inset)* eating, drinking and making music surround the Chinese House

temporary exhibitions. All of the pavilions are arranged around an internal garden planted with a multicoloured carpet of shrubs. A closer look will reveal that many of these colourful plants are actually vegetables.

⑧

Chinesisches Haus

🅐 Ökonomieweg (Rehgarten) 🚌 606, 695 🚊 91, 94 🕐 May–Oct: 10am–5:30pm Tue–Sun 🌐 spsg.de

The lustrous, gilded pavilion that can be seen glistening from a distance is the Chinese House. Chinese art was popular during the Rococo period – people wore Chinese silk, rooms were wallpapered with Chinese designs, furniture was lacquered, drinks were served in Chinese porcelain and Chinese pavilions were built in gardens.

The Chinesisches Haus was built in Park Sanssouci between 1754 and 1756 to a design by Johann Gottfried Büring. It is circular in shape, with a centrally located main hall surrounded by three studies. Between each of these are pretty *trompe l'oeil* porticoes. Ornaments, together with gilded figures of Chinese gentlemen and ladies, surround the pavilion. Originally the Chinesisches Haus served as a tearoom and a summer dining room. Today, it houses a collection of porcelain and has beautiful interior decoration featuring gilding and ceiling paintings.

⑨

Orangerie

🅐 Maulbeerallee (Nordischer Garten) 🚌 695 🕐 Apr: 10am–5:30pm Sat, Sun & hols; May–Oct: 10am–5:30pm Tue–Sun 🌐 spsg.de

Towering above the park is the Orangerie, designed in the Italian Renaissance style and crowned by a colonnade. The Orangerie was built to house guests, not plants. It was constructed between 1851 and 1860 by Friedrich August Stüler on the initiative and direction of Friedrich Wilhelm IV. The final design was partly based on the plans of Ludwig Persius. It served as a guest residence for the king's sister and her husband, Tsar Nicholas I. The rooms were grouped around the Raphael Hall, which was based on the Sala Regia in the Vatican and decorated with copies of the works of Italian artist Raphael. It is worth climbing up to the observation terrace for the view over Potsdam.

↑ The Bildergalerie, the first gallery built to house a ruler's art collection in Germany

(12) 〽 🏛
Historische Mühle

🏠 Maulbeerallee 5
🚌 695 🕐 Apr-Oct: 10am-
6pm daily; Nov & Jan-Mar:
10am-4pm Sat & Sun
🚫 Dec 🌐 historische-
muehle-potsdam.de

A mill has been located here since the early 18th century, although this is actually a reconstruction, dating from 1993. According to local legend, the original windmill was so noisy that Frederick the Great ordered it to be dismantled. However, a court upheld the miller's cause and the mill stayed. In 1790 a new windmill was built in its place, which lasted until 1945. The mill currently houses a museum of mechanical windmills.

(10)
Friedenskirche

🏠 Am Grünen Gitter 🚌 695
🚌 91, 94 🕐 Nov-Mar: 11am-
4pm 🌐 spsg.de

Close to Schloss Sanssouci (p254) is Friedenskirche, or the Church of Peace. The foundation stone was laid by King Friedrich Wilhelm IV in 1845 and the church was completed in 1848. Designed by Ludwig Persius, Friedrich August Stüler and Ludwig Hesse, the church is based on San Clemente in Rome.

Inside, the vaulted ceiling of the apse is covered by a 12th-century mosaic that depicts the figure of Christ as a judge. This Byzantine mosaic was originally located in the church of San Capriano on the island of Murano in Venice. Next to the church is a mausoleum containing the tombs of Friedrich Wilhelm I, Friedrich Wilhelm IV and Kaiser Friedrich III.

Surrounding Friedenskirche is the Marlygarten, created in the mid-19th century. The garden was also designed by royal architect Ludwig Persius.

(11) 〽
Bildergalerie

🏠 Zur Historischen Mühle
📞 0331 969 42 00 🚌 695
🕐 May-Oct: 10am-5:30pm
Tue-Sun

The Picture Gallery, housed in the building adjacent to Schloss Sanssouci was the first purpose-built gallery in Germany. It was constructed in 1764 to a design by J G Büring. The façade facing the garden is ornamented with an allegorical tableau representing Art, Education and Crafts, while busts of renowned artists have been placed in the windows.

The gallery contains an exhibition of Baroque paintings once owned by Frederick the Great, although part of the collection can be found in the Gemäldegalerie (p158). Highlights include Caravaggio's Doubting Thomas and Guido Reni's Death of Cleopatra', as well as a number of canvases by Rubens and van Dyck. The stunning interior has a floor inlaid with yellow marble complementing the gilded ceiling.

Did You Know?

Schloss Cecilienhof was the final palace built by the House of Hohenzollern.

⑬ 🎖️ 🖥️ 🛍️

Schloss Cecilienhof

🏠 **Am Neuen Garten**
📞 0331 969 42 00 🚌 692
🕐 **Apr-Oct: 10am-5:30pm Tue-Sun; Nov & Dec: 10am-5pm Tue-Sun; Jan-Mar: 10am-4:30pm Tue-Sun**

The Cecilienhof Palace played a brief but important part in history because the 1945 Potsdam Conference (p262) took place here. Completed in 1917, the palace is the most recent of the Hohenzollern dynasty buildings and was designed by Paul Schultze-Naumburg in the style of an English country manor. It is a sprawling, asymmetrical building with wooden beams making a pretty herringbone pattern on its walls.

The palace was the Hohenzollern family residence after they lost the crown; the family remained in Potsdam until February 1945. It now functions as a first-class hotel and restaurant, where visitors can relax amid carefully tended shrubbery. Most of the historic furnishings used during the famous Potsdam conference are on display.

---

⑭ 🎖️

Marmorpalais

🏠 **Am Ufer des Heiligen Sees (Neuer Garten)** 🚌 692, 695 🕐 **Nov-Mar: 10am-4pm Sat, Sun & hols; Apr: 10am-5:30pm Sat, Sun & hols; May-Oct: 10am-7:30pm Tue-Sun** 🌐 **spsg.de**

The Marble Palace is situated on the edge of the lake in Neuer Garten (p267), a park northeast of the centre of Potsdam. This small palace is a beautiful example of early Neo-Classical architecture and owes its name to its façade, which is clad in Silesian marble.

The square main body of the palace was the initiative of King Friedrich Wilhelm II. The original building was completed in 1791, but it turned out to be too small, and in 1797 it was extended.

An extra floor and two wings were added, which gave the Marmorpalais the character of a Palladian villa.

The main part of the palace contains Neo-Classical furnishings from the late 18th century, including furniture from the workshops of Roentgen and porcelain from the English firm Wedgwood. The interiors of the wings date from slightly later, from the 1840s. The concert hall in the right-hand wing is particularly beautiful. King Friedrich Wilhelm II died in this palace in 1797.

← The Italianate campanile, or bell tower, visible from the tranquil cloister of Friedenskirche

Schloss Cecilienhoff, scene of the Potsdam Conference

⑮
Nikolaikirche

🅰 Am Alten Markt
🚌 604, 605, 609, 610, 695
🚊 91, 92, 93, 94, 96, 99,
X98 🕐 10am–7pm Mon-
Sat, 11:30am–7pm Sun
🌐 nikolai-potsdam.de

This imposing church, built in a late Neo-Classical style, is the most beautiful church in Potsdam. It was designed in 1830 by Karl Friedrich Schinkel (p28) and the building work was overseen by Ludwig Persius. The main body of the church is based on a square cross, with a semicircular presbytery.

It was decided only in the 1840s to crown the church with a vast dome, supported on a colonnaded tambour (a wall that supports a dome). Schinkel had envisaged this from the beginning of the project, but it was not included in the orders of the king. Initially it was thought that the dome would be supported by a wooden structure, though ultimately it was built using iron, between 1843 and 1848, according to a design by Persius and Friedrich August Stüler. The interior decoration and the ecclesiastical furnishings of the church date back

to the 1850s, and in the main area of the church they were based on the earlier interior designs by Schinkel.

In front of the church stands an obelisk built between 1753 and 1755 to a design by Prussian architect Georg Wenzeslaus von Knobelsdorff. Initially it was decorated by medallions bearing the portraits of Prussian rulers, but during restorations carried out after World War II, they were replaced with portraits of renowned Prussian architects.

←
Architectural influence from the Netherlands seen in the Dutch Quarter

THE POTSDAM CONFERENCE OF 1945

On 17 July 1945 the heads of government of Great Britain, the United States and the Soviet Union met in Schloss Cecilienhof to confirm the decisions made earlier that year at Yalta. The aim of both conferences was to resolve the problems arising at the end of World War II. They decided to abolish the Nazi Party, to limit the size of the German military and monitor it indefinitely, and also to punish war criminals and establish reparations. The conference played a major part in establishing a political balance of power in Europe.

Stalin   Churchill
          Truman

⑯
Holländisches Viertel

🅰 Friedrich-Ebert-/
Kurfürsten-/Hebbel-/
Gutenbergstrasse 🚌 604,
609, 692 🚊 91, 92, 94, 96

Just as amazing as the Russian district of Alexandrowka (p266) is the Dutch Quarter. The area is popular with tourists, with numerous shops, galleries, cafés and beer cellars, especially along the central Mittelstrasse.

Dutch workers, invited by Friedrich Wilhelm I, arrived in Potsdam at the beginning of the 18th century. Between 1733 and 1742 a settlement was built for them, comprising 134 gabled houses arranged in four groups, according to plans by Johann Boumann the Elder. They were built from small red bricks and finished with stone and plaster details. These houses are typically three-storey, with picturesque roofs and gables.

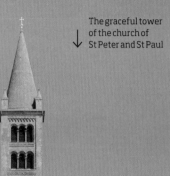

↓ The graceful tower of the church of St Peter and St Paul

café is a decent spot for a drink and a snack; book ahead if you want breakfast.

⑱ Peter und Paul Kirche

🏛 Bassinplatz 📞 0331 230 79 90 🚌 604, 609, 612 🚊 91, 92, 94, 96 ⏰ Mon–Sat; opening times vary, call ahead for details

This 19th-century church was the first large Catholic church built in Potsdam, at the initiative of Friedrich Wilhelm IV. The work of Wilhelm Salzenberg, it was built in 1870, in the shape of a Neo-Romanesque cross. Its slender tower is a copy of the campanile of San Zeno Maggiore in Verona, Italy. Inside are three beautiful paintings by French painter Antoine Pesne.

⑲ Französische Kirche

🏛 Bassinplatz 📞 0331 29 12 19 🚌 604, 609, 612 🚊 93, 94, 99 ⏰ Late Mar–Oct: 1:30–5pm daily

The French Church, which is reminiscent of the Pantheon in Rome, was built especially for the Huguenots in 1752. Following their expulsion from France, they were given the option of settling in Prussia in 1685. Those who settled in Potsdam initially benefited from the hospitality of other churches, then eventually the Französische Kirche was built for them. It was designed by Johann Boumann the Elder in the shape of an ellipse. The front elevation is supported by a grand columned portico. The side niches, which are the entrances of the church, are decorated with the allegorical figures of Faith and Knowledge. The interior dates from the 1830s and is based on designs by Karl Friedrich Schinkel.

EAT

Restaurant Juliette
Francophile spot Juliette is one of Potsdam's most popular dining spots thanks to its interesting range of dishes (from couscous to steak and *foie gras*) and great wine list.

🏛 Jägerstrasse 39 ⏰ noon–3:30pm & 6–10pm Wed–Sun 🌐 restaurant-juliette.de

€€€

⑰ Biosphäre

🏛 Georg-Hermann-Allee 99 🚌 604, 609, 638, 697 🚊 96 ⏰ 9am–6pm Mon–Fri, 10am–7pm Sat, Sun & hols 🌐 biosphaere-potsdam.de

This large glass-and-steel heated greenhouse was built to create a tropical rainforest environment that is now home to 20,000 different exotic plants and animals (including a butterfly house), waterfalls and more. Follow the various jungle pathways across mangrove swamps and up to the tree canopy, while learning about the various flora and fauna. The tropically themed

↑ The Marstall, a former stables and now a film museum

⑳ Ⓜ 🖵

Neuer Landtag

🏛 Alter Markt 1 🕐 Opening times vary, see website for details 🌐 landtag. brandenburg.de

Although this building now houses the parliament of the federal state of Brandenburg, its elaborate façade is a replica of the Potsdam Royal Palace that once stood here. Originally built in 1662, over time the palace was greatly enlarged and modernized to become a massive two-storey building with three wings, an elegant courtyard and a superb gateway crowned by a tower. A bombing raid in 1945 left the palace in ruins and it was finally demolished in 1960.

At the start of the 21st century, it was decided to construct a replica of the former palace façade, along with a modern interior. The works were finished in 2013 and the building now houses the Brandenburg parliament. Visitors are free to enter the inner courtyard through the entrance gate, the Fortuna Portal, as well as the entrance hall, with its famous Knobelsdorff staircase. There is also a roof terrace, a canteen and exhibition space.

㉑ 🚲 🖵 🛍

Marstall (Filmmuseum)

🏛 Breite Strasse 1A 🚌 605, 695 🚊 91, 92, 96, 98 🕐 10am–6pm Tue–Sun 🌐 filmmuseum-potsdam.de

This Baroque pavilion, once used as a royal stables, is the only remaining building of a former royal residence. It was first established in 1714 by refashioning an orangery built by Johann Nering in 1685. In 1746 it was extended and refashioned once more. It suffered extensive damage in World War II and in 1977, after major restoration, it was converted into a film museum. As well as mounting temporary exhibitions, the museum documents the history and work of the Babelsberg studios, Germany's earliest film studios. Exhibits include old projectors, cameras and other equipment as well as props used in some of the most famous German films.

㉒ 🚲 Ⓜ

Telegrafenberg

🏛 Albert-Einstein-Strasse 🚉 Potsdam Hauptbahnhof

The buildings on the Telegrafenberg hill are considered to be some of the best 20th-century structures in the world and attract many admirers of

---

GERMAN CINEMA

German cinema gained international prominence with the rise of Expressionism. The UFA film studios in Babelsberg became the heart of the film industry and rivalled Hollywood as a centre for innovation. Many famous films were produced here, including the Expressionist masterpiece *The Cabinet of Dr Caligari* (1920) by Robert Wiene, *Nosferatu* (1922) by Friedrich Murnau and Fritz Lang's futuristic *Metropolis* (1927). After Hitler came to power, many directors and actors left Germany.

modern architecture. The hill received its current name in 1832, when an optical telegraph station linking Berlin and Koblenz was built here. In the late 19th century, various educational institutes were located here, including the Institute of Astrophysics, for which the complex of buildings in yellow brick was built.

The meandering avenues lead to a picturesque clearing where the small Einsteinturm (Einstein's Tower) breaks through the surrounding trees. Specially designed to observe the solar system, the tower was intended to provide information that would support Einstein's Theory of Relativity. It was built in 1920 by Erich Mendelsohn and is regarded as one of the finest architectural examples of German Expressionism. Its fantastical appearance was intended to show what could be achieved with reinforced concrete. However, due to cost, everything above the first storey is brickwork covered in

→
The Wasserwerk Sanssouci, with its decorative dome and Moorish brickwork

plaster. The building is open from May to October for guided tours only, which must be prebooked (call 0331 749 94 69).

㉓

Filmpark Babelsberg

⌂ August-Bebel Strasse 26–53 (enter at Grossbeeren Strasse) **Ⓢ** Griebnitzsee **🚌** 601, 619, 690 **◷** Opening times vary, see website for details **✕** Nov-Feb **🌐** filmpark-babelsberg.de

This amazing theme park was established on the site of the film studios where Germany's first films were produced in 1912. From 1917 the studio belonged to Universum Film AG (UFA), which produced some of the most renowned films of the silent era, such as *Metropolis*. Nazi propaganda films were also made here.

The studio is still operational today, although part of the complex is open to visitors. There are plenty of sets from old films to explore, as well as behind-the-scenes professionals who demonstrate their skills to visitors – from set-building and makeup to handling animal stars. Older children can enjoy an explosive stunt show, 4D cinema, an interactive XD gaming arena and a spooky "submarine of horror"; for younger children there are gentler rides and activities, many featuring much-loved German children's characters.

㉔

Wasserwerk Sanssouci

⌂ Breite Strasse 28 **☎** 0331 969 42 25 **🚌** 605, 606 **🚊** 91, 94, X98 **◷** May-Oct: 10am-5:30pm Sat, Sun & hols

Designed by Ludwig Persius in 1842, the remarkable mosque of Sanssouci Waterworks was not built to serve the needs of an Islamic community, but to hide the special steam pump that serviced the fountains in Park Sanssouci *(p250)*. Inside you can see the preserved steam-powered machinery made by the Borsig company.

㉕

Altes Rathaus

🏠 Am Alten Markt 9 📞 0331 28 96 86 68 🚌 603, 605, 609, 631, 638, 639, 695 🚊 91, 92, 93, 96, 98, 99 🕐 10am–5pm Tue, Wed & Fri, 10am–7pm Thu, 10am–6pm Sat & Sun

The Old Town Hall is an elegant, colonnaded building, constructed in 1753 on the eastern side of Alter Markt. The uppermost storey, which features an ornamental attic roof, is decorated with the crest of Potsdam and allegorical sculptures. A glass passageway links the building to a neighbouring mid-18th-century building housing the Potsdam Museum. The museum's rich collection of artifacts tells the story of Potsdam's development. A nearby branch of the museum, Memorial Lindenstrasse 54/55, is a former prison and interrogation centre used by both the Nazi and East German regimes.

㉖

Alexandrowka

🏠 Russische Kolonie Allee/ Puschkinallee 🚌 604, 609, 692, 697 🚊 92, 96 🕐 Opening times vary, see website for details 🌐 alexandrowka.de

A trip to Alexandrowka takes the visitor into the world of Pushkin's stories. Wooden houses decorated with carved motifs and set in their own gardens create a very pretty residential estate. Although they appear to be traditional Russian houses, they were constructed in 1826 under the direction of a German military architect for the singers of a Russian choir. The choir was set up in 1812 to entertain the

↑ *Dacha*-style wooden house in former Russian estate of Alexandrowka

troops and was recruited from Russian prisoners of war who had fought with Napoleon. In 1815, when the Prussians and the Russians joined forces, the choir was retained by Friedrich Wilhelm III.

Peter Joseph Lenné was responsible for the overall appearance of the estate, and it was named Alexandrowka

after a Prussian Princess. It is based on the shape of the cross of St Andrew inscribed within an oval. In all, 12 houses were built here, as well as an outhouse which now contains a small museum on the choir. Some of the dwellings are still owned by the descendants of the choir. To the north of this estate stands the Russian Orthodox church of Alexander Nevski.

27 Ⓢ Ⓜ Ⓨ Ⓐ

Museum Barberini

Ⓐ Humboldtstrasse 5-6
Ⓢ Potsdam Hauptbahnhof
🚌 603, 605, 606, 609, 614, 631, 638, 650 🚋 91, 92, 93, 96, 98, 99 ⏰ 10am-7pm Wed-Mon ⓦ museum-barberini.com

This museum is located inside a stunning replica of Frederick the Great's 18th-century Barberini Palace. The exhibits on permanent display were built from a collection of French Impressionist landscape paintings donated by the museum's founder, philanthropist Hasso Plattner. The venue also hosts temporary exhibitions and events focusing on the history of art, from the Old Masters to the contemporary era.

Peter Joseph Lenné was responsible for the overall appearance of the estate, and it was named Alexandrowka after a Prussian Princess.

28

Neuer Garten

Ⓐ Am Neuen Garten 🚌 692

Running along the edge of Heiliger See lake, on what was once the site of palace vineyards, is the New Garden, a park laid out between 1787 and 1791. It was landscaped originally by Johann August Eyserbeck following the instructions of Friedrich Wilhelm II, while the current layout was created by Peter Joseph Lenné in 1816.

It is a Romantic park ornamented with numerous pavilions and sculptures. The charming Marmorpalais stands beside the lake, while the northern section contains the early 20th-century Schloss Cecilienhof (p261). Elsewhere you can see the red and green gardeners' houses, the pyramid-shaped ice-house and a Neo-Gothic library pavilion completed in 1794.

A belvedere, or viewing platform, giving views ↓ over the Neuer Garten

NEED TO KNOW

A train crossing the Oberbaumbrücke

BEFORE
YOU GO

Forward planning is essential to any successful trip. Be prepared for all eventualities by considering the following points before you travel.

AT A GLANCE

CURRENCY
Euro (EUR)

AVERAGE DAILY SPEND

SAVE	SPEND	SPLURGE
€60	**€125**	**€200+**

BOTTLED WATER	COFFEE	BEER	DINNER FOR TWO
€1.30	**€2.50**	**€3.50**	**€65**

ESSENTIAL PHRASES

Hello	Guten Tag
Goodbye	Auf Wiedersehen
Please	Bitte
Thank you	Danke
Do you speak English?	Sprechen Sie Englisch?
I don't understand	Ich verstehe nicht

ELECTRICITY SUPPLY

Power sockets are type F, fitting two-pronged plugs. Standard voltage is 230 volts.

Passports and Visas

For a stay of up to three months for the purpose of tourism, EU nationals and citizens of the US, Canada, Australia and New Zealand do not need a visa. For visa information specific to your home country, consult your nearest German embassy or check online.
Germany Visa Info
w germany-visa.org

Travel Safety Advice

Visitors can get up-to-date travel safety information from the **UK Foreign and Commonwealth Office**, the **US State Department** and the **Australian Department of Foreign Affairs and Trade**.
AUS
w smartraveller.gov.au
UK
w gov.uk/foreign-travel-advice
US
w travel.state.gov

Customs Information

An individual is permitted to carry the following within the EU for personal use:
Tobacco products 800 cigarettes, 400 cigarillos, 200 cigars or 1 kg of smoking tobacco.
Alcohol 10 litres of alcoholic beverages above 22% strength, 20 litres of alcoholic beverages below 22% strength, 90 litres of wine (60 litres of which can be sparkling wine) and 110 litres of beer.
Cash if you plan to enter or leave the EU with €10,000 or more in cash (or the equivalent in other currencies) you must declare it to the customs authorities.
If travelling outside the EU, limits vary so check the restrictions before departing.

Insurance

It is wise to take out an insurance policy covering theft, loss of belongings, medical problems, cancellation and delays.

EU citizens are eligible for free emergency medical care in Germany and should ensure they have an **EHIC** (European Health Insurance Card). Visitors from outside these areas must arrange their own private medical insurance.
EHIC
ⓦ gov.uk/european-health-insurancecard

Vaccinations

No inoculations are needed for Germany.

Money

Major credit, debit and prepaid currency cards are accepted in larger shops and chains. Contactless payments are becoming more widely accepted, although not on public transport. It is always worth carrying some cash, as many smaller businesses don't accept card payments. Cash machines are placed at various points throughout the city centre.

Booking Accommodation

Berlin offers a huge variety of accommodation to suit any budget, ranging from luxury five-star hotels to family run B&Bs and budget hostels.

Lodgings can fill up during the busy summer months, and prices are often inflated during peak season, so it's worth booking in advance.

A comprehensive list of accommodation to suit all needs can be found on **Visit Berlin**, the city's official tourism website (p277).

Travellers with Specific Needs

Free airport assistance at Tegel and Schönefeld airports can be requested through your airline or travel agency no later than 48 hours before your planned departure.

Most of the city's main sights are suitably adapted for disabled access. Call in advance to ensure your needs will be met.

Berlin's wide streets and open spaces make it a very wheelchair-friendly city. Most train stations are equipped with lifts, tactile guidance lines and mobile ramps. Buses and trains have wheelchair access doors. The tram network runs a mix of modern wheelchair-friendly low-floor trams and old carriages with stairs; look for wheelchair symbols on timetables for guidance. Plan your route with **accessBerlin** (p277), a free app detailing the most accessible route to Berlin's key tourist destinations.

A free door-to-door **VBB Bus & Train Escort Service** for individuals requiring assistance getting around the city, including to and from Schönefeld airport, is available 9:30am–5:30pm Mon–Fri. Call ahead to book: 030 34 64 99 40.

In the event of a wheelchair malfunction, the **RPD Berlin** wheelchair breakdown service will assist you or provide a temporary replacement.
RPD Berlin
ⓦ rpd.berlin/index.htm
VBB Bus & Train Escort Service
ⓦ vbb.de

Language

German is the official language, but Berlin is an international city. The use of English is almost as prevalent as German, particularly in business and tourism. Most staff and locals speak English, and you can easily get by without knowing a word of German, but it's appreciated if you can handle a few niceties in the local language before continuing the conversation in English.

Closures

Monday Some museums and tourist attractions are closed for the day.
Sunday Most shops and some small businesses close early or for the entire day.
Public holidays Schools, post offices and banks are closed for the entire day; shops, museums and attractions either close early or are closed for the day.

PUBLIC HOLIDAYS	
1 Jan	New Year's Day
19 Apr	Good Friday
22 Apr	Easter Monday
1 May	Labour Day
30 May	Ascension Day
10 Jun	Whit Monday
3 Oct	Day of German Unity
25 Dec	Christmas Day
26 Dec	St Stephen's Day

GETTING AROUND

Once divided between East and West, Berlin is now connected by an excellent public transport system that crisscrosses the city and beyond.

PUBLIC TRANSPORT COSTS
Tickets are valid on all forms of public transport in Berlin.

SINGLE

€2.80

(zones A–B)

DAY TICKET

€7

(zones A–B)

7-DAY TICKET

€30

(zones A–B)

SPEED LIMIT

MOTORWAY

130 km/h
(80 miles/h)

REGIONAL ROADS

100 km/h
(60 miles/h)

RURAL ROADS

70 km/h
(40 miles/h)

URBAN AREAS

50 km/h
(30 miles/h)

Arriving by Air

Schönefeld and Tegel airports are Berlin's main airports. Both are extremely well-connected and receive regular flights from Europe, North America and Asia.

The city centre is easily reached from Schönefeld by train or public transport using an ABC ticket or by taxi. Tegel airport has direct bus links to the city centre and outlying areas. Buses and taxis stop in front of the airport's main hall. Following ongoing delays, Berlin's Brandenburg airport is not expected to open until 2020.

For journey times and travel costs between the city centre and Schönefeld and Tegel airports, see the table opposite.

Train Travel

International Train Travel

International high-speed trains connect Berlin to other major cities across Europe. Reservations for these services are essential.

You can buy tickets and passes for multiple international train journeys from **Eurail** or **Interrail**. You may need to pay an additional reservation fee depending on which service you travel with. Always check that your pass is valid on the service on which you wish to travel before boarding.

Eurostar runs a regular service from London to Brussels via the Channel Tunnel, where you can change for Berlin. **Deutsche Bahn** also runs a regular high-speed service to and from many other European destinations.

Students and those under the age of 26 can benefit from discounted rail travel both to and in Germany. For more information on discounted tickets and passes, visit the **Eurail** or **Interrail** website.

Deutsche Bahn
w bahn.de
Eurail
w eurail.com
Eurostar
w eurostar.com
Interrail
w interrail.eu

GETTING TO AND FROM THE AIRPORT

Airport	Transport to city centre	Journey time	Price
Schönefeld	Airport Express (RE7/RB14)	30 mins	€3.40
	S-Bahn (S9/S45)	50 mins	€3.40
	Taxi	30 mins	€25–30
Tegel	Bus (TXL)	40 mins	€2.80
	Bus (X9)	20 mins	€2.80
	Taxi	25 mins	€20–25

Domestic Train Travel

Germany's railways are operated by Deutsche Bahn (DB). The Regional Bahn and Regional Express (RB and RE) trains service the wider Berlin-Brandenburg region and beyond. Use this service for day trips to Potsdam and other smaller towns near Berlin.

Tickets can be bought from automatic machines on station platforms or from ticket offices. Special offers include a five-person ticket that is valid for one day.

Berlin has a universal ticketing system. This means that tickets for RB and RE services are also valid on the S-Bahn and U-Bahn, as well as on other public transport services in Berlin.

Public Transport

The **Berliner Verkehrsbetriebe (BVG)** is Berlin's main public transport authority and service provider. Timetables, ticket information, transport maps and more can be found online.
BVG
w bvg.de

Tickets

Berlin is divided into three travel zones for the purposes of ticket pricing: A, B and C. Zone A covers the city centre, Zone B the outskirts of town, and Zone C includes Berlin's suburban areas, Potsdam and its environs, as well as Schönefeld airport. Tickets are available for each combination of zones.

A single ticket is valid on all forms of public transport, including S-Bahn, U-Bahn and ferries, for two hours, with as many changes as required.

Tickets are validated in the red or yellow time-stamping machine near the ticket machine at platform entrances or on board buses.

Travel is only valid in one direction, so a second ticket is required for the return journey.

Short-trip (Kurzstrecke) tickets are cheaper, but can only be used for three stops on trains and six stops on buses and trams. If caught without a valid ticket you may face a €60 fine.

Daily (Tageskarte) and seven-day tickets (7-Tageskarte), costing €7 and €30 respectively for zones A–B, are much better value for those planning on making multiple journeys.

Seven-day tickets also allow you to travel with one extra adult or up to three children for free after 8pm, as well as on weekends, public holidays and on 24 and 31 December.

Discounted tickets are available with some tourist cards that combine public transport with museum entry (p277).

U-Bahn

Don't be confused by the name, these "underground" trains also run on elevated tracks above ground. There are ten U-Bahn lines in total, each connecting with S-Bahn and other U-Bahn lines at various points across the city.

The service usually closes down between 12:30am and 4am. On weekends all lines are open 24 hours except the U4 and U55.

U-Bahn stations are marked by a rectangular blue sign, featuring a large, white letter U.

S-Bahn

The S-Bahn is faster than the U-Bahn, and its stations are further apart from one another. Berlin has 16 S-Bahn lines in total, running well beyond the confines of the city. Trains run every 10 or 20 minutes, or more frequently during peak travel times.

S-Bahn stations are marked by a round, green sign, featuring a large, white letter S.

Buses

Several bus services operate in Berlin, and conveniently they all use the same ticket tariffs.

Regular buses are marked by three-digit route codes and operate every 20 minutes between 5am and midnight. Important routes are serviced by Metro buses (marked by a letter "M" before the route number), operating 24 hours a day, and running every 10 to 20 minutes, whilst express buses (marked by a letter "X") run every 5 to 20 minutes.

The night bus service operates every half an hour from midnight until 4am when the U-Bahn service resumes. Regular tickets are not valid on this service. Night bus tickets can be bought directly from the driver (cash only).

All bus routes have a detailed timetable on display at each stop, and inner-city bus stops are equipped with digital screens indicating waiting times. Consult the BVG website (p273) for specific route information.

Long-Distance Bus Travel

Eurolines offers a variety of coach routes to Berlin from other European cities. Fares start from £19, with additional discounts for students, children and seniors. Other services include **Berlin Linien Bus**, **Student Agency Bus** and **Ecolines**.

The **Central Bus Station** (Zentraler Omnibusbahnhof) is Berlin's largest long-distance bus station with connections to towns all over Germany and the rest of Europe. Check their website for timetables and tickets.

Berlin Linien Bus
ⓦ berlinlinienbus.de
Central Bus Station
ⓦ zob.berlin
Ecolines
ⓦ ecolines.net
Eurolines
ⓦ eurolines.eu
Student Agency Bus
ⓦ studentagencybus.com

Trams

Despite only servicing the eastern parts of the city, trams (Strassenbahn) are a popular way to get around for locals and tourists alike, particularly if you are travelling from Mitte to any part of Prenzlauer Berg.

Important routes are serviced by Metro trams running every 10 or 20 minutes, 24 hours a day. Some run a reduced service on weekends. Other tram services run every 20 minutes between 5 or 6 am and midnight.

Berlin's integrated transport system allows the use of tram tickets on buses, S- and U-Bahn train services, and vice versa. Tickets can be purchased at the usual vending points, or by using machines (coin only) on board.

Taxis

Official Berlin taxis are cream, have a "Taxi" sign on the roof and have a meter on the driver's dashboard. Taxi apps such as UBER also operate in Berlin.

Taxis can be hailed on the street, picked up at an official taxi rank (Würfelfunk), usually situated in popular locations, or booked in advance online or over the phone.

If you are travelling 2 km (1 mile) or less, ask for a short trip (Kurzstrecke) for €5 – this can only be done in taxis you have hailed from the street. The following services can be booked by phone or online:

Taxi Funk Berlin
ⓦ funk-taxi-berlin.de
Würfelfunk
ⓦ wuerfelfunk.de

Driving

Driving licences issued by any of the European Union member states are valid throughout the EU. If visiting from outside the EU, you may need to apply for an International Driving Permit. Check with your local automobile association before you travel.

Driving to Berlin

Berlin is easily reached by car from most European cities via E-roads, which form the International European Road Network.

Germany's regional roads (Landesstrassen) are marked with yellow road signs, whilst motorways (Autobahnen) are marked with blue road signs. Although some stretches of motorway have variable speed limits depending on weather and road conditions, others have no enforced speed limit at all. German drivers therefore tend to zoom along at high speeds reaching up to 200 km/h (125 miles/h).

Berlin is surrounded by a circular motorway called the Berliner Ring, which has numerous signposted exits into the city centre.

Drivers must carry their passport and insurance documentation if driving their own foreign-registered vehicle in Germany.

In the event of a breakdown, accident, or if you require assistance on the road contact **ADAC Auto Assistance**.
ADAC Auto Assistance
ⓦ adac.de

Car Rental

You must be 21 or over and have held a valid driver's licence for at least a year to rent a car in Germany. By law, drivers aged 21–22 must purchase a Collision Damage Waiver (CDW). Drivers under the age of 25 may incur a young-driver surcharge.

Driving in Berlin

Berlin is relatively straightforward to navigate by car; road layouts are clear and streets are well signposted. Parking is not hard to find and relatively cheap compared to other major European cities.

If you are flying to Berlin and staying within the metro area the most efficient way to travel is by public transport. There are also park-and-ride facilities on the outskirts of the city, which are a lot cheaper than inner-city parking.

Beware of cyclists and trams in the city. Trams take precedence; take care when turning; and allow cyclists right of way.

Rules of the Road

Drive on the right. Unless otherwise signposted, vehicles coming from the right have priority.

At all times, drivers must carry a valid driver's licence, registration and insurance documents. Seatbelts are compulsory in a hired car, lights must be used in tunnels and the use of a mobile phone while driving is prohibited, with the exception of a hands-free system. The drink-drive limit *(p277)* is strictly enforced.

All drivers must have third-party insurance *(Haftpflichtversicherung)* – it is the minimum insurance requirement in Germany. Also compulsory is an environmental badge for vehicles driving within **Environmental Green Zones** *(Umweltzonen)*. Most of downtown Berlin is classified as an *Umweltzone*. Certification can be purchased online for a small fee.

Environmental Green Zones
🔲 umwelt-plakette.de

Cycling

Berlin is generally a bike-friendly city, with many designated cycle lanes and traffic lights at intersections.

Should you get tired of pedalling, bicycles can be taken on the U-Bahn, S-Bahn and trams, but they are prohibited on buses, except night buses, which can carry up to two at the driver's discretion. For all public transport an additional *Fahrrad* (bicycle) ticket is required.

Bicycle Hire

Deutsche Bahn operates an excellent public bicycle system called **LIDL Bike**. Bikes can be picked up from train stations and major intersections. They can be dropped off at any of the LIDL Bike stations conveniently dotted throughout the city.

To rent a LIDL Bike, you must register by providing your credit card details. A one-off registration fee of €3 applies. The first 30 minutes cost €1.50, and you will be charged €1 for every additional half hour.

You can also hire bikes at many cycling shops for similar or cheaper rates; one of the most reliable is **Fahrradstation**. Be aware that drink-drive limits *(p277)* also apply to cyclists.

Fahrradstation
🔲 fahrradstation.com
LIDL BIKE
🔲 lidl-bike.de

Bicycle Safety

Ride on the right. If you are unsure or unsteady, practise in one of the inner-city parks first. If in doubt, dismount: many novices cross busy junctions on foot; if you do so, switch to the pedestrian section of the crossing. Beware of tram tracks; cross them at an angle to avoid getting stuck.

For your own safety, do not walk with your bike in a bike lane or cycle on pavements, on the left side of the road, in pedestrian zones or in the dark without lights. The locals usually don't bother, but wearing a helmet is recommended.

BERLIN BY BOAT

An extensive system of canals and lakes links Berlin's city centre with Potsdam, Spandau, Charlottenburg and the area of Müggelsee.

Public Ferries
Six ferry lines operate in Berlin as part of the integrated public transport system. Marked by a letter F, they provide cross-river connections in locations to the east where there are no bridges. The F10 provides a particularly charming trip from Wannsee (near Potsdam) to the beautiful lakeside village of Alt-Kladow.

Boat Tours
For those who wish to explore the city by boat, regular river tours along the Spree river and the Landwehrkanal are available. The following companies offer tours in English and German:
Reederei Bruno Winkler
🔲 reedereiwinkler.de
Reederei Riedel
🔲 reederei-riedel.de
Stern und Kreisschiffahrt
🔲 sternundkreis.de

Boat Hire
Potsdam and its lakes and rivers make for an excellent day out on the water, and the town is teeming with boat rental companies offering various rental opportunities. Book in advance online or you can make enquiries at the tourist information centre on the day.
Potsdam Tourist Information Centre
🔲 potsdam-tourism.com

PRACTICAL
INFORMATION

A little local know-how goes a long way in Berlin. Here you will find all the essential advice and information you will need during your stay.

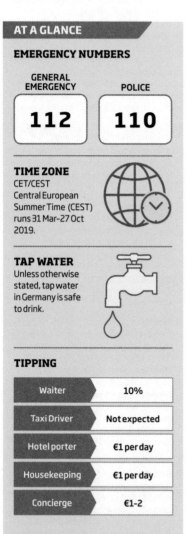

AT A GLANCE

EMERGENCY NUMBERS

GENERAL EMERGENCY	POLICE
112	**110**

TIME ZONE
CET/CEST
Central European
Summer Time (CEST)
runs 31 Mar–27 Oct
2019.

TAP WATER
Unless otherwise
stated, tap water
in Germany is safe
to drink.

TIPPING

Waiter	10%
Taxi Driver	Not expected
Hotel porter	€1 per day
Housekeeping	€1 per day
Concierge	€1–2

Personal Security

Pickpockets are known to work crowded tourist areas. Use your common sense and be alert to your surroundings.

If you have anything stolen, report the crime as soon as possible to the nearest police station. Get a copy of the crime report in order to claim on your insurance.

Kottbusser Tor U-Bahn station is notorious for its drug pushers, so be careful there late at night. Panic buttons on platforms at S- and U-Bahn stations can be used in an emergency.

Contact your embassy if you have your passport stolen, or in the event of a serious crime or accident.

Health

For minor ailments and prescriptions go to a pharmacy *(Apotheke)*. Details of the nearest 24-hour service are posted in all pharmacy windows, or can be easily obtained by checking the **Apothekerkammer** website.

You may need a doctor's prescription to obtain certain pharmaceuticals, and the pharmacist can inform you of the closest doctor's practice.

EU citizens can receive emergency medical treatment in Germany free of charge *(p271)*, but you may have to pay upfront for medical treatment and reclaim on your insurance later.

For visitors from outside the EU, payment of hospital and other medical expenses is the patient's responsibility. It is therefore important to arrange comprehensive medical insurance before travelling *(p270)*.
Apothekerkammer
🅦 www.akberlin.de

Smoking, Alcohol and Drugs

Germany has a smoking ban in all public places, including bars, cafés, restaurants and hotels. However, many establishments circumvent these laws by naming themselves a *Raucherkneipe*, or smoking pub.

The possession of narcotics is strictly

prohibited and could result in prosecution and a prison sentence.

Unless stated otherwise, it is permitted to drink alcohol on the streets and in public parks and gardens. Germany has a strict limit of 0.05 per cent BAC (blood alcohol content) for drivers.

ID

There is no requirement for visitors to carry ID, but in the event of a routine check you may be asked to show your passport. If you don't have it with you, the police may escort you to wherever your passport is being kept so that you can show it to them.

Local Customs

Germany has strict laws on hate speech and symbols linked to Hitler and the Nazis. Disrespectful behaviour in public places can warrant a fine, or even prosecution. Be respectful when visiting Berlin's historical sights.

Visiting Churches and Cathedrals

Dress respectfully: cover your torso and upper arms; ensure shorts and skirts cover your knees.

Mobile Phones and Wi-Fi

Free Wi-Fi hotspots are widely available in Berlin's city centre. Cafés and restaurants are usually happy to permit the use of their Wi-Fi on the condition that you make a purchase.

Visitors travelling to Berlin with EU tariffs will be able to use their devices abroad without being affected by data roaming charges; instead they will be charged the same rates for data, SMS and voice calls as they would pay at home.

Post

German post offices and post boxes are usually easy to spot with their distinctive yellow *Deutsche Post* signs.

Stamps (*Briefmarke*) can be bought in post offices, newsagents, tobacconists and most major supermarkets. There are usually self-service stamp machines conveniently placed outside post offices.

Taxes and Refunds

VAT is 19% in Germany. Non-EU residents are entitled to a tax refund subject to certain conditions. In order to do this, you must request a tax receipt and export papers (*Ausfuhrbescheinigung*) when you purchase your goods. When leaving the country, present these papers, along with the receipt and your ID, at customs to receive your refund.

Discount Cards

Berlin Welcome Card free entry to 30 of Berlin's major tourist attractions and discounted entry for nearly 200 more. This card also includes unlimited use of public transport for the duration of your trip. Available from tourist offices and online.

Berlin Pass free entry to over 60 attractions, tours and museums and the option of an integrated travel card. Prices vary depending on your needs and the duration of your stay. Available from tourist offices and online.

Berlin City Tour Card save up to 30% on Berlin's top 10 tourist attractions and enjoy unlimited free travel on public transport for the duration of your stay. Available from most tourist offices and online.

Berlin Welcome Card
ⓦ berlin-welcomecard.de
The Berlin Pass
ⓦ berlinpass.com
Berlin City Tour Card
ⓦ citytourcard.com

WEBSITES AND APPS

www.visitberlin.de
Visit Berlin, the city's official tourist information website
accessBerlin
A free app detailing the most accessible routes around the city
BVG FahrInfo Plus
Live departures and travel updates from the city's local transport operator BVG
Berlin Free WiFi
This app can be used offline to direct users to free Wi-Fi hotspots throughout the city centre.

INDEX

Index

Page numbers in **bold** type
refer to main entries

PHRASE BOOK

IN AN EMERGENCY

Where is the telephone?	Wo ist das telefon?	voh ist duss tele-fon?
Help!	Hilfe!	hilf-uh
Please call a doctor	Bitte rufen Sie einen Arzt	bitt-uh roof'n zee ine-en artst
Please call the police	Bitte rufen Sie die Polizei	bitt-uh roof'n zee dee poli-tsy
Please call the fire brigade	Bitte rufen Sie die Feuerwehr	bitt-uh roof'n zee dee foyer-vayr
Stop!	Halt!	hult

COMMUNICATION ESSENTIALS

Yes	Ja	yah
No	Nein	nine
Please	Bitte	bitt-uh
Thank you	Danke	dunk-uh
Excuse me	Verzeihung	fair-tsy-hoong
Hello (good day)	Guten Tag	goot-en tahk
Goodbye	Auf Wiedersehen	owf-weed-er-zay-ern
Good evening	Guten Abend	goot'n ahb'nt
Good night	Gute Nacht	goot-uh nukht
Until tomorrow	Bis morgen	biss morg'n
See you	Tschüss	chooss
What is that?	Was ist das?	voss ist duss
Why?	Warum?	var-room
Where?	Wo?	voh
When?	Wann?	vunn
today	heute	hoyt-uh
tomorrow	morgen	morg'n
month	Monat	mohn-aht
night	Nacht	nukht
afternoon	Nachmittag	nahkh-mit-tahk
morning	Morgen	morg'n
year	Jahr	yar
there	dort	dort
here	hier	hear
week	Woche	vokh-uh
yesterday	gestern	gest'n
evening	Abend	ahb'nt

USEFUL PHRASES

How are you? (informal)	Wie geht's?	vee gayts
Fine, thanks	Danke, es geht mir gut	dunk-uh, es gayt meer goot
Until later	Bis später	biss shpay-ter
Where is/are?	Wo ist/sind...?	voh ist/sind
How far is it to...?	Wie weit ist es...?	vee vite ist ess
Do you speak English?	Sprechen Sie Englisch?	shpresh'n zee eng-glish
I don't understand	Ich verstehe nicht	ish fair-shtay-uh nisht
Could you speak more slowly?	Könnten Sie langsamer sprechen?	kurnt-en zee lung-zam-er shpresh'n

USEFUL WORDS

large	gross	grohss
small	klein	kline
hot	heiss	hyce
cold	kalt	kult
good	gut	goot
bad	böse/schlecht	burss-uh/shlesht
open	geöffnet	g'urff-nett
closed	geschlossen	g'shloss'n
left	links	links
right	rechts	reshts
straight ahead	geradeaus	g'rah-der-owss

MAKING A TELEPHONE CALL

I would like to make a phone call	Ich möchte telefonieren	ish mer-shtuh tel-e-fon-eer'n
I'll try again later	Ich versuche es später noch einmal	ish fair-zookh-uh es shpay-ter nokh ine-mull
Can I leave a message?	Kann ich eine Nachricht hinterlassen?	kan ish ine-uh nakh-risht hint-er-lahss-en
answer phone	Anrufbeantworter	an-roof-be-ahnt-vort-er
telephone card	Telefonkarte	tel-e-fohn-kart-uh
receiver	Hörer	hur-er
mobile	Handy	han-dee
engaged (busy)	besetzt	b'zetst
wrong number	Falsche Verbindung	falsh-uh fair-bin-doong

SIGHTSEEING

library	Bibliothek	bib-leo-tek
entrance ticket	Eintrittskarte	ine-tritz-kart-uh
cemetery	Friedhof	freed-hofe
train station	Bahnhof	barn-hofe
gallery	Galerie	gall-er-ree
information	Auskunft	owss-koonft
church	Kirche	keersh-uh
garden	Garten	gart'n
palace/castle	Palast/Schloss	pallast/shloss
place (square)	Platz	plats
bus stop	Haltestelle	hal-te-shtel-uh
national holiday	Nationalfeiertag	nats-yon-ahl-fire-tahk
theatre	Theater	tay-aht-er
free admission	Eintritt frei	ine-tritt fry

SHOPPING

Do you have/ Is there...?	Gibt es...?	geept ess
How much does it cost?	Was kostet das?	voss kost't duss?
When do you open?	Wann öffnen Sie?	vunn off'n zee
close?	schliessen Sie?	shlees'n zee
this	das	duss
expensive	teuer	toy-er
cheap	preiswert	price-vurt
size	Grösse	gruhs-uh
number	Nummer	noom-er
colour	Farbe	farb-uh
brown	braun	brown
black	schwarz	shvarts
red	rot	roht
blue	blau	blau
green	grün	groon
yellow	gelb	gelp

TYPES OF SHOP

antique shop	Antiquariat	antik-var-yat
chemist (pharmacy)	Apotheke	appo-tay-kuh
bank	Bank	bunk
market	Markt	markt
travel agency	Reisebüro	rye-zer-boo-roe
department store	Warenhaus	vahr'n-hows
chemist's/ drugstore	Drogerie	droog-er-ree
hairdresser	Friseur	freezz-er
newspaper kiosk	Zeitungskiosk	tsytoongs-kee-osk
bookshop	Buchhandlung	bookh-hant-loong
bakery	Bäckerei	beck-er-eye
post office	Post	posst
shop/store	Geschäft/Laden	gush-eft/lard'n

film processing shop	**Fotogeschäft**	fo-to-gush-**eft**
self-service shop	**Selbstbedienungs-laden**	selpst-bed-**ee**-nungs-lard'n
shoe shop	**Schuhladen**	shoo-lard'n
clothes shop	**Kleiderladen/ Boutique**	klyder-lard'n boo-**teek**-uh
food shop	**Lebensmittel-geschäft**	lay-bens-mittel-gush-eft
glass, porcelain	**Glas, Porzellan**	glars, port-sell-ahn

STAYING IN A HOTEL

Do you have any vacancies?	**Haben Sie noch Zimmer frei?**	harb'n zee nokh tsimm-er-fry
with twin beds?	**mit zwei Betten?**	mitt tsvy bett'n
with a double bed?	**mit einem Doppelbett?**	mitt ine'm dopp'l-bet
with a bath?	**mit Bad?**	mitt bart
with a shower?	**mit Dusche?**	mitt doosh-uh
I have a reservation	**Ich habe eine Reservierung**	ish harb-uh ine-uh rez-er-**veer**-oong
key	**Schlüssel**	shlooss'l
porter	**Pförtner**	pfert-ner

EATING OUT

Do you have a table for...?	**Haben Sie einen Tisch für...?**	harb'n zee tish foor
I would like to reserve a table	**Ich möchte eine Reservierung machen**	ish mer-shtuh ine-uh rezer-**veer**-oong makh'n
I'm a vegetarian	**Ich bin Vegetarier**	ish bin vegg-er-**tah**-ree-er
Waiter!	**Herr Ober!**	hair oh-bare!
The bill (check), please	**Die Rechnung, bitte**	dee resh-noong bitt-uh
breakfast	**Frühstück**	froo-shtock
lunch	**Mittagessen**	mit-targ-ess'n
dinner	**Abendessen**	arb'nt-ess'n
bottle	**Flasche**	flush-uh
dish of the day	**Tagesgericht**	tahg-es-gur-isht
main dish	**Hauptgericht**	howpt-gur-isht
dessert	**Nachtisch**	nahkh-tish
cup	**Tasse**	tass-uh
wine list	**Weinkarte**	vine-kart-uh
tankard	**Krug**	khroog
glass	**Glas**	glars
spoon	**Löffel**	lerff'l
teaspoon	**Teelöffel**	tay-lerff'l
tip	**Trinkgeld**	trink-gelt
knife	**Messer**	mess-er
starter (appetizer)	**Vorspeise**	for-shpize-uh
the bill	**Rechnung**	resh-noong
plate	**Teller**	tell-er
fork	**Gabel**	gahb'l

MENU DECODER

Aal	**arl**	eel
Apfel	**upf'l**	apple
Apfelschorle	**upf'l-shoorl-uh**	apple juice with sparkling mineral water
Apfelsine	**upf'l-seen-uh**	orange
Aprikose	**upri-kawz-uh**	apricot
Artischocke	**arti-shokh-uh**	artichoke
Aubergine (eggplant)	**or-ber-jeen-uh**	aubergine
Banane	**bar-narn-uh**	banana
Beefsteak	**beef-stayk**	steak
Bier	**beer**	beer
Bockwurst	**bokh-voorst**	a type of sausage
Bohnensuppe	**burn-en-zoop-uh**	bean soup
Branntwein	brant-vine	spirits
Bratkartoffeln	brat-kar-toff'ln	fried potatoes
Bratwurst	brat-voorst	fried sausage
Brot	brot	bread
Brötchen	bret-tchen	bread roll
Brühe	bruh-uh	broth
Butter	boot-ter	butter
Champignon	shum-pin-yong	mushroom
Currywurst	kha-ree-voorst	sausage with curry sauce
Dill	**dill**	dill
Ei	**eye**	egg
Eis	**ice**	ice/ice cream
Ente	ent-uh	duck
Erdbeeren	ayrt-beer'n	strawberries
Fisch	**fish**	fish
Forelle	for-ell-uh	trout
Frikadelle	Frika-dayl-uh	rissole/ hamburger
Gans	ganns	goose
Garnele	**gar-nayl-uh**	prawn/shrimp
gebraten	g'braat'n	fried
gegrillt	g'grilt	grilled
gekocht	g'kokht	boiled
geräuchert	g'rowk-ert	smoked
Geflügel	**g'floog'l**	poultry
Gemüse	g'mooz-uh	vegetables
Grütze	**grurt-ser**	groats, gruel
Gulasch	goo-lush	goulash
Gurke	**goork-uh**	gherkin
Hammelbraten	hamm'l-braat'n	roast mutton
Hähnchen	haynsh'n	chicken
Hering	**hair-ing**	herring
Himbeeren	him-beer'n	raspberries
Honig	hoe-nikh	honey
Kaffee	kaf-fay	coffee
Kalbfleisch	kalp-flysh	veal
Kaninchen	ka-neensh'n	rabbit
Karpfen	karpf'n	carp
Kartoffelpüree	kar-toff'l-poor-ay	mashed potatoes
Käse	kayz-uh	cheese
Kaviar	kar-vee-ar	caviar
Knoblauch	k'nob-lowkh	garlic
Knödel	k'nerd'l	noodle
Kohl	koal	cabbage
Kopfsalat	kopf-zal-aat	lettuce
Krebs	**krayps**	crab
Kuchen	kookh'n	cake
Lachs	lahkhs	salmon
Leber	**lay-ber**	liver
mariniert	mari-neert	marinated
Marmelade	marmer-lard-uh	marmalade, jam
Meerrettich	may-re-tish	horseradish
Milch	**milsh**	milk
Mineralwasser	minn-er-**arl**-vuss-er	mineral water
Möhre	**mer**-uh	carrot
Nuss	**nooss**	nut
Öl	**erl**	oil
Olive	o-**leev**-uh	olive
Petersilie	payt-er-**zee**-li-uh	parsley
Pfeffer	**pfeff**-er	pepper
Pfirsich	**pfir**-zish	peach
Pflaumen	**pflow**-men	plum
Pommes frites	pomm-**fritt**	chips/ French fries
Quark	kvark	soft cheese
Radieschen	ra-**deesh**'n	radish
Rinderbraten	**rind**-er-brat'n	joint of beef
Rinderroulade	**rind**-er-roo-lard-uh	beef olive
Rindfleisch	**rint**-flysh	beef
Rippchen	**rip**-sh'n	cured pork rib
Rotkohl	roht-koal	red cabbage
Rüben	**rhoob**'n	turnip
Rührei	**rhoo**-er-eye	scrambled eggs

Saft	zuft	juice
Salat	zal-aat	salad
Salz	zults	salt
Salzkartoffeln	zults-kar-toff'l	boiled potatoes
Sauerkirschen	zow-er-**keersh'n**	cherries
Sauerkraut	zow-er-krowt	sauerkraut
Sekt	zekt	sparkling wine
Senf	zenf	mustard
scharf	sharf	spicy
Schaschlik	shash-lik	kebab
Schlagsahne	shlahgg-zarn-uh	whipped cream
Schnittlauch	shnit-lowhkh	chives
Schnitzel	**shnitz**'l	veal or pork cutlet
Schweinefleisch	shvine-flysh	pork
Spargel	shparg'l	asparagus
Spiegelei	shpeeg'l-eye	fried egg
Spinat	shpin-art	spinach
Tee	tay	tea
Tomate	tom-art-uh	tomato
Wassermelone	vuss-er-me-lohn-uh	watermelon
Wein	vine	wine
Weintrauben	vine-trowb'n	grapes
Wiener Würstchen	veen-er voorst-sh'n	frankfurter
Zander	tsan-der	pike-perch
Zitrone	tsi-trohn-uh	lemon
Zucker	tsook-er	sugar
Zwieback	tsvee-bak	rusk
Zwiebel	tsvee**b'l**	onion

NUMBERS

0	null	nool
1	eins	eye'ns
2	zwei	tsvy
3	drei	dry
4	vier	feer
5	fünf	foonf
6	sechs	zex
7	sieben	zeeb'n
8	acht	uhkht
9	neun	noyn
10	zehn	tsayn
11	elf	elf
12	zwölf	tserlf
13	dreizehn	dry-tsayn
14	vierzehn	feer-tsayn
15	fünfzehn	foonf-tsayn
16	sechzehn	zex-tsayn
17	siebzehn	zeep-tsayn
18	achtzehn	uhkht-tsayn
19	neunzehn	noyn-tsayn
20	zwanzig	tsvunn-tsig
21	einundzwanzig	ine-oont-tsvunn-tsig
30	dreissig	dry-sig
40	vierzig	feer-sig
50	fünfzig	foonf-tsig
60	sechzig	zex-tsig
70	siebzig	zeep-tsig
80	achtzig	uhkht-tsig
90	neunzig	noyn-tsig
100	hundert	hoond't
1,000	tausend	towz'ht
1,000,000	eine Million	ine-uh mill-yon

TIME

one minute	eine Minute	ine-uh min-oot-uh
one hour	eine Stunde	ine-uh shtoond-uh
half an hour	eine halbe Stunde	ine-uh hullb-uh shtoond-uh
Monday	Montag	mohn-targ
Tuesday	Dienstag	deens-targ
Wednesday	Mittwoch	mitt-vokh
Thursday	Donnerstag	donn-ers-targ
Friday	Freitag	fry-targ
Saturday	Samstag/ Sonnabend	zums-targ zonn-ah-bent
Sunday	Sonntag	zon-targ
January	Januar	yan-ooar
February	Februar	fay-brooar
March	März	mairts
April	April	april
May	Mai	my
June	Juni	yoo-ni
July	Juli	yoo-lee
August	August	ow-goost
September	September	zep-tem-ber
October	Oktober	ok-toh-ber
November	November	no-vem-ber
December	Dezember	day-tsem-ber
spring	Frühling	froo-ling
summer	Sommer	zomm-er
autumn (fall)	Herbst	hairpst
winter	Winter	vint-er

ACKNOWLEDGMENTS

The publisher would like to thank the following for their kind permission to reproduce their photographs:

Key: a-above; b-below/bottom; c-centre; f-far; l-left; r-right; t-top

123RF.com: Mesut Dogan 172bl; Shanti Hesse 13cr; iloveotto 10-1b, 31tr, 150-1t; Anton Ivanov 260-1; lauradibias 19t, 142-3; marina99 220-1; Jaroslav Moravcik 195tl; Karl-Heinz Spremberg 12-3b, 240-1b; Lothar Steine 44tl; Anibal Trejo 132-3t; T.W. van Urk 202t; vvoennyy 173tl; Velislava Yovcheva 257cra.

4Corners: Luca Da Ros 19bl, 152-3.

500px: Vladan Radivoja 242-3.

akg-images: Album / Prisma / Antonin Mercie *Gloria Victis* (1874) 67cra, Brazalete de bronce. Siglo III d. 86crb.

Alamy Stock Photo: 500px 60-1; A Media Press 86clb; zAF Archive 107crb, 264br; Agencia Fotograficzna Caro 58-9t, / Andreas Teich 32bl, / Muhs 97br, 228br; allfive 49ca; Artexplorer 158br; Berlin-Zeitgeist 182cla; Walter Bibikow 122; Bildagentur-online / Schoening 264t; bilwissedition Ltd. & Co. KG 245br; Eden Breitz 40b, 41tl, 47tl, 184cra, 237t; Bridgeman Images 58tl; Chronicle 57bc; colaimages 106clb; Collection Christophel 107clb; Ian G Dagnall 49cl; Digital-Fotofusion Gallery 37cl; dpa picture alliance 45tr, 46tl, 58br, 147tr, / Britta Pedersen 47cl, / Bernd Settnik 253bl; Adam Eastland 34-5b, 156-7b, 159, 161t, 182-3b, 226cra, 226-7b, 244-5tc, / © 2018 The Andy Warhol Foundation for the Visual Arts, Inc. / Licensed by DACS, London 2018 Andy Warhol *Chairman Mao* 124-5b; EyeEm / Oliver Byunggyu Woo 36-7t; Alexandre Fagundes 250t; Falkensteinfoto 55tr; Stephane Gautier 106cla; Scott Goodno 109tl; hanohikirf 184br; hemis.fr / Eric Planchard 26bl, René Mattes 158clb; Juergen Henkelmann 244bl; Historical image collection by Bildagentur-online 54t; Peter Horree 56bc, 92bl, 125cra, 164-5t; imageBROKER 50-1b; 59bl; 183tl, / Helmut Baar 228tl; INTERFOTO 56cr, / Karl Johaentges 169t; Masterpics 30tl, 160br; Iain Masterton 38-9t, 166b, 183tr, 185, 188b, 192t, 248cra, / Karl Schmidt-Rottluff © DACS 2018 30-1b, / Bernhard Heiliger © DACS 2018 *Tor der Kugel* at Kunsthaus Dahlem 246t; mauritius images GmbH / Torsten Elger 115br; MISCELLANEOUSTOCK 96-7t; Niday Picture Library 54br; PAINTING 158cb; Pictorial Press Ltd 262cra; Prisma Archivo 90cra; Ricardo Ribas 213; TravelCollection / Inga Wandinger 216bl; travelpix 149tr; travelstock44.de / Juergen Held 20tl, 178-9; United Archives GmbH 55tl; UtCon Collection 160tl; Lucas Vallecillos 28-9t, 90cb; Scott Wilson 35cla; Julie g Woodhouse 29crb, 67cla, 158cra, 177br; World History Archive 56-7, 58bc.

AWL Images: Sabine Lubenow 2-3, 4, 17cb, 102-3.

Berlin Story: 50tl.

Berliner Ensemble: Lovis Ostenrick 129br.

Berliner Fernsehturm: Marco Wendt 24t.

BerlinerFestspiele: Daniele Baldi 53tl; Camille Blake 47br; Mutesouvenir / Kai Bienert 46b.

Berlinische Galerie / BG Gebäude: © Foto: Nina Straßgütl 190cla, 190-1t.

Bridgeman Images: Berlinische Galerie / Otto Dix © DACS 2018 *The Poet Iwar von Lücken* (1926) 31br.

C/O Berlin: 205t.

Daimler Art Collection; Stuttgart/Berlin: V.l. Marius Glauer, Monika Brandmeier, Ulrich Erben, José Heerkens, Ding Yi, You Honglei *Last Night's Fortune Teller* - Daimler Contemporary, Berlin 2018. / Hans-Georg Gaul 42-3t.

DDR Museum: 24br.

Depositphotos Inc: chrissi 225cb; claudiodivizia 247crb; Elnur 29cla; Konrad Kerker 21, 208-9; S Kohl 212br; philipus 217t; terroa 135br; whatslove 262b.

Dorling Kindersley: Dorota and Mariusz Jarymowicz 127tr, 130bc, 215br.

Dreamstime.com: 12ee12 175br; 22tomtom 108bl; Andersastphoto 73br; Andreykr 239tr; Andrey Andronov 253crb; Anticiclo 111tl; Anyaivanova 53br; Michal Bednarek 75t; Blitzkoenig 265br; Vladimir Bondarenco 12clb; Bred2k8 33cla; Boris Breytman 109tr, 219br, 251tr; Andrea Calistri 17tl, 82-3; Carolannefreeling 110b; Claudiodivizia 22bl, 86cr, 125tl; Creativeimpression 170cb; Dedi57 256bl; Delstudio 146cra; Demerzel21 81cra, 133br; Draghicich 232b; Eddygaleotti 76-7t, 123ca; Eldadcarin 234tl; Elenaburn 117tl; Elenasfotos 263tl, 266tr; Alexandre Fagundes De Fagundes 86cra, 212cla; Eugene Feygin 248-9t; Alessandro Flore 89br; Franz1212 191br; Gekaskr 16, 62-3; Guadapad 45cla; Hanohiki 172tr; Ixuskmitl 106cl; Jdm512 28-9b; Marek Jelínek 230t; Katatonia82 51tr, 167tr, 214t; Kerrick 78-9b; Vassiliy Kochetkov 229t; Sergey Kohl 52bl; Patryk Kosmider 218cla; Oleksandr Kovalenko 26cr; Ivan Kravtsov 253clb; Anna Krivitskaia 86bc; Laudibi 256tr; Axel Lauer 52cl; Madrabothair 174t; Markwaters 53bl, 139tr, 148tr, 241tr; Vasilii Maslak 114tr; Meinzahn 18, 24cr, 118-9, 266-7b; Merlindo 68br; Mijeshots 69t; Minnystock 6-7b, 107tl, 170-1b, 268-9; Jaroslav Moravcik 89cr, 93tr, 187b; Yurii Moroz 76bc; Moskwa 49cr, 258tl; Oanap24 147cla; Sean Pavone 234-5t; Plotnikov 251t, 258-9b; Radiokafka 224c; Rfoxphoto 201; Rosshelen 94t; Rphstock 225tl; Rumifaz 70bl; Jozef Sedmak 109br; 200cra; Snake81 255tl; Stefan Baum 204bl; Tomas1111 112tl; Tupungato 78tl, 134-5t; T.w. Van Urk 32-3t, 101tl; Xantana 140bl; Yorgy67 212clb; Velislava Yovcheva 255cra; Yuryz 236bl.

Festival of Lights: Morten Carlsson 52br; Frank Hermann 89tr.

Gedenkstätte Berlin-Hohenschönhausen: Thomas Weber 231b.

Georg Kolbe Museum; Berlin: Enric Duch 238t.

Getty Images: age fotostock / Reiner Elsen 149cra; Alinari Archives 55bc; Jon Arnold 8-9b; Adam Berry 26crb; Estate of Emil Bieber / Klaus Niermann 56tl; Peter Bischoff 107cb; Bloomberg / Jochen Eckel 37cb; Corbis Documentary / Ruggero Vanni 31cla; DEA / Biblioteca Ambrosiana 57bl; Eye Ubiquitous 55br; Sean Gallup 42bl, 43b, 67bl; Carsten Koall 193bl; Benjamin Matthijs Lichtwerk 252tr; The LIFE Picture Collection / Hugo Jaeger 58cla; Moment Open / Federica Gentile 146-7b; NurPhoto 52cla; Popperfoto / James Jarche 58cr; ullstein bild 55cra, 56br, 57tr, 106clb, / Drescher 35tr, / Heilke Heller 123bc, / Koch 254bl; Universal History Archive 54bc.

iStockphoto.com: Antonistock 24clb; bluejayphoto 163bl; Martin Dimitrov 100b; Giflishtih 138-9b; golero 13t; hanohiki 33br; holgs 52cr, 200bl; kavunchik 72t; Jonny Kristoffersson 40tl; lechatnoir 11br, 41br, 227tr; lesart777 116bl; lubilub 81cl; lucamato 194bl; MarioGuti 41cl, 164bl; Maxlevoyou 192br; mikkelwilliam 59br; Mlenny 13br; Nellmac 48-9t; Nikada 22t, 22cr, 59tr, 130-1t, 163tr; Max Ozerov 52cra; Leonardo Patrizi 43cla; pixelprof 141tl; querbeet 38-9b, 44-5b, 99bl; SeanPavonePhoto 8bl; suteishi 136; Terroa 39cla; VFKA 22crb; Ziutograf 90cl.

Mary Evans Picture Library: Sueddeutsche Zeitung Photo 106crb.

Museum der Dinge: Armin Herrmann 51br, 189br.

Museum fur Kommunikation Berlin: Michael Ehrhart 34tl.

Museum fur Naturkunde: Carola Radk 126b.

Nola's am Weinberg: 137t.

Courtesy Peres Projects; Berlin: Matthias Kolb 148b.

Pierre Boulez Salle: Volker Kreidler 70-1.

Rex by Shutterstock: EPA / Alexander Becher 53cl, / Hauke-Christian Dittrich 53tr.

Robert Harding Picture Library: Stefan Huwiler 74br; Yadid Levy 10cla; 48bl; Travel Collection 20cb, 196-7.

Salt n Bone: 39crb.

Sammlung Boros: Installationsansicht mit Arbeiten von Michel Majerus / © NOSHE 128-9t.

Science Center Spectrum Stiftung Deutsches Technikmuseum Berlin: Clemens Kirchner 186tr.

SO36- Sub Opus 36 e.V.: © Prokura Nepp 11clb, 12t, 189tl.

Staatliche Museen Zu Berlin: Kunstgewerbemuseum / Achim Kleuker 176bl; David von Becker 87.

© Stadtmuseum Berlin: David von Becker 11t, 90-1, 92cr, 93b; Achim Kleuker 157cra, 157tl; Foto Setzpfandt 113b; Christina Sieber 98t.

Stasimuseum/ASTAK e.V.: John Steer 51cl, 231tr.

SuperStock: DeAgostini / Adolph Menzel *The Artist's bedroom in the Ritterstrasse (Das Schlafzimmer Des Kunstlers)* (1847) 95tc.

Tanz im August: Dajana Lothert 53cr.

Tim Raue Restaurant; Berlin: Wolfgang Stahr 36bl.

Urban Nation Museum for Urban Contemporary Art: Sabine Dobre 168bl.

Urban Spree Galerie: 150bl.

Zeiss Grossplanetarium © SPB: F.M. Arndt 233t.

Zeughaus (Deutsches Historisches Museum): Thomas Bruns 66, 80clb.

Zoologischer Garten Berlin AG: Steffen Freiling 35br; Frank Roesner 207cra; Tierpark Berlin / Steffen Freiling 230cla; Zoo Berlin 203bl.

Front flap:
Depositphotos Inc: Konrad Kerker cb; **Getty Images:** Sean Gallup cra; ullstein bild / Drescher bl; **iStockphoto. com:** Nikada cla; Noppasin br; SeanPavonePhoto t.

Sheet map cover:
Alamy Stock Photo: Sean Pavone

Cover images:
Front and Spine: **Alamy Stock Photo:** Sean Pavone
Back: **123RF.com:** lauradibiase c; **Alamy Stock Photo:** Sean Pavone b; **AWL Images:** Sabine Lubenow cla, tr;

For further information see: www.dkimages.com

Penguin
Random
House

Main contributers Paul Sullivan, Małgorzata Omilanowska
Senior Editor Alison McGill
Senior Designer Laura O'Brien
Project Editor Robin Moul
Project Art Editors Bess Daly, Tania Gomes, Ben Hinks, Hansa Babra, Bharti Karakoti, Ankita Sharma, Priyanka Thakur
Design Assistant William Robinson
Factchecker Solveig Steinhardt
Editor Louise Abbott
Proofreader Samantha Cook
Indexer Zoe Ross
Senior Picture Researcher Ellen Root
Picture Research Harriet Whitaker, Marta Bescos
Illustrators Andrzej Wielgosz, Lena Maminajszwili, Dorota Jarymowicz, Pawel Pasternak
Cartographic Editor Casper Morris
Cartography Simonetta Giori, Subhashree Bharati
Cover Designers Maxine Pedliham, Bess Daly
Cover Picture Research Susie Peachey
Senior DTP Designer Jason Little
DTP Coordinator George Nimmo
Senior Producer Stephanie McConnell
Managing Editor Rachel Fox
Art Director Maxine Pedliham
Publishing Director Georgina Dee
This edition updated by Hansa Babra, Elly Dowsett, Petra Falkenberg, Casper Morris, Robin Moul, Susie Peachey

MIX
Paper from responsible sources
FSC™ C018179
www.fsc.org

First edition 2000

Published in Great Britain by Dorling Kindersley Limited, 80 Strand, London, WC2R 0RL

Published in the United States by DK Publishing, 1450 Broadway, Suite 801, New York, NY 10018

Copyright © 2000, 2018 Dorling Kindersley Limited
A Penguin Random House Company
19 20 21 22 10 9 8 7 6 5 4 3 2 1

A CIP catalog record for this book is available from the British Library.

A catalog record for this book is available from the Library of Congress.

ISSN: 1542 1554
ISBN: 978 0 2413 6871 8

Printed and bound in China.

www.dk.com